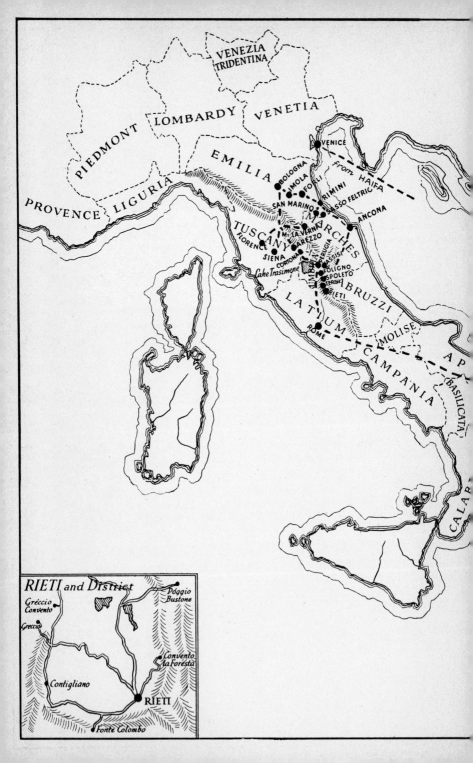

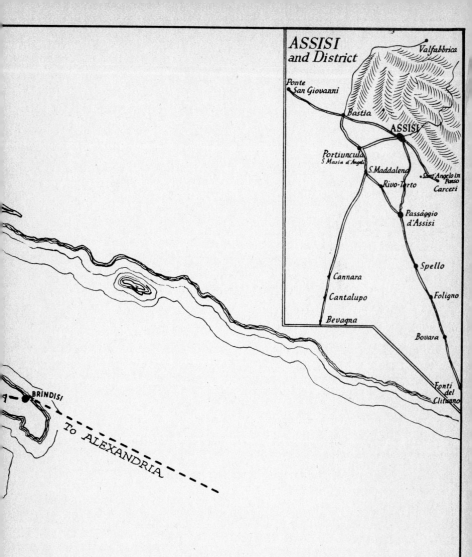

ASSISI
and District

Valfabbrica

Ponte
San Giovanni

Bastia

ASSISI

Portiuncula
S. Maria d'Angeli

S. Maddalena

Rivo-Torto

Sant'Angelo in
Panso
Carceri

Passággio
d'Assisi

Spello

Cannara

Foligno

Cantalupo

Bevagna

Bovara

Fonti
del
Clituano

BRINDISI

To ALEXANDRIA

ITALY

Author's Route

IN THE STEPS OF
ST. FRANCIS

IN THE STEPS OF ST. FRANCIS

IN THE STEPS OF
ST. FRANCIS

By

ERNEST RAYMOND

*Illustrated with Photographs
by the Author*

FRANCISCAN HERALD PRESS

1434 WEST 51st STREET • CHICAGO, 60609

New edition published by agreement with the Estate of the late Ernest Raymond and the agents of the Estate, Collins-Knowlton-Wing, Inc. and A. P. Watt, London, England. Copyright © 1975, The Estate of Ernest Raymond. New edition copyright © 1975 Franciscan Herald Press, 1434 West 51st St., Chicago, Illinois, U.S.A.

LIBRARY OF CONGRESS CATALOGING IN PUBLICATION DATA:

Raymond, Ernest, 1888-
    In the steps of St. Francis.

    Reprint of the 1939 ed. published by H. C. Kinsey, New York.
    1. Francesco d'Assisi, Saint, 1182-1226. 2. Franciscans. 3. Italy—Description and travel—1901-1944. 4. Levant—Description and travel. I. Title.
BX4700.F6R3 1975   271'.3'024 [B]   74-17076
ISBN 0-8199-0551-8

MADE IN THE UNITED STATES OF AMERICA

INTRODUCTION FOR SCHOLARS ONLY

IF any learned students of St. Francis' life should glance into these pages of mine, they may feel some scholarly irritation that I should have dealt with one or two aspects and incidents of the life as if there were no dispute about them at all. They will remark, for instance, that I have stated without comment that Francis' mother, Domina Pica, was of Provençal origin and high birth, that the Third Order sprang from a sermon at Cannara, that Bernard of Quintavalle led the first mission to Spain, and that the "Chapter of Mats" was held in 1219. Not a mention of Alviano as the possible scene of the beginning of the Third Order, nor of 1221 as a likely year for the "Chapter of Mats"!

But my justification must be that my book is not an argument, but an effort at an imaginative recreation of Francesco di Pietro Bernardone; and that it would have been fatal to my purpose to burden the text with disputations or to damage its musical flow (if it has any) with the halts and hesitations of footnotes. For the same reason I am keeping most of my acknowledgments within this preface. They are simple enough: my thanks to every book in the bibliography at the end of this volume, for though I cannot claim to have read all these mighty works, I am indebted either directly or indirectly to them all; and my gratitude to Harriet Waters Preston for her translations of Provençal poems, and to Arthur Symons for his translation of *En una Noche Escura* by St. John of the Cross.

Those who desire the full arguments must go to the standard biographies of Sabatier, Jörgensen, and Father Cuthbert, to a fine, forgotten book, *Sons of Francis*, by Anne Macdonell, and to the other works in the bibliography. Writing on a humbler level than these great students, I have just made my decision as to which of the disputants seemed to have the better of the argument, and then got on with the tale. In the few cases where the balance between them seemed to swing level, I have deliberately chosen the more dramatically effective of the alternatives, because it served my purpose better: that purpose being, I repeat, to make as vivid and memorable as possible the impact of Francis upon this modern age of ours, which, if I mistake not, is more sadly disillusioned than any period within the last seven centuries and more sick for a God and a sanctity.

ILLUSTRATIONS

CHAPTER I

I

SOMEWHERE near where the old bridge spans the Tiber at
Ponte San Giovanni, in the year 1202, a young man came
running into history. It was into a battle that he came
running, a lively skirmish between the soldiers of two
Italian cities, with good blows given and received; and
that is the first thing to notice with some interest, in view
of his later career. That he also came laughing as he
plied his sword or his fists I have little doubt: it was fun
to be fighting by the side of his brothers of Assisi against
their traditional enemies, those conceited bullies of
Perugia. Probably the *carroccio* of Assisi was in the field
among the knights and the pikemen, for every proud little
city in those days had its *carroccio*, a huge car bearing an
altar and priests, with the standard of the borough flying
above them; and nearly always the *carroccio*, with oxen
inspanned, went into battle among its children, like the
ark of the covenant of the Lord. Who can doubt that the
young man studied to belabour the Perugians as skilfully
as he might in defence of this Assisan mascot? One has
seen the studentry of our medical schools absorbed in
much the same studies along the pavements of London or
Edinburgh.

This skirmish among the vines (for it was little more)
went on throughout the day; and the old Roman bridge,
spanning an immortal stream at precisely the point of
strategic value between the two cities, watched it cynically
enough: it had felt the feet of the Legions in its time, and
seen during the centuries the marching and counter-
marching of imperial armies. It alone knew that these
boys were fighting over buried Etruscan tombs and

I

stumbling over Etruro-Roman fragments in the fields. It dubbed their quarrel an insignificant affair; and in this it was right: the battle of Ponte San Giovanni would have had no importance at all if it hadn't held the moment in which a youth of laughing and careless demeanour came stumbling into history, with much of the future of the world upon his shoulders.

The lads of Assisi lost the fight, as they always did; and the young man, with many of his friends, was taken prisoner and marched over the old bridge and up into the walled city of Perugia. He laughed at the disaster; he made a joke of it, as he was thrust into an underground prison. His airy, confident manner, together with his fine clothes, so impressed the gaolers that they concluded he must be a gentleman and pushed him in with the nobles and the knights instead of with the common citizens and men-at-arms. As a matter of fact his position, as a wealthy tradesman's son, seems to have been somewhere between the two. And in that prison he was held for more than a year, and almost all the time he persisted in being cheerful with a kind of Mark Tapley jollity, so that his companions were astonished and inquired if he was mad.

But he was not mad. It was simply that a gush of high spirits, a surge of creative gaiety within him, refused to be quenched and was shaping itself for the present in clowning and raillery. I hazard a guess that he greeted his fellow-captives every morning with the words, "Good morning, good people," which later he was to use on his first entrance into the mountain village of Poggio Bustone, as its citizens remember with celebrations to this day. "Buon giorno, buona gente." It is a greeting that fills with significance when we remember that he was destined, just because he persisted in seeing people as good, to lead them out into a new and better morning. I think too that he gave nicknames to his companions, because this was a habit of his to the end of his days. And beyond doubt he sang often in the daytime, because he loved singing, especially the ditties of the troubadours; and in a later chapter we shall have occasion (or we will make it) to consider the songs he may have sung.

Always with such a surge of spirits goes a soaring optimism, and when the more *blasé* of the young men asked if he was off his head to be so lively in a prison, he answered them, his eyes impudent and merry, "Why shouldn't I be lively? One day the whole world will bow down to me."

"Sanctissima Madonna!" exclaimed the young men and, despairing of him, turned away.

He had quite made up his mind that the world was going to bow down to him, but he knew himself so little in these early years that he supposed they would bow down to him as a great soldier or a great troubadour or a great prince. He did not perceive that another side of his character was so strong that it must balk this crude ambition or convert it into something completely different; that it must grow and grow in strength till it commandeered for its own ends all his goodwill towards his fellows, all his gay creativeness, and all his dreams of success.

And yet this other aspect of him showed itself in some power during that incarceration at Perugia. Among the young officers was one of a type we know well: a shy and awkward creature, born to be unpopular in any company, a "bad mixer," and as certain to be the odd-man-out as that happy youth, Francesco di Pietro Bernardone, was certain to be the centre of the fun, and yet a fellow who would have liked to be loved and who suffered deeply from the slights and the japes of his companions. Francis saw the suffering in his face and felt something go through his heart like the stab of a stiletto. He went to him and talked to him and let him feel that he was his friend. And leaving him and hurrying to the others, he compelled them to say some kind words to him and to welcome him into their fellowship.

Francis, old Pietro Bernardone's son, was subject to pity.

2

A year ago I went on a pilgrimage. I went to all the places in Italy, Egypt, and the Holy Land which I knew this young man to have visited in the course of his extraordinary life. I went hoping to get a little deeper into his meaning by wandering with my thoughts among the places where he had been. It was a pilgrimage in search of his meaning.

And there is every reason why I should ask you to share this pilgrimage with me as I describe it, because this young man in his out-dated clothes, moving among people who have been seven hundred years dead, still embodies a challenge to the whole world. And to say "a challenge to the whole world" is really to say little more than "a challenge to *you*." To you, to me, and to the next man, because individual intelligences are the only doors through which his challenge can reach the world. And since I am going to suggest that this challenge may be nothing lessthan the call of Reality to you, the invitation to us all to become real, it should be interesting matter enough. I believe that if you are honest with yourself you will admit that you are catching a whisper

4

of this tremendous call in everything you hear about him. All the way his actions will whisper to you of that real self which you will not allow to come to full life. I believe that, as you follow his steps with me, your experience will be mine: you will know within you little leaps of affirmation, little flashes of intuition that he was right, little heart-cries of "Yes! Yes!", little moments of vision that there is a better way of living, a nobler set of values, and even, possibly, a finer and higher form of consciousness—a consciousness as different from our present limited consciousness as that is different from the consciousness of animals. And you will experience all these intuitive assurances just because a part of you is like him. "All knowledge comes by likeness," said Plotinus; and the people of all nations and sects could not have glimpsed that the truth was in Francis, and fallen down and worshipped it, if a little portion of that truth had not slept uneasily in themselves.

Sanctity—or, if that word carries for you too heavy an odour of stale incense, let me say "the spirit of old Bernardone's boy"—is violently contagious, just because there is an inherited susceptibility to it in us all. You see, there are three latencies in us, not two only. Not Dr. Jekyll and Mr. Hyde only, but Dr. Jekyll, Mr. Hyde, and Young Francis. I dare almost assert that this has been proved in the clinics when the doctors have studied the phenomenon known as dissociated personality. The classic case is that of Miss Beauchamp. The normal, everyday personality of Miss Beauchamp disintegrated into three component and warring parts, which Dr. Prince, who was in charge of the case, labelled respectively the woman, the devil, and the saint. One of these "persons" would fade right out of consciousness with all

5

her train of memories, and another with quite different memories and motives would take command of Miss Beauchamp. By hypnotism Dr. Prince was able to dismiss one personality at will and open the chamber of consciousness to another, though I think I am right in saying he could never quite put the "devil" to sleep. The "devil" stayed always in the background watching and ridiculing the other two. I mention this famous case simply as an extreme pathological instance of something we all feel to be true: that within us contend three potential people, Dr. Jekyll, an ordinarily decent fellow, Mr. Hyde, an unspeakable person, and—very small, very little, very poor, a Poverello indeed—Young Francis.

Of course we could call the young and saintly one by another name than Francis if we could find in the calendar another saint whose life embodies so well all that we really believe to be the Perfect Reality of ourselves—that reality which, alas, remains for most of us always potential and unattained. The mystics of the Christian colour have not hesitated to call this highest potentiality in themselves by the name of Christ, and actually to identify it with Him.

A sentence of Rudolph Eucken may help us here. "Man," he says, "is the meeting-place of two orders of Reality." That is to say, Man alone of all the creatures in this world is visited by gleams from, or is possessed by a portion of, that invisible, eternal, ultimate Reality which is Perfection, and which lies behind the vivid but illusory "reality" of this imperfect, temporal sphere; and the result of this strange visitation or possession is that his present consciousness stands midway between an old, moribund, lower self which cleaves to the imperfections of the lower world from which it has sprung and a young, emergent higher self which is happy only when it is approximating towards the perfections of Eternity.

His present consciousness stands there like a captain able to direct its will towards one or other of these two. Most mystical writers have called this directing consciousness the Soul, the higher self the Spirit, and the lower self the Body; and if we had only grasped that this was what they meant by Body, we should have been saved a deal of misunderstanding. Soul, then, our present consciousness; Spirit, that which we long to be; and Body, that which we desire to escape: these terms have never been wholly satisfactory, but there are none better, and we shall use them on this our exciting pilgrimage, when we are getting a bit mystical.

That it is bound to be exciting I reaffirm. First, because of this personal reference which will be implicit in our talk all the way. No talk quite so interesting as that which we can relate to ourselves! And secondly, because the life-story which it will compel us to re-tell is just about the most human and the most moving in the libraries of Christendom. There never was a more dramatic tale lying to the hand of a novelist. Francis would have used none of these large words written above, Ultimate Reality, Temporal Sphere, Directing Consciousness, and what not; he would not have understood them, for there was never a saint less well read in the lives of the saints, never a teacher more happily ignorant of most of the teachings of the Church that he loved, never a preacher more likely to be tripped up over a passage in the Bible; he just did with simplicity and ignorantly what you and I won't do; he dared, in the end, to let the Real come through. He dared to let the eternal truth in him conquer all; which is simply to say that he dared

to let the surging love in him determine his every movement and thought. And if a man does this, he must stir
up drama like dust at every step.

It is what every saint does, of course; but Francis did
it more impressively, more graciously, and more amusingly
than any other. A born artist, a natural, unconscious
dramatist, a wit, he showed forth this greatest of all
dramas, the clash of the Eternal on the things of Time,
in a life-story so stirring in its ascent to an awful climax
that the world has been able to match it only with that
played out by his Master twelve hundred years before.
Strange young man, too full of love! There has been one
Francis, and one only.

3

You will see something of what I mean if we open our
pilgrimage by sitting on the top of Assisi's hill, with
the ruin of the old castle behind, the city shackled to
the slope below, and the wide vale of Spoleto filling up
the floor of the world.

Before us now is the theatre in which most of the
drama was staged. It all looks extraordinarily peaceful to-
day. We sit among tall grasses and wild flowers, in
an air pungent with the smell of mint, while innumerable
butterflies flit about us—which seems to fit, somehow, the
opening of a Franciscan tale. Lizards dart across the
stones, and a lark, descendant perhaps of one of Francis'
larks, sings its office in the limpid Italian sky. The grey
olive trees go shimmering down the slope, all round and
below the city walls. They carry our eyes to the great
flat plain which is a patch-work of maize-fields and
clover-fields, with the vines festooned from maple to
elm between them. In the farthest distance run fold

after fold of mountains, each a lighter grey than the last. And the last has a mysterious light above it like the light of another world.

Looking down on the city, we can see right into the streets along which Francis went rioting at midnight with his boon companions, his lute slung before him and his voice lifted in troubadour songs, to the disturbance of graver citizens in their sleep. That was before the sword pierced him deep enough. We can see into the open piazzas where in his lifetime excited and gesticulating crowds must have discussed one sensation after another. "What's happened to Francis? He's quite different from what he used to be." "Have you heard of the awful row that is developing between that young idiot, Francis, and his father?" "Listen, all of you: old Bernardone is haling his son before the bishop for trial." "Have you heard the latest?—would you believe it?—Bernard of Quintavalle—Bernard of all people, that sober and sub-stantial townsman!—has thrown up everything and is going to join young Bernardone in his mad game. And Dr. Peter Cataneo too, a lay canon of the cathedral, if you please—he's caught the disease. He and Bernard are giving all their goods away to the poor now in the Piazza San Giorgio." One shift of our eyes, and we can see the Piazza San Giorgio. Then: "Listen, everybody: young Clare, the lovely daughter of Count Favorino of the Scefi—and she only eighteen!—eloped from her home at midnight last night and ran to young Francis' crazy establishment in the forest. What are children coming to?" Eighteen days later: "Agnes, Clare's sister, and only fifteen years old, has run off to join her! Her father and uncle are going with a strong force to get her back."

Yes, down there in houses whose remains are still to be found, there developed and detonated battles between children and parents not a whit different from those beneath the roofs of England to-day.

Far away to our right, down there in the plain, do you see a grey chapel against some cypresses? That is San Paolo in Bastia, where Clare clung to the altar when her family came to drag her home again. Look left: do you see those haystacks against a farmhouse high up on the steep slope? That farmhouse holds the remains of the Benedictine nunnery of Sant' Angelo in Panzo, where Francis put Clare till he could find a home for her. Can you distinguish the path winding up to it? Up that path ran little Agnes to join her beloved sister. Up that path galloped knights and men-at-arms, determined to recover her. Do you see that file of cypresses marching down the hill to the left of the Porta Nuova? They mark the road to the little convent of San Damiano. There Francis installed Clare with her clinging sister, Agnes. There she founded the order of the Poor Clares, and there she lived, perhaps the most complete of all the creations of Francis. To San Damiano they brought him dying, and there she looked after him, mending his habit and making sandals for his wounded feet. There in the garden one day—do you see the garden?—he burst into his Song of Brother Sun and All the Creatures, though the sun of the East had blinded him and he could hardly see the creatures any more. To San Damiano his brothers, knowing how Clare had loved him, brought his dead body that she might weep over it for a little and say Addio.

And now leave San Damiano and see, right in the centre of the picture, as it ought to be, the dome of the great basilica that enshrines the Portiuncula, the tiny chapel of the "Little Portion" by which Francis chose to live and to die, and in which he dreamed such dreams of us men as we have not yet been great enough to fulfil—but there is time. "Good morning, good people."

Sitting up here beneath the old ruined Rocca, are we not indeed gazing over a country where once upon a time (as Angela of Foligno said of herself with the unblushing truth of the saints) some men and women of our race, like early envoys seeking an alliance, "walked with the Holy Spirit among the vines"?

CHAPTER II

I

FRANCIS limped to the gate of Assisi and stared out at the same country. Overtures for peace between Assisi and Perugia had released him from prison, but immediately an illness had confined him for weeks to a sickroom—evidence that his slight frame had not the resistance he would wish for it—and now, on his first day out, he had struggled as far as the gate that he might look once more on the familiar scene. And lo! a landscape which in the past used to thrill and trouble him with its beauty could give him to-day no pleasure at all. It was just a flat valley furnished with forests and farmlands and bordered by dull mountains. Try as he might to love it, he couldn't; the love wouldn't come. The loss of a love is always a sickly experience, and according to the depth of our nature so will it affect us. Francis in later years must have thought this a crucial experience, because it is set down as such in all the first biographies, and he alone could have told the tale of it and impressed his friends with its importance.

It was a kind of post-influenza depression, no doubt, but a Francis can do a lot with post-influenza depression. He frowned, and, turning his gaze inward, tried to analyse his sadness. And in momentary flashes he saw many things about himself. Let us try to see steadily and clearly what he was seeing only in flashes and with difficulty and couldn't have put into words.

It was something like this. When Francis was born to Pietro Bernardone and his wife, Madonna Pica, there was born a lover, an artist, and a mystic. Now a lover craves always the permanent, an artist craves always the perfect, and a mystic craves always the One, the Whole, the Timeless and the Still. And to-day the lonely lover in this boy was hungering for something that endured, and he could see nothing but impermanence everywhere. *Panta chorei,* all things change, all things pass and perish, and one can never step into the same river twice. The artist in him was hungering for perfection, and he could see nothing that wasn't somewhere flawed or dirtied or discordant or incomplete. The mystic in him longed for unity with God and the whole universe, and he could feel only his apartness from God and his utter separateness and solitariness in the world of created things. He could see nothing that met his needs anywhere. He could see nothing perfect between the plain, the mountains, and the sky.

And therefore all meaning and all charm seemed to have been drained off from the world. (And yet San Damiano was there, and the Portiuncula was there, and a girl child of ten, in a house not far behind him, was playing somewhat blasphemously with a row of pebbles for a rosary.)

Fame! He had wanted fame, and he wasn't famous yet, and his youth was going. (He was twenty-two.) Never did fame keep pace with one's mounting ambitions, and, in the end, like all else, it decayed and perished. For one quick moment he saw that he could never find happiness by seeking his own glory and profit, but only by uniting himself with the still, eternal God and spending all his life in the service of Him and His children. But he couldn't do it. No, never: his nature was too divided. He was his father's son as well as his mother's. From his mother, Madonna Pica, a lady of Provence, he had drawn, not only his love for the troubadour songs of her homeland and for the exciting tales of chivalry, but also his thoughts of God; and he knew that she cherished a hope that he would be a "man of God" one day. But Pietro Bernardone had also played a part in his creating, and a big part too. And Pietro, a good, honest, strenuous cloth merchant, commonplace and vulgar in his values, was a man who measured all success with his merchant's yard-stick and gloried in the wealth, fine clothes, and social opportunity which he could give his sons. And the unfortunate thing was that Francis gloried in them too. He loved his full purse, his showy doublets, and his place in the best society of the town. He rejoiced in his reputation as a wit and as the most popular of the riotous youths of Assisi. He liked to think of himself as their chosen leader when they sallied forth on some new rag at midnight. And (yes, let us have the truth) he delighted in his singing voice whose beauty all men spoke of. Had he not, in the service of this voice, and in his craze to be a troubadour, ordered a minstrel's suit like Blondel's, with parti-coloured hose and pointed shoes and a hooded tunic and a lute slung behind? And in this picturesque attire had he not swaggered with his friends down the streets of Assisi, to the amusement of the frivolous and the scandal of the staid? Yes, he was thoroughly vulgar, thoroughly contemptible. There was nothing in him that was unspoiled and wholly good.

He had forgotten his outrush of goodwill to anyone he chanced to meet. Or perhaps this was so natural to him that he thought no more of it than of the air he breathed. And he had forgotten that thrust of pity which he felt at the sight of pain. Or did he perhaps remember it in this self-examination by the gate and wonder if it was good? Did he recall how once in his father's warehouse, when he was displaying some cloth to a distinguished customer, a beggar had come in and asked an alms in the name of

14

God, and how, angry at the disturbance, he had told the wretch to be off? The beggar had turned and gone sadly to the door, and at the sight of that disappointed back Francis had taken such a stab that he could know no healing till he had run after the fellow and pushed money into his hand. Yes, I think he must have considered his feeling for the outcasts as he thought how wonderful it would be to give himself in service to the world. But he couldn't do it: he hadn't the strength to follow the nobler things he saw. With a sigh he turned and limped back towards his home.

Seven hundred years ago this happened, and it might have been written of any boy or girl of to-day. It might have been written of you and me when we were young and dreamed one moment of being famous and the next of being good. And then, perhaps, of some method by which we could be both. Paul Sabatier has a fine sentence to describe this despair of Francis: it was, he says, "the solitude of a great soul in which there is no altar." You and I may not be great souls, but we approach to greatness in so far as we are lonely for want of an altar.

Francis limped back to his home. For a moment that higher self, the Spirit, had stirred restlessly within him and tried to rise upon his arm. For a moment the sword of God had been drawn before him, and he had looked upon it. Dimly he recognised it. It was the sword that pricked him at the sight of pain. It was a very terrible weapon. He knew that if he let it pierce him to the heart, it must slay all his shining ambitions and change them into something that terrified him. He knew also that if he recoiled from it, it would leave him a coward, a refuser and a failure. He turned and went through his door (possibly that old rotting door that they still show you in the Chiesa

Nuova) and shut it behind him. And the sword was sheathed again.

2

When I was in Nazareth, the things that moved me most were not the grotto of the Annunciation or the cave of Joseph, Mary, and Jesus' house, but the sight of a fat baby playing alone on the cobbles and, a minute after, the sight of a handsome, lively boy climbing the street to the family home. So too one warm, soft night in Assisi. I stood with the crowd in the Piazza della Chiesa Nuova, watching a choir of Assisan youths and girls singing Bella Porta di Rubini by the light of a single hanging-lamp, and beneath the vigorous arms of their conductor. The gaping and listening crowd packed the little square right up to the baroque walls of the Chiesa Nuova, which is the church covering the sight of Bernardone's house and shop. More people watched and listened from the lighted windows of the houses around and from the high loggia at the top of the Municipio. And the single cone of light fell on the upturned faces of the choristers and of the lads who were accompanying them with stringed instruments. The lads with the mandolins seemed cheerful enough, and so did those with the guitars; the player with the double bass, on the other hand, seemed to be feeling the largeness of his responsibility. The grey-haired old maestro, fervently conducting, was perhaps the happiest lad of them all, especially when they sang a madrigal of his own composition, and the multitude applauded it to the Umbrian stars.

This merry concert, attended by the Podestà himself, was in honour of the Felibri Provenzali, a community of Provençal poets and artists who had come on a pilgrimage

16

to Assisi under the leadership of their "Queen," because the mother of Francis was a lady of Provence. There had been a little outpost of Provence in this house of Bernardone, and the son of the house, they liked to think, was almost a native of their own land. The Queen and all the women were in ancient Provençal costume and made a pretty show, standing in a phalanx by the singers and the band. The Queen was a kind-faced woman in middle life, tall and dark; and that is all that I will say about her, for her elaborate costume was such as I have not the hardihood to describe.

After half an hour of songs in the piazza we all ran and skipped and pushed down the Via Bernardo da Quintavalle to where another bright lamp awaited us. First went the singers and the band, then the smiling maestro, then the Provençal women with their tall, dark Queen, then the most pushing of the people, including the present author, then the double-bass player, who, after all, had something to carry, and lastly the streaming tail of the crowd. And again under a cone of light, before Bernard of Quintavalle's door, the picture was re-created: the boys and girls singing, the band striking on their strings, the maestro conducting, the tall, dark Queen watching, and the dense black crowd framing all.

And suddenly my eye fell on one of the youths in the choir. He was spare in body to the point of delicacy, but his shirt, opened at the throat, disclosed a healthy, brown, Italian skin. His face was less handsome than lovable, with its neat features and large Southern eyes. He was singing so triumphantly that it was easy to isolate his voice, a strong Italian tenor of which I am sure he was by no means ashamed. My eyes swung to the Queen of the Provenzali, and the scene dissolved, and the past re-

17

turned. . . . Francis . . . and the lady his mother from Provence . . . and the sound of singing and stringed instruments in the streets of Assisi. A sound that faded and was lost in a night of seven hundred years ago.

3

"When the devil was ill, the devil a monk would be. When the devil was well, the devil a monk was he!" In the resilience of youth Francis quickly recovered his strength and his good opinion of himself; and that moment of disillusion by the gate was forgotten. The old zest and gaiety returned, the parti-coloured minstrel's suit came out of the cupboard and amused the piazzas of Assisi, the lute was struck again and the rich voice led the singers as they left the small square in front of his home and went down the narrow street opposite, past Bernard of Quintavalle's door. The old dreams of fame were inflating his days again and pumping their excitement through his heart.

And at last opportunity opened. For some time past a war fever had been raging in Italy. A real Duce had arisen for Catholic Christendom in the person of Pope Innocent III, and under his leadership the totalitarian state of the Church was resurgent, exultant, aggressive. The enemy was the well-hated German army of the Empire, and the prize the kingdom of Southern Italy, or "The Two Sicilies," as they called it then. Of this kingdom Innocent had claimed the regency on behalf of himself and Holy Church, and had ordered his battalions to march. It was 1204 in Italy, but if we call it 1914–15 in England, or, better still, 1936 in Italy with the Duce issuing orders from Rome and Badoglio marching on Addis Ababa, we shall have said enough.

At first, and indeed for a long time before this hour of enthusiasm, the papal forces had been dealing more in defeat than in success, but now—and the enthusiasm was all the greater for the previous disappointment—a brilliant leader had appeared above the crowd of mediocre captains, and he seemed incapable of anything but victories. He was Duke Walter of Brienne, but, again, let us say Marshal Foch sweeping forward at last over the liberated earth of France and we shall know all about the elation in the piazzas of Assisi. Every well-to-do young man there, for it was the very top of the age of chivalry, was restless to be riding in the army of Walter of Brienne. Quickly, lest it should be too late, a young noble organised his own troop of horse. Francis was one of the first to join it; and his next few days were filled with delight as he ordered himself the best equipment that money could buy. He was always lavish in his spending, and Pietro Bernardone set no limits to it, so long as he was buying distinction for the family. We can imagine the interest and pride with which the family examined the articles of equipment as they came in: hauberk, I suppose, and surcoat and chausses of banded mail; helm and buckler; belt and sword. Francis tried them all on, and the Lady Pica thought he looked lovely in them, and old Pietro was quietly proud, and the younger son Angelo gaped, and Francis was more pleased with his appearance than he cared to say. He paid one or two secret visits to the mirror, just as we did in 1914, when we first sported riding-breeches and top boots, sam-brownes and swords; for we too were twenty then.

And had we the least doubt that our side was right and the other fellows were deluded criminals? That it was God's own cause and the Germans were the agents of the

Devil? It was the same with Francis. Simple and un-critical to the end of his life, for his talents were all of the heart, he believed that he was setting out on a crusade, and was happier than he had been for years. The clashing motives within him had found a point of harmony—or he liked to think they had. He could be both famous knight and man of God. He could please both father and mother. He could enjoy both adventure and hardship, both applause and service. Service, surely, because he was quite ready to die for Christ and Walter of Brienne. He had the best of both worlds. The split nature had closed along a line of healing, and he was a-brim with the energy that comes from mental peace. "Now God be thanked who has matched us with his hour, And caught our youth . . ." "Blow, bugles, blow. Nobleness walks in our ways again."

Yes, his joy in life was high. It turned his days into a tense exhilaration and lit up his sleep at night. Most striking, in these days of psycho-analysis—more striking than he or his first biographers believed—he dreamed one night a dream. He was standing alone in his father's shop, and somehow it had enlarged itself into a great house, a palace worthy of a noble or a king. The shelves along the walls were all transfigured: they were much larger, and instead of holding grey, unopened bales or rolls of coloured cloth with the sample ends hanging down, they held casques and shields and lances, and their edges were hung with knightly banners. And now he was not alone, for by his side—I think the young body stirred with desire—stood a bride who in her perfection fulfilled his every wish. And she was *his* bride, and this palace was theirs, and a voice told him that the armour was the armour of his liegemen and followers. A house, a bride, shields and spears and swords—I leave the interpretation to the analysts, but I know what I think.

And a few mornings after, the men of the troop, with every last gift hung about them, paraded for departure, most certainly in the great piazza opposite the Temple of Minerva, for what other was large enough? And the townspeople cheered them as at the word of command they turned and went with waving hands down the street that is now the Via Santa Chiara. It was then the natural way out of the city towards Spoleto and the South. And so they must have gone jingling by that palazzo against the old gate, and (if the tradition that it was hers is true), the ten-year-old daughter of the Scefi must have come excitedly to the window, to watch the noisy, laughing, colourful troop go by. How little she knew! Nothing told her to look for one lithe youth with large black eyes, brown skin, and the buckler of a page upon his arm.

The cavalcade passed under the old gate, and on to the new one beyond the Piazza San Giorgio, and so down the open road that led to Spoleto.

4

Let us go ahead of them. We pass under a third Porta Nuova, built since Francis' time, and now we too are on the open road that twists and turns on itself because of the steepness of the side of Mount Subasio. It winds down through the olives and the vines, and we know that it will soon find the high road and put us on our way to Spello. As we go down it, we give a thought to the Blessed Angela of Foligno, one of the greatest of Francis' followers, since this is the path, "the narrow road that leads upward to Assisi and is beyond Spello," where, as she says so pleasantly, she "walked with the Holy Spirit between the vines."

At the junction called Passagio d'Assisi it drops us on to the dusty high-road where we take to the fringe of the maize-fields, that the motors and ox-carts may spare us their contributions as they pass. We walk dead straight for an hour, and all the while Spello is ahead of us, clambering up the side of its mountain—or tumbling down it, we are not sure which. A kilometre this side of Spello we see a few jagged ruins, like monoliths of brickwork, rising behind a green bank, and since we are not going to miss any sights, we climb the bank to learn what they may be. Immediately we recognise the ring of a Roman amphitheatre, tumbled among the grasses and the weeds; we can just distinguish the entrance where the crowds from Hispellum would go funnelling into the games.

Leaving this Roman arena, we pass the Roman gate of Spello, and then we have but a short way to go before Foligno looms behind the trees. Our road takes us right through the centre of Foligno, about which we shall have a story to tell later, and, Foligno passed, our feet are on the old Flaminian Way. The old Flaminia Via that went from Rome to Rimini to keep the Gauls in order! We pass the city of Trevi plunging down its mountain-side, and there at its foot is Bovara, whose very name tells us that we are getting near to the holy river Clitumnus——

It tells me nothing of the sort, you object: what has Bovara to do with Clitumnus?

Only this, that it is called Bovara because they would assemble the oxen here before taking them to drink of the sacred water and have skins for ever after as white as their udders' milk.

Then must every ox in Italy, you say, have drunk of

22

THE OLD BRIDGE AT PONTE SAN GIOVANNI

the water of Clitumnus, because I have never seen one whose skin wasn't as white as the soutane of the Pope.

Certainly, sir; you are right; and there is no point of controversy between us.

Clitumnus! Virgil sang of it, and Propertius sang of it, and Pliny warbled about it in his own way. Byron, lover of classical times, came to look into its dark, slow water, and lifted up his voice and sang. Carducci too. What, then, are we going to see? What is it that so stirred the heart of the ancient world, and inspired the poets to sing?

A sign-post thrills us: it is pointing so casually to Campello sul Clitunno. Poplars marching in Indian file from the hinterland to the Flaminian Way, with here and there a weeping willow to break their ranks, tell us that we are coming to our meeting with Clitumnus. The road skirts or leaps the low feet of the mountains, and suddenly, just beneath its embankment, we see a graceful little temple built of pagan stones in the classical style. We are near a holy place of the ancient world. Women stoop over a bank between the poplars, washing their clothes, as they did two thousand years ago. They shake their drooped hands to let the drips fall from their fingers, back into the stream. Now another signboard points us towards the trees: it bears the words "Fonti del Clitunno." A plain board, inadequate, uninspired, disappointing as the voice of a man who has no ear for the verse he is speaking. Obedient to it, we go down from the road, pass through a fence—and immediately we wonder no more; with the least encouragement we too would lift up our faces and sing.

Out of the limestone mountain, spurting from under the leap of the Flaminian Way, a score of springs form themselves straightway into pools so silent and untroubled that you would swear they have no movement at all; and yet the water, after enfolding grassy islands, runs away into the fields, a full-grown river at the very point of its birth. Poplars guard the solitude everywhere, and willows bend like Melisande to weep over the dark water. Gnats and flies wheel above the rushes; and pasturing sheep, so rare in Umbria, wander over plank bridges from one peace to the next. One moment we liken the water to polished ebony reflecting all things, but then, looking into its deeps, we see the white stones from the mountain as clear as through glass, except that they have changed their colour to blue. I see my own face mirrored there, and I remember that this water reflected the face of Virgil as he looked in. It is Clitumnus, and we have left Francis a thousand years in the future.

5

Francis rode with his squadron past the springs of Clitumnus and into Spoleto. And at Spoleto something happened to him, no one knows what. But it drove him to an action most difficult to explain. Some have read it as one of the most courageous of his life, others as one of the most self-centred. For my part, I think self-love and self-offering were mingled in it. He was not ready yet for acts of pure heroism. Sabatier suggests that the young nobles of the troop, now that they had got the better-dressed and uppish young shopkeeper into their power, proceeded to take him down a peg. This seems to me a brilliant guess, and if it is right, no greater hurt could have been inflicted on a lad who suffered from the weakness of wanting to be loved. The official biographers, good unimaginative men, who knew him at a later date and wanted him to have been a saint from the beginning, would have us believe that the old fever struck him down and that in his sleep he heard a voice asking him why he wanted to serve a servant of the Lord when he might be a knight of the Master himself. This may express the second half of the story but not, in my view, the first. After the injury to his pride he may well have been feverish and dreamed of God. A deep humiliation before now has broken up the hard soil of a man and enabled the things of the Spirit to come through. It may well be that when all his delight in being a soldier faded from him, he hungered for God again, and that, suddenly, in the small grey hours of the morning, a wonderful choice presented itself to him: "You want dissipation, do you not, Francis? Well, why not dissipate yourself in the service of God rather than in the vulgar fashion of men? You know that it would be wonderful to do so; why then continue to kick against the pricks?"

One's mind can be very clear at three o'clock in the morning; and we may hold that Francis saw at last that, in putting on his armour to follow Walter of Brienne, he had really been arming himself against that awful sword. In the cold, clear light he saw the sword again; and it was too clean and straight for mercy. Walter of Brienne or Christ? How wonderful to answer Christ! To give up all —all!

Well, it is mostly guesswork, I suppose. What we know for certain is that the next morning he left the troop and rode home to Assisi and to whatever jeers might await him there.

He may have gone with sadness, or with a high but rather tremulous hope, or with both. Since he was incapable of being purely sulky, I shall believe that his unknown lodging at Spoleto had seen him make a tremendous effort to follow his ideal, and that his will for that effort had been strengthened by the injury he had received. How it all reminds us of our own youth, with its swaying motives and swiftly interchanging moods!

I planted myself a little way up the mountain outside Spoleto. I was standing there (if you will understand me) to see Second Lieutenant Francis ride home. And there below me, straight as a taut string, was the road he must have taken, because it was, even in his day, the ancient Flaminian Way. I saw him in his fine accoutrements passing behind the olive trees. He was moving slowly: of that I was sure, because whether he was sad or exultant, he must have been asking himself, What had he done? What had he done? What terrible step had he taken in turning from all his dreams and leaving them behind him?

And he rode on towards Clitumnus, Foligno, Spello, and the ruined amphitheatre in the fields. I am purposely stressing the Roman origins of the road because I have this in mind: the road itself was Roman; yesterday, in the midst of his troop, Francis rode along it, a child of the Middle Ages; to-day he was riding back along it, a very lonely cavalier, but the herald of an age that was to be.

CHAPTER III

I

READING the biographies, one can only conclude that Francis backslid very quickly from his high resolve at Spoleto. The swaying motives of youth do not find their balance after one violent effort or after two. But he is not quite the same as he was before he went to Spoleto; he is shaken; he is, as it were, bruised and confused and somewhat lacking in energy, as if a conflict were draining his vitality again. He still leads the revels, but not with the old zest. Sometimes he is abstracted in the midst of them. And often in the daytime he goes right into himself and wanders out into the country alone. And the beauty of the landscape, like the richness of the banquets, has lost its savour, almost as it did before. Empty again, the valley, the mountains, and the sky; and withered the joy of dreams. "All things betray thee, who betrayest Me."

It is hard, very hard, when you are Francis, to kick against the pricks.

But to give up all! Oh, the curse of being granted spiritual vision, the curse of being able to see too much! If he were to be loyal to his vision, Fame must go, and the delight of dress and ostentation and parade, and the pleasures of the flesh—yes, if he were to follow to the farthest point he could see, if he were to respond to the most distant call, he must give up the sweetness of having his own bride. This last surrender would be the most difficult of all to an affectionate, passionate, and hungry nature. (That this hunger was with him almost to the end we know from the temptations of which he frankly told. Once, harried by it, he rushed out into the wintry night and made figures in the snow, one large and the others smaller,

27

and with his usual wit, he said, "There, Francis, thou vile son of Pietro Bernardone! There are thy wife and thy children." And on another occasion, still merry, he told his worshippers not to be so sure that he was a saint since he might yet present them with a wife and children. And I am glad that he was tempted thus, because it takes him out of the stained glass window and puts his hand in ours.)

But why must he give up everything, even the hope of a woman and a home? We know by his founding of the Third Order that he didn't think the pleasures of home to be wrong for the majority of men. Why must *he* give up all? Because his nature was such that it could not halt this side of perfection, and he was hearing a call to nothing less than the mystic's unity with all created things. And in flashes of vision he was seeing, as possibly no man before him except his Master had seen, that all possessiveness, all acquisitiveness, meant a deliberate separating of himself from others. To pursue fame and wealth was to separate himself from common men by his superiority. And, more subtly, it was possible to separate himself from them within the wall of a single, monopolising love. The only way to be one with the poor and the outcast, who so clutched at his heart, was to be their equal in poverty and to cast himself out.

That was the truth for him. If he were to let all the love in him have its way, *that* was the end to which it was driving him. It was urging him to deal with poverty as Christ with pain: Christ desired that no man living should be able to say, "I have suffered more than you"; and Francis, wandering along the footpaths round Assisi, desired that no man, whether living then or yet to live, should be able to say, "But, Francis, I have been poorer than you."

It was one of the most dazzling visions that have ever come to a man.

"But I was at the bottom of the world," someone might protest, rejecting his offered hand.

"I too," must Francis answer.

The bottom! So only could he be true to the highest in himself. So only could he be *real*. We are real only when we find the truth of ourselves and create it; in anything less we are in error and have only a lower kind of reality. Francis felt that he would be less than real until his love was as deep as degradation itself, and his pity as wide as the compassion of the sun.

To be real! Ah, yes, this showed him the positive aspect of the matter; the business of giving up all was its negative side. One arm of the eternal paradox took everything from you, but the other added all things unto you. By giving up all he would inherit the earth. By losing his life he would save it. The same merciless blade which killed him would let in, for the first time, the fullness of life. For the first time he would be free. Extraordinary that upon the heart of this unintellectual young tradesman there should have broken the brilliantly clear vision that property meant not only separateness but imprisonment; that all men everywhere were shutting themselves up in prisons of gold; that the more they grasped, the more they lost; and that, as far as possible, one must give up "to have" if one desired "to be."

The vision is worth examining further, and we shall restate it again and again as we go along, because it is one part of the challenge of Francis to all the ages, and most notably to our own. It is his pitying laugh at our scales of measurement. It was Christ's challenge too, of course, but Francis was almost the only man in history who dared to take Christ at his word and act the principle out. "Let me once be quit of the desire for property and praise, and I shall be free. Free from the nagging ache of envy. Free from the sick hurts of resentment. Free to love all and forgive all. Free to do and say the right, regardless of unpopularity. Free to wander everywhere as my inspiration guides me, and to enjoy the whole world of plain and forest and mountain, because I own no blade of grass in it anywhere. Only by having nothing of my own to look at anxiously shall I be able to see all. Pure contemplation is only for the unconfined."

And confound him, confound him, for he disturbs us with the fear that he may be right! Listen: does not the same fear disturb us every time the excellent hobo goes by? The hobo may be a very bad man, and probably is, but one aspect of him always troubles us, if we are worth anything at all, as we all are. He brushes our shoulder in the highway, the symbol of something we have missed. It is because we all have the tramp in us, as we all have the saint and the artist—aye, all—even that lamentable creation, the hard-headed business man, who knows it in strange moments of wistfulness and nostalgia.

So watch Francis carefully now. He has the bold notion that he would like to set free the artist, the saint, and the tramp in him. He is troubled by the desire to incarnate a vision in which tramp, saint and artist are one.

Unity with all the world, and freedom to be real; and the key-word was poverty. He could achieve both if he wed poverty. Wed? *Wed?* Francis stood still on the path. A lovely fancy had presented itself. A fancy that thrilled through him as the discordant forces ran to it to find their harmony. An idea that would sublimate (as we say nowadays) instead of combating his desire to be a lover and his dream of himself as a knight who vowed allegiance to "Dieu et ma dame." A fancy that would give him the best of both worlds far better than his service in the ranks of Walter of Brienne. Had he found his peace at last?

These thoughts of his solitude Francis had hidden, up till now, from his flighty companions. One only he is known to have taken into his confidence, but no one knows who that one was. Before the others he was keeping intact the façade of ribaldry and song. Or nearly intact, because sometimes they detected a crack in it or a ring of hollowness behind. They would observe a remoteness in his eyes or the lines of strain on his brow. And one night the ferment within him found utterance in a strange word.

A very fine banquet was just over, and the lads full or wine and merriment, resolved to go in procession through the streets with a Lord of Love at their head. The Bright Young People of that day, drawing their inspiration from the elegant courts of Sicily and Provence, they decided to brighten Assisi that night with a song or two of love. With acclamations that brooked no refusal they elected Francis Lord of Love and put the wand of that office in his hand. They lit their torches, slung their lutes, and went out into the night. With the golden tresses of the torches streaming above their heads, they went singing, shouting, pushing, and swaying, down the middle of the piazzas and up this steep street and round the corner and down the next. The beggars asleep on the doorsteps lifted their heads out of their rags to see the expensive young gentlemen go by. I think that the glance of Francis, Lord of Misrule, fell upon those beggars, because he stopped singing, halted for a second, and after a time fell behind the others and sank into a reverie. Rioting along, his friends did not immediately observe this, but then one of them, perceiving that their Lord was no longer leading them from in front but from behind, shouted back at him (for the jokes of young men were much the same then as to-day) : "What's the matter, Francis? Buon Dio, he must be in love!"

And the others took up the quip. "Who is she, Francis? Have you found your fair lady at last? Who is she?"

Francis smiled back at them. "She is someone **more** beautiful and richer than any you can imagine."

2

But it is one thing to see a vision, and another to amass the courage to create it. Wondering if he could ever, *ever* conquer his need of applause, his love of self-decoration, and his fastidious recoil from dirt and disease, he wandered more and more frequently alone. He took to climbing the mountains till he was far away from men and alone with the leaves. He found a cave where he could sit with his thoughts or kneel unperceived in prayer. He was praying much these days, praying for strength to conquer the body and let the spirit win.

I went in search of this cave or grotto because it seemed to me a place of some importance in our human history. Here, after all, Francis faced and fought the Third Temptation which whispers always to anyone who has talents and a gift for success, "I will give you all the kingdoms if you will fall down and worship me, your lower ideal." And again and again this youth must have answered it in his cave, "Get thee behind me, Devil, for I must worship only my higher ideal, which is God in me, and Him only must I serve." The fruits of his final victory were not small for us men, so I set out to look for the field of battle.

There is a mountain over against Subasio, on the other

32

side of the Torrente Tescio, and as its empty slopes must certainly have drawn him, I wandered up there looking for grottoes. I was much encouraged by the name of a region half way up and now farmed, which is Le Grotte. Passing some bright-eyed mountain children, I asked if they knew of any caves hereabout, and either they didn't or, hearing my Italian, they thought I was of the devil and best answered with a safe, "No, signore." I took my question to a labouring man hard by (the children following) and he pointed up to the part called Le Grotte but assured me that he didn't know why it was called that, because there were no grottoes there. At this point a tall and strapping barefoot woman, magnificent creation of the mountain side, came hurrying down, confident that she could manage trouble better than any man or child (in which she was right) and inquired of everybody what the clamour was about. And on everybody informing her at once, and on my elucidating the perplexities further, she half shrugged and half nodded and pointed up the slope to two little copses of oak and ilex. There were caves or hollows there, she said, which might account for the name.

I waited for no more. I hastened towards them with increasing excitement and, so steep the way, increasing breathlessness; and in the first of them, right under the roots of an ilex tree, I did come upon a large natural hollow. I did not suppose it was Francis' cave, but—it might have been. And if so . . .

I stood there some time in the silence of the mountain. All the kingdoms of Francis' world were before me. All the vale of Spoleto, that old lake-floor, lay spread below, bordered by its mountain ranges, with Assisi scrambling up a knee of Monte Subasio to the left, and, far away to the right, proud Perugia astride its peaks and lifting its

33

towers into a sunlit mist. Down in the middle of the plain ran the white road, southward past the Portiuncula, to Foligno, to Spoleto at the gates of the valley, and so onward to Rome.

It was the Portiuncula, the Little Portion, that won.

I was to remember this panorama later when I stood in the wilderness by the Dead Sea.

3

Francis' next manœuvre in the long-drawn-out battle was to hurry to Rome. With all the impetuous suddenness of his nature he started off for Rome. Perplexed and discouraged, but struggling still, he went there in the spirit in which we go into a church, hoping for some miracle of help. Still a child of the Middle Ages, as in his head he always was, no matter where his heart might lead him, he made the pilgrimage to Peter's Tomb as to an oracle.

And now, instead of travelling with me in space, I want you to come on a journey through time. Leaving 1938 behind us, we will walk back down the highways of twelve centuries till we reach the year 774. We shall pass Francis on the way, so to speak, and leave him in his thirteenth-century highway. Having made the long journey, we shall come upon a church which no longer exists. It is the basilica of St. Peter's, Rome, as it was in 774 and for another seven hundred years.

As we approach it, we see a broad flight of white marble stairs, above which is a noble four-arched porch, flanked by a high campanile. This porch, however, does not lead into the basilica itself but into the atrium, which is a great courtyard paved with marble and framed with colonnaded cloisters. In its midst is the Pilgrims' Fountain

34

whose metal roof bears a huge bronze pine-cone, put to rude use by Dante when he described the face of one of the giants in hell as "lunga e grossa Come la pigna di San Pietro a Roma."

We pass the fountain and come to the pillared façade of the church itself. Entering through the central door of solid silver, we exchange at once the sunlight of this day in 774 for the half-darkness of a vast cathedral. Beneath the flat beamed roof we see the parallel avenues of Corinthian columns, eighty-eight columns in all, stretching away towards the altar and the apse. Above the altar is a canopy resting on four pillars of porphyry, and just beneath it is the Confessio, or grating through which the pilgrim may look down into the low chapel that holds the apostle's tomb.

That is all for the moment. After this peep into the church let us return to the white marble stairs and the Porch before the atrium. It is Eastertide in 774, and a very great occasion. The authorities for this scene are the *Liber Pontificalis*, Gregorovius, Gibbon, Villari and Cotterill. On the top of the stairs, attended by a throng of cardinals, choristers, and city dignitaries, stands Pope Hadrian I. All these persons in their many and various vestments are looking down the long road that stretches to Hadrian's Mausoleum, in obvious expectation of some exalted person who will come as nobly attended as the holy father himself. A stir in the assembly on the steps, a swaying and a murmur of the crowd on either side of the road—and the head of a procession has appeared. First come file after file of Roman students carrying branches of palm and olive and loudly singing; then some of the nobles and chief men of the city; then the clergy carrying their crosses and their banners; then the tall, fair Frankish

35

warriors, all on foot because of the sacredness of the ground; and lastly—see how the crowd sways, and hark how the cheering becomes a roar!—Charlemagne himself. He is walking on foot, but he is taller than all his paladins, almost by the length of his great golden head. Built on this imperial scale and soon to be crowned Emperor of the World, he has come to visit the Pope and kneel before Peter's Tomb.

Reaching the marble stairs, he ascends them on his knees, kissing each step until he is at the feet of the Pope, who bends graciously, lifts him up and embraces him.

With their hands still joined, and preceded by the clergy and the choir singing *Benedictus qui venit in nomine Domini*, they cross the atrium, pass through the silver door, and enter the half-darkness between the marching columns. Charlemagne goes up the nave towards the tomb of the saint.

It is the Berlin–Rome axis of that day.

And now, with the mere breath of our wish, we disperse four and a half centuries—but the stout old building stays; and here we see another figure coming up the same marble stairs, crossing the same atrium, and passing through the silver door into the same half-darkness which has been held between the columns during all the centuries. He too goes straight up the nave to the Confessio before St. Peter's tomb. But he is quite unattended and unnoticed; just a youthful stranger in whom something new is astir.

Do you see? The gigantic imperial figure, and the slight dark youth. The man who was ambitious to be at the top of the world, and the one who had a mind to be on the bottom.

Francis knelt by the grating and looked down the shaft.

He prayed there for a long time. And every few seconds his praying was disturbed by the approach of rich and well-dressed people who came to the fenestrella, muttered a prayer, and flung down their small offerings. He found himself examining the size of their offerings. How niggardly they were! What Christianity was this that could spend pounds on self-decoration and offer pence for the help of others? What could their minds be like who thought to salve their consciences thus? When would they learn the first thing about Christ and His teaching? Irritation swelled, and at last in an angry protest, generous in the main but not empty of ostentation, he thrust his hand into his purse, took out all its contents, and flung them through the fenestrella.

The action exactly expressed Francis at the time. He was only half-way in his spiritual development. Not yet had he shed the impatient superiority of youth; not yet had he learned the stupidity of wrath and punishment; not yet had he learned to use his dramatic instinct in the cause of love instead of contempt; but at least he had shown the clear perceptions, the impulsive munificence, and the sense of completeness which would carry him the whole way; at least he had revealed his inability to do less than give all.

He left the church and went across the sunlit atrium to the parvis before the porch. And here on the white marble stairs he suddenly noticed the beggars raking with their mummied hands the sleeves of those who approached the doors and whining, "Un soldo, signore . . . per amor di Dio. . . ."

"Per amor di Dio:" that was what the beggar had said to him in his father's shop. Beggars. He moved off a little way and turned to watch them. They were

37

touchstones by which he could test the strength of his love. With his heart he wanted to love them, but his senses were shuddering away from their ugliness and their rags. What nonsense to suppose he could ever identify himself with them! Could he, a scented dandy, bear to wear rags and exchange the admiration of the vulgar for their contempt? It didn't seem very likely. And yet—why not try? Why not try, here and now? Why not make an experiment to see what it felt like to be a beggar? Why not defeat his fastidiousness and throw it down, as it deserved? *Could* he?

Impetuously he decided that he could and would. He might not be equal yet to doing challenging things in Assisi where all knew him, but in Rome, where he was unknown, he could do a dramatic thing and challenge himself.

One beggar had a surprise that morning. Not often when one stands in a public place does a Francis come up to one. Francis offered the beggar money for the use of his clothes! Festival for the beggar! And Francis, in some place of retirement, put on the unpleasant rags, fighting his own over-delicate sensibilities. If he were to wed his fantasy bride, the Lady Poverty, then the clothes of a beggar were the suit of the groom. And all that day he stood in rags on the steps that the richly robed Charlemagne had kissed, begging alms from the people of God, and from the tourists. The biography written by the Three Companions tells us that he begged in French "because he loved to speak the French tongue, albeit he spake it not aright." That dear, troublesome language!

The experience in Rome, both of impatience at the smug mediocrity of professing Christians and of angry conviction that the outcasts were his people, carried him a little way nearer his goal. But the decisive moment had not come

THE BISHOP'S PALACE, ASSISI

COURTYARD OF THE CASA GUALDI

yet. He knew it when it came. That he recognised it as such all his life we see from the first sentence of his Will, which he wrote on his death-bed for his sons. After his return to Assisi he still mooned about the mountains or rode along the bridle-tracks, with the puzzle behind his eyes: could he ever finally defeat himself? And one day, as he was riding towards Assisi along the old Perugia–Foligno road, he came near the crossways where stood the leper hospital of San Salvatore. San Salvatore delle Pareti was a lazar-house administered by the Order of the Crucigeri who, like the Knights of Lazarus, devoted themselves to the care of lepers. It was one of the nineteen thousand houses for lepers known to have existed in the thirteenth century all over the Western and Eastern Empires. To Francis it was a dreadful place, and usually he went past it quickly or made a detour through the fields to avoid it, because the sight of the lepers and the odour from the walls stirred in him both nausea and fear. But to-day, before he could do this, he was startled by a quick, frightened swerve of his horse. A leper stood in the path before him.

His first impulse was his lowest, to swing round his horse's head and escape the sight, after flinging a coin at the man. But immediately—perhaps he remembered the meagre offerings of the rich men of Rome or the happy fact that he had been able to force himself into the clothes of a beggar—a loftier impulse cancelled the first and told him that his test stood before him. If he survived this test, he would conquer indeed; if he ran from it—but he mustn't. Was not the leper with his eaten face and his outcast's uniform the very symbol of poverty? A better symbol than the beggars of St. Peter's?

Before the nobler resolve could disperse, before he could think again, leaping from his horse, forcing himself all

39

the time, he went to the leper, put all his money in his hand, and lifted the hand and kissed it. And in Italy the kiss of the hand is the kiss of reverence to the representative of Christ.

The leper, touched to the heart, and encouraged to do by Francis, gave him the kiss of peace; and Francis as his brother kissed him felt a sweetness fill his whole being like the sweetness of the first kiss of love. Happier than he had ever been, he leapt on to his horse and galloped up into Assisi. His happiness was greater than that of an accepted lover because it combined the joy of self-conquest with the excitement of love. He had enabled the spirit in him to conquer the body, and he was going to wed himself to the poor.

In such a manner was it that to young Francis of Assisi the Spirit and the Bride said, "Come."

CHAPTER IV

I

"WHEN I lived in sin, it was very painful to me to see lepers," wrote Francis in the first sentence of his Will, "But God led me into their midst, and I remained there for a little while. When I left them, that which had seemed to me bitter had become sweet and easy."

It is a happy period of Francis' life that opens now. Most of us can remember periods of quiet blessedness in our youth. when for a little we tried to be good. Francis was experiencing all that blessedness and more, because his dedication was surer.

He filled up with energy. He had the spiritual energy to lift weights which yesterday he could hardly have moved from the ground. He had the physical energy to drive himself to anything. Now, this access of energy is a significant phenomenon, most worthy of emphasis. It derived, I feel certain, from his achievement of a sense of unity with the whole world. He had destroyed that hampering, draining separateness, and felt one with everyone everywhere. And to understand what springs of energy this sense of unity can release I commend you to the studies of Mr. Richard Gregg. Listen to this from his book, *The Power of Non-Violence*:

> The invigorating effect of a great realisation of unity may account in part for the original flaming energy of Islam. It perhaps explains the great flowering of Buddhist civilisation. It may also account in part for the energy of the French Revolution, whose watchwords were Liberty, Equality, and Fraternity, and for the subsequent sweep of the political idea of democracy. Doubtless it accounts partly for the tremendous vigour of Communism in Russia.

He might well have included Francis in his enumeration,

for History has witnessed few more spectacular successes than the first advance of Franciscanism.

But for the present Francis foresaw nothing of all this. He just wanted to be good by himself. And the very next morning he walked into the hospital of San Salvatore to visit and show love to the lepers. That elegant villa, the Casa Gualdi, stands now on the site of the old lazaretto, and there is nothing in its battlemented façades to suggest the dreadful place whose smell offended the people of Assisi as they passed the cross-roads, going down into the plain. From its walls to-day comes only a strong smell of wine, as if you were passing the bonded vaults by the Thames. But its young padrone is a kindly man, and he was very ready last year to open his door to a traveller who came knocking. And very ready, on hearing the stranger's business, to declare that the inner façade of his stately little quadrangle was nothing less than the façade of the old hospital of the Crucigeri.

I do not know if he was right. Monsignor Pronti, librarian of Assisi, assured me that he was, so with the ready consent and help of the padrone, I took for you the accompanying photograph. If these gentlemen are right, then the arches in the picture are those through which a young gallant in rich clothes and vigorous health passed to minister to his brothers the lepers. Through them the young Dives passed in to Lazarus.

That they are very old is certain, because you may find behind them an old sacristy, and an old chapel with its early mediæval frescoes still traceable over the apse. Did Francis kneel here with his new brothers? On the site certainly, if not on the present floor. To-day that floor holds the padrone's wine in some of the biggest barrels I have ever seen, and the smell of wine is so strong that it cannot be contained within the chapel but flows out over the roadway and the fields.

When he was not ministering to the lepers, Francis would saunter about the fields and the hillsides as before, but as elated now as he was disheartened then. All his old delight in Nature was restored to him. No longer did it hurt him with its transience and imperfection. Instead it had a new and brighter light upon it, because he felt one with it, and with the Purpose working through it.

And one day he walked out of the very gate by which he had stood in such disillusionment, and, strolling down the hill, came upon a little field-chapel with a tiny priest's house against its wall. It was dedicated to San Damiano. Attracted always by these little shrines in the solitudes, he wandered in and knelt down to pray. The chapel was in a sorry condition: it seemed to be falling to pieces for want of money, but apparently it was still used for worship sometimes, because a big Byzantine crucifix hung above its altar, and the candles looked as if they had been burning that morning. But not a sound disturbed its quiet as Francis knelt and stared up at the crucifix.

Now, the face on that crucifix was unusually alive, with wide-open, questioning eyes (you can go and look at it to-day in the jealous custody of the nuns of Santa Chiara). And, staring up into those strange eyes, Francis meditated long on the crucifying of Christ and what it meant.

What did it mean? That Love could reach the world only through pain? That the greater the love the greater the pain? That Love, because it was unity, had to clash with evil, which is all forms of separateness: getting, despising, hating, hurting, slaying? And that, because it was the only reality, one must let it come to birth

43

in one's heart and grow to its full stature, even though it led one to a place of crucifixion by the adversary? Yes, the cross was the picture of Love, and of Man's high stature achieved.

And he wanted to achieve no less. Staring up at it, he prayed, "Love, what can *I* do? Show me something that *I* can do."

A small acquaintance with the writings, not only of mystics, but of rational philosophers also, will make credible to the severest rationalist what happened now. Gazing fixedly at any object, repeating the same sentence a thousand times—either of these, or both together, may induce a trance, or, at any rate, hypnotise the mind into a highly suggestible state. Many psychiatrists will tell you that they employ these methods when it is desirable to hypnotise a patient. And Evelyn Underhill, in her detailed and scrupulous study, *Mysticism*, gives us the following paragraph:

That these proceedings do effect a remarkable change in the human consciousness is proved by experience: though how and why they do it is as yet little understood. Such artificial and deliberate production of ecstasy is against the whole instinct of the Christian contemplatives; but here and there amongst them also we find instances in which ecstatic trance or lucidity, the liberation of the "transcendental sense," was inadvertently produced by purely physical means. Thus Jacob Boehme, having one day as he sat in his room "gazed fixedly upon a burnished pewter dish which reflected the sun with great brilliance," fell into an inward ecstasy, and it seemed to him as if he could look into the principles and deepest foundations of things. The contemplation of running water had the same effect on St. Ignatius Loyola. Sitting on the bank of a river one day, and facing the stream, "the eyes of his mind were opened, not so as to see any kind of vision, but so as to understand and comprehend spiritual things . . . and this with such

clearness that for him all these things were made new."
This method of attaining to mental lucidity by a narrowing
and simplification of the conscious field finds an apt parallel
in the practice of Emmanuel Kant, who "found that he
could better engage in philosophical thought while gazing
steadily at a neighbouring church steeple."

Francis, gazing fixedly on those strange painted eyes,
and asking, "What can *I* do?" felt the love and joy-in-
unity swell to an ecstasy, and suddenly was aware of
words being spoken. Their sense was simple enough,
like himself at this stage, and humble enough; it did not
deal with the principles and deepest foundation of things.
Doubtless, they really came from his heart, but in this
trance-like condition he externalised them and believed
they came from the figure on the cross. But what matter?
That was only the mediæval way, as distinct from the
modern way, of believing they came from God. *Somewhere*
in that chapel of San Damiano that day the words were
heard, "Francis, go and repair my church which, as
you see, is falling into ruin."

Exultant, he jumped up. By this miracle Christ had
clearly accepted him. He had a Master to follow and love,
in whose service no danger could be too great. What
with Poverty for his Lady and Christ for his Lord, the
old idea of knighthood had now a perfect sublimation.
Francis was the squire of Christ. The Eternal had broken
through and found a page.

Have we called him impetuous? I know no more
impetuous figure in history. He is the Hotspur of religion.
He ran out of the chapel, saw an old priest standing in the
sunshine, realised that he came from the little house
attached to the chapel, put all his money into his hand
telling him that it was to buy oil for a lamp that must

burn always before the crucifix, and left him standing there, somewhat bemuddled. He ran home, ran into Pietro Bernardone's store, chose some bales of scarlet cloth, slung them across his horse, jumped into the saddle, and cantered off to Foligno.

Foligno was the market for his wares. It stands where the road from Perugia and the north meets the Flaminian Way on its journey from Rome to the port of Ancona and the East. They were selling cloth in its market square as Francis cantered past Spello, with his bales swinging. They are selling it there still. They were selling it when I walked into the market-square one Saturday evening and took the photograph that faces this page. Francis dismounted in that market-place and held aloft Pietro's best cloth, and very soon sold it at a good price. Then, since he could do nothing by halves, he decided that he must also sell his horse; he sold it; and, as far as I can see, no book in the vast Franciscan bibliography has made anything of this fact, beyond merely mentioning it.

But what did it cost Francis, who so loved animals, to sell his horse? What was his parting with that companion of his loneliness? What were his last words to the purchaser? "Be kind to him"? What were his feelings as he saw the patient beast led away? But—he must love without possessing, so he gave up the horse and, with a purse full up for God, trudged the ten miles back to Assisi.

We can imagine his excitement as he climbed the slope to San Damiano and pictured himself showing his money to the old priest. We can also imagine the confusion of that old gentleman when he saw the money in the boy's hand and realised that he had met somebody who wanted to do something and do it quick. I have seen vicars in England confused by laymen who really wanted to get something

46

THEY STILL SELL CLOTH IN FOLIGNO MARKET

VESTIBULE OF THE BISHOP'S PALACE, ASSISI

done. He asked how he had come by this money and, when he heard, refused to have anything to do with it; perhaps with some relief. Francis laid it sadly on a window-sill, and the heart of the old priest was moved to pity (everything in the tales suggests that he was a kindly disposed if indolent and peace-loving man), so that, when Francis asked if he might come and live with him while he repaired his chapel for him, he could distress the youth no more, and answered, Why, yes, he saw no reason why he shouldn't.

So Francis settled himself in the home of the priest of San Damiano, happy as a child in having some building to do, and in imagining himself a religious.

2

But, after all, there was such a person as Pietro Bernardone. Francis apparently supposed that there was nothing that Pietro would like better than that his best cloth should be sold to provide money for the Church. Pietro quickly revealed that there was nothing he liked less. The incident brought to a head his festering annoyance with the recent aberrations of his son. It had pleased his good-hearted, vulgar mind when Francis dressed lavishly, displayed the family wealth, and walked with the best people in Assisi. But when the boy argued the desirability of giving up all and living like a beggar—and be sure there were stormy arguments over the dinner-table —the words painfully overturned his paternal pride and, worse still, lunged straight at his conceit of himself. An impatient, domineering man, such opinions whipped him to fury. And when he learned that the young fool had carried his freak to the point of selling the firm's cloth,

47

selling one of the horses, and leaving home to live with a poverty-stricken old mass-priest, he decided that it was time to put his foot down.

So begins the great tussle between father and son. Another genius in religion, though a humourless and unattractive one, Madame Guyon, has a fascinating title for a chapter in her autobiography. "Diverses Croix chez M. son Père," she heads it sadly. It is the plaint of every wilful daughter in the home of a wilful father. It is also the perfect title for the chapter of quarrels that here ensues.

Justice has never been done to Pietro Bernardone.

In the first place, he has had far too bad a press. All the mediæval writers and artists seized upon his fine boorish figure as the obvious villain to set in black relief against their hero. The poor old devil fills this niche in every Franciscan fresco in Italy. And yet his chief crimes were that, like ninety fathers in a hundred, he had an immense pride in his boy, an immense conviction that he knew better than the young fool, and an immense desire to have his own way. As a father myself, with a strong feeling that I am generally right, I am jealous that a plea should be put in for Pietro. It is not easy for a good-hearted but crude and conceited man to have a genius for a son. It must be the deuce and all to have begotten a Francis.

Pietro Bernardone was of a type that can still be found in our own street, and even in our own shirt. He had virtues, but they were all tethered by longer or shorter ropes to his egotism and could not stray far from that rooted centre. He was an energetic merchant, eager to make money for his wife, his children, and his house, because they were his. To this end he journeyed long distances

48

with his pack-horses and sumpter mules—over the Alps into Provence and northward into Normandy. And this must have demanded bravery in the age of Cœur de Lion, Ivanhoe, and King John, when the barons practised piracy on the trade-routes, and the outlaws roamed the greenwood. It was on one of these journeys that he found his bride, the Lady Pica, in a great house of Provence, and there is little doubt that he loved her soft nature as much as, and probably more than, her social rank. I like to think that England saw his tall figure with its furlined *cotte* reaching to his calves and its capuchon drawn over his dark head, to keep out the disgusting cold. Is it not more than likely that he came to the great Stourbridge Fair, in the early days of October, with the other cloth merchants from Flanders, Normandy, and Italy? He was affectionate and generous to all who belonged to him. Overjoyed at the birth of a boy when he was abroad in Provence, he insisted on calling him Francesco—the little Frenchman—after a dear land which had given him a good wife. And he denied the boy nothing so long as his extravagances worked honour for the name of Bernardone. To his native town of Assisi he made large benefactions, though not, apparently, with such modesty that his right hand did not know what his left hand was doing. In an age of ruthlessness and rape there were many worse men than Pietro Bernardone.

In the second place, no one has pointed out that Pietro was in great part the real creator of St. Francis. No one has pointed out that Francis' life is one long reaction against his father. Pietro was vain and violent; Francis became a passionate believer in humility and the crass stupidity of force. Pietro liked to be master; Francis called himself always a servant, "less than the least of the

49

servants of God." Pietro was acquisitive and money-loving, a faithful esquire of My Lord Wealth; Francis enthroned the Lady Poverty as his inspiration and his "toast," and developed a hatred of money that at times seemed over-stressed (though of this over-stressing I am far from sure). Pietro was a snob and a tuft-hunter; Francis threw up all such social measurements, insisted that his brothers should remain *minores*, and aligned them with the poorest of the poor. Pietro worked for every privilege he could get; Francis forbade his brothers to seek from Pope or magistrate any privilege whatsoever, "except the privilege of the most high poverty." It was a hundred-per-cent. reversal, and thus, to a great degree, Pietro gave us Francis. Thank you, Pietro.

However, that the old gentleman was a loud-voiced bully is shown by the fact, distressing to those who want their hero to be perfect from the beginning, that Francis was palpably afraid of him. One unperceived reason for remaining with the old priest was, I surmise, a dislike of meeting his father. And when in due course his father came storming down the hill to know what all this buffoonery was about, Francis quickly slipped from sight. He ran to a secret cave (he always loved secret caves) and hid there for days till the sad, angry father had given up the hunt. I am sorry to have to report such unheroic behaviour, but this is to be the truest book that ever was written.

How potent must have been this fear of his father, since it lingered longer than his fear of the lepers and was a bigger hurdle to surmount! What shoutings and beatings it suggests in his childhood! In his youth he must have been more afraid of his father than of the formidable Perugian bravos or of the notoriously ferocious

German armies, and now, for the first few laps of his new course, he was more afraid of him than of God.

But what a man does once he will do again : the youth who forced himself to kiss a leper will certainly force himself to face a father. And Francis, struggling with his weakness in the cave, decided that poltroonery had no place in the armour of a knight. He must go and meet Pietro. More, he must proclaim before all Assisi, no matter what the ridicule, his new service and his new Master. And so one day, pale with sleeplessness, haggard after combat, and deliberately dressed, it would seem, in a beggar's livery, so as to make the task as difficult and the success as convincing as possible, he emerged from his hiding-place and climbed the hill to Assisi. He was setting his face steadfastly to go to Jerusalem. It was his second strong effort of self-purgation, and the first dramatic act by which, in the public places, he challenged the values of the world.

And of course the mob crucified him. That is to say, he had hardly passed under the city gate before the children were running after him and yelling, "Pazzo! Pazzo!" "A loony! A loony!" One flung a stone, and immediately the others picked up stones and dirt and flung them too. Loafers followed behind to see the fun, and occasionally shouted their waggeries. A *via dolorosa*, indeed, for one who had loved to be admired and acclaimed, but he must tread it : remembering his Master, he answered nothing, but walked on steadily, with the hooting, jeering crowd behind. The stones cut his face, the mud bespattered his clothes, and his persecutors increased in number and noise. Faces appeared at windows and doors; and as the strident hubbub approached Bernardone's shop, he himself strolled to the door with a faint curiosity to learn what was afoot. And he saw.

51

Oh, good people, spare a tear for Pietro, for this was his crucifixion too! Let us forgive him that he did not behave with dignity. He was terribly hurt, and he was not a great man. He ran out in a blind, sobbing fury, and, dragging his son into the house and out of the dreadful daylight, beat him like a madman, hurled him into a cellar, and locked the door. And Francis, faithful to his Captain, offered neither resistance nor protest. But this humility did not undo the father; not on the surface, at all events (it is the all-conquering method, but it works slowly), and Pietro, when he was obliged to travel again on business, thought to secure his house from further humiliation by putting manacles on the unresisting boy. And then, utterly miserable in the aftermath of anger, he went angrily away. He went off with his pack-mules and his porters, wreaking his impatience on both because he had no heart to be kind to them. He had left his heart, somewhat broken, in his house at Assisi.

And when Pietro was gone, there happened that which shows that the essential human relationships were precisely the same in 1207 as they are in 1938. No sooner was Pietro out of sight than the Lady Pica—that poor, pleading lady—came to the cellar, drew the bolt, and set the boy free. And, taking him to her, she argued that surely he could find a way that would please both Christ and his dear father; and when he protested that he couldn't compromise with the truth, she let him convince her. Sighing, she disputed no more, but accepted his kiss and watched him starting off again for San Damiano.

History does not tell what happened between husband and wife when Pietro returned. We can suspect that he had come home troubled by remorse and ready to contend more gently with his son, but when he found that his orders had been defied and his authority set at naught, his accursed *amour propre* (how wise Francis was to be done with it!) swept his head clean of anything but fury. The woman—pooh! She wasn't so much to be blamed. The boy had argued her round: women were ever soft creatures at the mercy of their children. The boy was the criminal; and the last conclusive battle must be joined.

And so we come to a scene for which modern and northern minds will need preparation. In it Francis does that which will shock our ideas of decorum, unless we realise that this sort of thing was much more popular in the Middle Ages, that Francis was an Italian and not an Englishman, that he was a dynamic genius and not a timid conventionalist, that he had an astonishing gift of dramatising truth in unforgettable actions, and that it is not possible to do this and remain an English gentleman. We must realise that Francis, strangely, and quite unconsciously—for no one was ever more truly self-effacing—had a magnificent flair for publicity. Dynamically original and independent, he advanced his cause throughout his career by keeping it front-page news. He couldn't help doing it. And lastly, it will be enlightening to ask ourselves this question: is it possible that the point where we draw the line in the matter of demonstrative gesture is not necessarily the point where it is drawn by God?

There is nothing absolute in the proprieties of gesture: they are relative to the time, the place, and the man. We in these days allow ourselves a quantity of gestures which only familiarity saves from absurdity. We open wide our mouths and cachinnate through them like horses when we are amused: Lord Chesterfield, on the other hand, held

53

that all laughter was unbecoming to a gentleman. We sit and bang our palms together, like seals flapping their fins on the rocks, in order to produce a succession of childish reports, as evidence that we appreciate a performance: Lord Chesterfield, I am sure, considered all such bewildering percussion to be excessively ill-bred. Is there not a possibility that we may be as supercilious as he if we hastily condemn an exceedingly expressive gesture by Francis?

The maddened father ran down the hill to San Damiano. Poor man! he did not know that he was beating out a track for a million pilgrims since—a track that they have since planted with cypresses. Finding Francis, who no longer avoided him, he rained furious words upon him and, afterwards, blows. That the boy resisted not at all only infuriated him the more. The young thief and renegade could either return home and restore all the money he had got from the sale of his father's goods, shouted Pietro, or he could go his own lunatic way and be disinherited for ever. Francis replied that he was ready and even eager for disinheritance, but the money was not his to restore because he had given it to the Church. The argument does not sound convincing, and we can guess an unconscious obstinacy in the presence of his father. It takes more than a year to make a saint; and the most difficult knot to cut may be the secret nexus between father and son.

"Very good!" exclaimed Pietro. "Very good!"

And he swung round and hurried up the path, breathlessly, for it was steep, and he was a high-living man. But temper will always defeat breathlessness or fear of blood-pressure, and he went straight to the Palazzo del Commune opposite the Temple of Minerva, and demanded the arrest and banishment of his son. "The Mayor looked blue; so did the Corporation too." After his liberal benefactions to the borough, the consuls of Assisi were anxious to please him, but they very much disliked this present suggestion. They temporised. They dispatched a herald to Francis ordering him to appear before them. In modern terms, a policeman knocked at the door of the little priest-house of San Damiano with a summons for Francis to appear before the local bench. Francis refused the summons on the ground that he was now a religious (boyish pleasure here?) and no longer subject to civil jurisdiction. How he could have sustained this objection I do not see, but fortunately for him the consuls seized upon it with relief and sent word to Bernardone that they were sorry, but they seemed to have no jurisdiction to proceed in the matter.

Did this check Pietro? No. He was of that red-necked substance which brags less of its humanity than of its he-manity and is therefore incapable of giving in. It can never know the sweetness of resentment abandoned, but must always suffer the ache of vanity craving revenge. "All right! If the civil courts cannot act, the Church courts shall!" And he bundled round the corner to the Bishop, his near neighbour in the Piazza del Vescovado, and demanded the trial of his "religious" son in the episcopal court.

So Bishop Guido comes on the scene. And Bishop Guido is a most interesting minor character in the Franciscan tale. His character emerges from the chronicles with unusual clearness: a kind, confused, commonplace, and most litigious gentleman. Kind, because he gave affection and support to Francis till his death; confused and commonplace, because he would never see what Francis was aiming at, and would always recommend to him the safe and conventional course; litigious, because if anyone

55

so much as trod upon the outer hem of his rights, or the rights of Holy Church, he went to law about it, rejoicing. Throughout the tale he is helping Francis with one hand and arranging a forensic quarrel with the other. And now here was a case in which he could smell at once a chance to assert the legal authority of the Church and perhaps to defend the interests of a young man whom he already knew and liked, or, at the least, to enjoy a most attractive juridical argument. He convened his court straightaway, and summoned Francis to appear before it. Francis accepted service of the writ without hesitation. "Gladly will I appear before my Bishop," he sent word, "for he is the father and lord of souls." And at this the Bishop loved him even more. (The naïve Legend of the Three Companions says so, in as many words.)

What of the gossip now in the streets and homes of Assisi? Bernardone, one of the town's most prominent burgesses, and Francis, till yesterday the leader of its Smart Set! A family quarrel in its Mayfair! It was the *cause célèbre* of the hour, and, thanks to Francis' gesture, it has been a *cause célèbre* ever since. I wish I were sure where the famous scene was enacted. Certainly it was somewhere against the church of Santa Maria Maggiore, which was then the pro-Cathedral, but was it out in the piazza or within the Bishop's palace which stood beside the church? The early frescoes place it outside; the later students seem to prefer the vestibule of the palace; the Bishop's chaplain who opened the palace door to your investigator last year would not hear that it took place anywhere but on the very floor where we were standing. He pointed to the Bishop's throne against the side wall and to a picture at the end of the long chamber portraying the scene on the actual tiles beneath us.

If it really took place in this chamber (or, rather, in a predecessor of this chamber, because restoration has changed the Bishop's palace almost entirely), then we can be sure that the people were crowded to the walls, and that a much larger crowd thronged the garden and the piazza outside, either peeping through the windows or waiting for news. Bishop Guido took his seat upon the throne, and Pietro stood on one side of him, and Francis on the other, dressed, for his own reasons, in the bright clothes of his rank. And the audience fell to silence, their eyes swinging from Bishop to plaintiff and defendant, their lips apart. Bishop Guido opened the proceedings with a suitable address from the chair; Pietro then stated his case; Francis kept silence like his Master; and there was nothing left for the Bishop to do but to sum up. He did so with his usual kindness and good sense.

"Your father," said he to Francis, "is very much vexed with you. Now, if, as you say, you want to be God's servant, I advise you to give him back his money, because if there has really been any irregularity in your taking of it, then, my boy, God will not want it used for the service of His Church. Only hand it all back, and I am confident your father's anger will be allayed. And, as for your desire to help the Church, and rebuild the chapel of San Damiano, God can raise up for you in other ways all the money you need."

Francis immediately obeyed him. He did very much more than obey him. He acted with such decision that it is plain he must have been planning his action during his incarceration in his father's house or during his walks around San Damiano.

"My lord," he said, "I give him back the money gladly; and not only the money, but my clothes also."

57

And he stripped himself of all his clothes and, standing naked, laid them with the money at the feet of his father.

The action was to symbolise his break with property and rank, his adhesion to utter poverty, and his complete trust that God would honour His promises to those who dared take Him at His word. And these he supposed to be his only motives, but can we doubt that, unperceived by him, the hostility to his father had slipped in and was hiding behind the nobler company? Unperceived in this solemn moment, I feel certain, but there notwithstanding: if all his subsequent career is in part an unconscious protest against his father's values, we must expect this note to ring clear at its opening. And if there was unkindness in the action, it was almost his last unkindness.

"Listen, everybody," he added, turning to the people. "Until now I have called Pietro Bernardone father: henceforth I desire to say only, 'Our Father which art in Heaven.' "

Unfortunately we can only read the words as they have been given to us, and cannot hear his voice as he uttered them. But some quietness in his voice, some dignity in his manner, some sadness in his large eyes, seems to have swung all the people's sympathy towards him. Many wept.

Bernardone alone was unmoved—unless he was moved to greater indignation as he felt the court-room turn against him. In him self-pity must always be stronger than parental pity, and he stooped down, picked up all the clothes so that nothing was left for the naked boy, and pushed his irate way through the people to the door. "For by reason that he had loved him much," say the Three Companions, "he did so grieve over him that he would curse him." I see him going up the hill to his home with that bundle of clothes under his arm.

Ah, poor Pietro: good-bye; we shall not see you again; but we have understood.

Bishop Guido, in the meantime, had risen and put his own cloak round the naked figure. Here was another symbolic action, though unwittingly so—a perfect picture of all that was to happen: Francis, naked, was a prophetic figure, disturbing in its suggestion of a new, clean start; and the Church, compassionate, admiring, but fearful, quietly folded its ancient vesture around it. Have no fear, all ye faithful: new, naked prophet is now old vested priest.

The trial was at an end, and the people pressed out to publish the thrilling story.

Guido took Francis into the inner rooms and found for him the cast-off suit of a labourer. This would be the single short tunic, coarse *chausses*, and rough felt boots worn by all labourers throughout the Middle Ages. Francis asked for nothing better, for was it not the uniform of his new rank? The good Bishop offered him a temporary home in the palace, but Francis declined, because, if faithful to poverty, he must go out and sleep under the sky or in some rough lodging earned by hard work. Moreover, a glow within him was driving him out into the sun. A great decision was past, a great step had been taken, all sides of his nature had found integration in it, and therefore energy was filling him to start upon the new adventure.

And what an adventure it was to be! The adventure of trusting utterly in God. Had anybody ever really made this adventure for a thousand years? Christ had promised that God would care for a man who trusted in Him as He cared for the flowers of the field. Had any man since the Apostles really put that promise to the test? He had preached, "Take no anxious thought for the morrow. . . . Seek ye first the Kingdom of God, and all these things shall be added unto you." How many had really obeyed Him? He had said, "Resist none. Condemn none. Love your enemies and bless them that curse you, and to him that would take away your coat give your cloak also." How many had accepted this without a gloss? Not the Poor Men of Lyons, or the Humiliants, or the Cathari, or any of those earlier reformers, who had fought and quarrelled and condemned. Francis was ready for the experiment of utter dependence, obedience, and acceptance. He was going to model his life in every tiniest detail on the pattern of Christ. He was going to give himself as completely as Christ to love.

What would happen? What would happen if a man said, "I accept God's word. I cast all my needs upon Him. He is here, and He will provide for me day by day"? What would happen if he let love go to its supremest, most illogical end, far beyond common sense : if, linking himself without salvo or proviso to the Father, he made himself "to the Eternal Goodness what his own hand is to a man"?

Excited, happy, Francis went out from the Bishop's palace to see.

He did not guess that much more must happen in such a case than he could imagine now, who had no thought of a great work, but only of quiet service. Far more : even to the conquering of the heart of the centuries. He went out in his old labourer's suit, and when he was clear of the city, he began to sing. A very different soldier, this, from the one who rode out in a gay uniform to join Walter of Brienne in Apulia! A madder than Quixote here! He was out to make the world's completest offering. Nothing withheld; nothing qualified; nothing explained away. Done with property. Done with praise. Done with power. Done with the ties and cares of a single dwelling-place. "The world was all before him, where to choose his place of rest, and Providence his guide." There he goes, climbing beneath the Italian sky, exultantly happy and singing, because he has taken the final step and is free at last. Free and empty: he has emptied himself of all, that he may be nothing but a vehicle for God's love.

> I am the gilly of Christ,
> The mate of Mary's son. . . .

CHAPTER V

I

ONE morning I left the western gate of Assisi, descended
to the gorge of the Tescio, and began to climb the mountain opposite. I had a plan to cross the ranges and drop
down to Valfabbrica in the valley of the Chiagio. My
rucksack slung, I bent myself to the steep incline. The
first half-hour I passed (and apparently entertained)
many women and children, for the lower slopes were
terraced with olive orchards and dotted with farm-
houses. I had to climb a good way higher before I found
the loneliness of the summits. And, even then, not perfect
loneliness: I could always hear the distant voices of
labourers ploughing, because the struggling Italian peasant
cultivates his country to the very base of the rocks and the
foot of the sky.

And all the time vaster and vaster views were unrolling
before me: parts of them in sunlight, and parts in shadow.
Assisi lay under me on my right, a toy town on the knee
of Monte Subasio. Behind me the whole Umbrian vale
from Perugia to Spoleto seemed to be a basin in the
mountains into which one could hurl a stone. And, far
ahead of me, beyond crest after crest, I could see the
mountains of Gubbio, like the grey clouds of England.

Was it exhilarating? It was. Sweat damped my brow,
thirst narrowed my throat, and the air was like mountain
water ministering to both. Flowers peeped everywhere:
cyclamen, scabious, and pimpernel; and when for a little
I tossed off my pack and sat on a rock, feeling the perfect
tramp at last, I saw everywhere the tiny creatures pursuing
their busy day: independent of man, the lizards hurried
over the stones, the snails scaled the leaves, and the

butterflies and gnats drifted about the air. And in this high solitude, for a moment—a very happy moment—I felt my kinship with them all; and not more with the animals than with the plants. Then, slinging my pack again, I rose and toiled onward. And presently a lark opened his song above me; and I felt as free as he, and almost as high.

I sang a little, too. The parts below had been too steep for me to sing lustily (though that had been part of my design), but once I was on these level ridges, it seemed really the best thing to do. I met a pedlar, complete with trestle and tray, who had come over the passes from Gubbio, and he was of the same mind. In his silvery, southern voice he was singing "Ah, che la morte . . ." with more vigour than aptness. We gave each other good-day, for all men are brothers on the mountain tops, whatever they may be in the city. I clambered on to the last pass of all, and here I found a wayside shrine sheltering a fresco, which showed Francis stretching out his arms to the mountains of Gubbio, now fully in view. For in all the Umbrian and Sabine country they mark with such shrines the steps of Francis.

Now I had nothing more to do but to drop down into Valfabbrica. With its toy walls and towers it looked but an hour's descent below me; it proved, of course, to be nearer three hours'. I went down and down through the changing woods, from pine to oak, and from oak to the olive and poplar in the meads. My path all the way was down those stony tracks and twisting stairways worked out for me by the winter rains. In the early afternoon, footsore, aching, and yet alight with the strange exhilaration of fatigue, I tumbled on to the highroad and entered Valfabbrica.

63

Now, had I not the authority of Goad's scholarly work *Franciscan Italy* to show that he had trodden precisely this route before me, I should have supposed that I was the first Englishman to enter Valfabbrica. Much of the population came to study me closer. And, studying, they seemed bemused. I asked them if there was a *trattoria*, or restaurant, and they not only told me where one was to be found, but came too. And, as I passed through the fly-blown bead curtain into the restaurant, they formed a semicircle about the door to watch me order a meal.

The restaurant seemed no less excited than they that a stranger should come in and ask for a meal. The large, fat padrone, his plump wife, and a little hunchback woman converged upon me from different quarters of the small room in search of larger information. I expounded my long walk and my great hunger, and they all undertook, with one voice, to do their best. The padrone hastened out into the street and returned with a couple of steaks in a newspaper; the little hunchback, chattering to herself all the time, went to the back parts and returned with some twigs, which she kindled under a wide "Elizabethan" chimney; the comely housewife set a gridiron on the smouldering sticks and the steaks on the gridiron; the padrone, in the meantime, and to cater for my first urgencies, put before me salt ham, garlicky sausage, coarse bread, and, best of all, a litre of wine; beams, four hundred years old (but painted a salmon pink for better cheer), looked down upon the general activity—and, in truth, there was nothing different in the scene from the days when the beams were new.

Francis, leaving the Bishop's palace, took the road to Gubbio. Tradition sends him over the passes that I had crossed. More than tradition affirms that he sang as he went his favourite Provençal songs. All the biographers tell us that when he left the Bishop's house, he went on his way singing in the French tongue that he loved. And that was why, many times as I climbed, I tried to imagine a voice echoing among these rocks long ago, and wondered what were the words it sang. Which were Francis' favourites from among the Provençal songs of his day? We know that Bernard of Ventadour, Pierre Vidal, Peirol of Auvergne, and other troubadours toured the northern courts of Italy in Francis' most impressionable years, and that their songs swept over the country like the songs of their successors, the dance-band singers of to-day.

Bernard of Ventadour. Francis would have known his more famous compositions. Did he then, full of joy in his new adventure and allegiance, entertain the mountain with:

> No marvel is it if I sing
> Better than other minstrels all,
> For more than they I am Love's thrall
> And all myself therein I fling. . . ?

Or did he perhaps, remembering his own fantasy bride, chant a *chanso* of Jaufre Rudel to his Lady of Tripoli? Or, since Arnaut Daniel was the most celebrated of all the troubadours, did he sing his:

> Softly sighs the April air
>   Ere the coming of the may . . .
>
> Gladness lo! is everywhere
>   When the first leaf sees the day
> And shall I alone despair
>   Turning from sweet love away?

> Something to my heart replies
>   Thou too wast for rapture strung;
> Wherefore else the dreams that rise
>   Round thee when the year is young?

Everything around him as he walked might have suggested this song, because it was April as he came this way. And everything in him, because he was free. Free as the air and the lark overhead. Free to roam the world that unfolded itself in one broad view after another as he came over the crests. And when he sat down to rest on a rock, feeling the perfect tramp at last, and saw, all about him, the little creatures of the earth and the wild flowers, he felt his brotherhood with them as never before. I know he did, because in a small way I had felt it, and, unlike him, I had not given myself that morning with perfect completeness to the Order and Purpose of things. He called that Eternal Order, that ultimate Reality, God, and he believed—later he was to *know*—that it was Love. Does it matter, then, what were the actual words of his songs? Here is the spirit of them, sung, a few years after him, by the Persian Moslem, Jalalu'd Din:

> Thy love has pierced me through and through,
>   Its thrill with bone and nerve entwine.
> I rest, a flute laid on Thy lips,
>   A lute, I on Thy breast recline. . . .

And here it is, sung with great felicity in our own day by Anna Bunston:

> No excuse and no invention
>   Makes me less unworthy Thee,
> No prostration, no pretension
>   Of unique humility,
> But Thy glorious condescension
>   Blazes through my misery,
> And Thy love finds full extension
>   In the nothingness of me.

66

Dark my soul, yet Thou hast sought her,
My night allows Thy day to shine,
Thou the grape art, I the water—
Both together make the wine.
I the clay, and Thou the craftsman,
I the boat and Thou the strand
I the pencil, Thou the draughtsman,
I the harp, and Thou the hand.

This is what was singing in his heart, as he came over the crests and dropped down by the water-courses into Valfabbrica.

CHAPTER VI

I SHALL pass over his visit to Gubbio because its incidents are lost in a fog, and I shall treat lightly of his rebuilding of San Damiano because it is so well known; so that I may come quickly to his finding of the Portiuncula.

When he returned from Gubbio to the old priest of San Damiano he was not in the labourer's clothes. Some unknown friend at Gubbio, the cause perhaps of his journey there, had entered heartily into his plans and readily given him, who must now beg everything, a complete pilgrim's outfit: tunic, belt, sandals, and staff. And I am sure that Francis, in whom the element of make-believe was always strong, got as real a pleasure from putting on these as he had from putting on the banded mail and belted sword of a soldier.

In this kit we may picture him very clearly, because his own convert, Thomas of Celano, has etched for us his portrait with all the care of an enthusiast.

> He was of middle height, inclined to shortness; his face was long and prominent, but of cheerful countenance and kindly aspect; his eyes black, his hair dark, his nose symmetrical, his lips thin and fine, his teeth white and even, his beard black and rather scanty, his hands attenuated with long fingers, and his voice powerful, sweet-toned, clear, and sonorous.

To be to the Eternal Goodness what his right hand is to a man. What was that exalted Intelligence instructing Its right hand to do? Nothing very big as far as he could see, or hear: just to continue his repairing of San Damiano, and to serve the lepers at San Salvatore. From wealthy Assisans he begged stones for the restoration. It was part

of the extremity of his indictment against Society that he
refused, as a general rule, to handle money. Money, we
must remember, had not in his day become the universal
currency it now is, and most services were paid in kind.
Francis, with extraordinary foresight, saw in it a symbol
of enslavement, and, with habitual drama, expelled it as
untouchable. But the people, not sure what to make of
him, because he had strangely impressed them at his trial,
gave him all the material he needed. One or two must
have given him money because we read of his exchanging
it with a priest for stones. And some of his old companions,
stirred to pity or amusement, came jovially down the hill
and joined in the fun of mixing mortar and laying stone
upon stone. They were young too. Francis must have
enjoyed it more than any, because for him it held both play
and service. You may see, unless I am quite in error, the
result of their hard work in the time-darkened walls and the
ancient barrel vaulting of the present chapel of San
Damiano. The same design, the same barrel vaulting, are
seen in all the churches Francis is said to have rebuilt.

A homely little incident shows that the old priest discovered gradually that he loved this lad who had come to
live with him. There is no record of a single person, man
or woman, exalted or lowly, pope or peasant, who, coming
close to Francis, did not love him, even though sometimes
disagreeing with him completely. What was this charm
that once walked in Umbrian ways, and now lies buried
in San Francesco? I can suggest only that to the old
gaiety, impulsiveness, wit, and flattering affectionateness,
he had now added humility and eager service. He won
the heart of the old priest, who began, out of his scanty
means, to take pleasure in surprising him, after the day's
work, with his favourite dishes. At first Francis ate them

with gratitude and a relish, but then, after thought, and protestations of thankfulness, he said, "No. I must go and beg my meals."

Ridiculous? Possibly; but here is the point where Francis has you on the hip: he hadn't the least objection to being ridiculous. To be sure, he couldn't make his challenge in any other way. You cannot indict a civilisation which you believe to be enslaving humanity by methods of common sense or good form. To say nothing of the fact that, from his viewpoint, it was civilisation that was ridiculous, and not Francesco di Pietro Bernardone. No feather-bed preaching for him. Logic might whisper, "Accept the father's kindness, and don't be a fool." Spiritual intuition said, "No, beg, else you are not being faithful to Poverty. This, thou vile son of Pietro Bernardone, is Comfort, not Poverty. Is this to be equal with the lowest? Get out and beg, and purge yourself of the last trace of superiority and softness. To beg is the touchstone of your loyalty to the poorest."

So Francis ate at the father's board only that which he had begged at the doors of his friends, though, in the beginning, this solicitation hurt him more than anything he had set himself to do.

Going too far? Possibly; but wait till you hear the poem he composed about this food given generously. It is the first of his lyrics, and is of three words only. He called all food given in charity "the Lord's table." What did he mean? That God had spread the world with food for His family, but men had turned it into property and fenced it from the poorest; or that, when a man gives generously to the poor, it is the actual love and bounty of God working with his hand? "This is what I call treasure," said Francis to a companion one day, as they sat on a rock by a stream, eating some bread that had been given to them, "when we have nothing but what is given by God's providence, like this table of stone so fine, and this fount so clear, and this bread that we have begged."

Having completed San Damiano—and one likes to think of his pleasure as the last touch was given, to see him stepping six paces back where the courtyard now stands and examining the work with his head on one side —what next? "Francis, repair my church . . ." the voice had said. Well, there was that church of San Pietro which he could restore in the intervals of visiting the lepers. It does not seem to have occurred to him that he should preach, and still less that he should become captain of a band of followers. He restored San Pietro, and then one day—it is really a moment of capital importance— he wandered into the forest which lay on the flat of the valley, and saw a little ruined chapel among the trees: a little oblong stone chamber with a pointed gable at each end. The trees stood all around it, and the grass and the brambles beat up against its crumbling walls.

A page or so back I called this moment his "finding" of the Portiuncula. Actually he may have known it always, but it is just to say that he only found it in this moment when he fell in love with it. We do not discover anything or anyone till we love them. He stood looking at it. Near by were the remains of a small Benedictine settlement, because St. Benedict, seven hundred years before Francis, had seen it (or its predecessor) among the trees, and, believing the legend that it had been built by some pilgrims from Palestine to hold a relic of the Madonna, had cleared a small portion of the forest, settled some of his monks there, and called it St. Mary of the Little Portion.

The name Portiuncula applies really to the little portion of land; the chapel was St. Mary's: either St. Mary of the Portiuncula or, by a later christening, St. Mary of the Angels. But the settlement had long gone back to desolation when Francis came to it, for the Benedictine monks, in these times of warfare, loot, and outlawry, had left it for a new stronghold high upon Mount Subasio.

And there under the trees Francis stood, looking at the old shrine beleaguered by the high grasses and the underbrush—and he knew nothing of the ground on which he was standing. He did not know that within a few years five thousand knights of his army, wearing his peculiar livery, would encamp here to confer with him how best to carry their conquest beyond the confines of Italy, and even beyond the confines of the Catholic world. He did not know that for centuries after him, in the first days of August, the multitudes would come and press in dense, slow-moving throngs towards the chapel, to obtain the Perdono of San Francesco. Nor that the tiny building would be revered for all time as the *caput et mater omnium ecclesiarum universi ordinis Seraphici*, the head and mother church of the universal Seraphic Order.

You may see the chapel now almost exactly as Francis restored it, but all the trees around it have been changed as by an enchantment into lofty columns, and all the grass has given place to a vast cathedral floor, and high above its little gabled roof, shutting out the sky which once looked down upon the clearing, hangs a dome that seems hardly smaller than St. Peter's or St. Paul's. A colossal basilica, built by the piety of the years, now surrounds and enshrines St. Mary of the Little Portion, like a very large casket holding a very small toy. And a sad, lost look has the little field-chapel in those broad, cold, echoing aisles.

In its superb prison it seems to look at you with wistful eyes, as if it wondered what had happened. It is like a woodland creature caged.

Such was the silence of the trees, such was the seclusion of the clearing, that Francis decided at once that here was the ideal estate for Lady Poverty. He would make this shrine, in a very special sense, his own place of worship. Plans tumbled over one another in his head. He would rebuild it, and during the work he would bivouac in the woods at its side. Perhaps he would always make his home here: the quiet and the remoteness were sweet as water to his thirst for solitude, and yet it was not a mile away from his friends the lepers at San Salvatore.

So Francis left the priest of San Damiano and made himself some sort of shelter in the wood and began to rebuild St. Mary of the Little Portion. At night, work ended, he slept beside it.

2

And I, striving to get a little deeper into the thoughts of Francis, went down on to the plain one midnight, when darkness had rubbed out all the buildings that now surround the Portiuncula, and the elms and the vines might have been the trees of the lost forest, and the silence was just as it was when Francis lay down to sleep. Apart from the stars powdering the sky and the lights of Assisi on the distant hill, the things that bore on my senses were the insistent whirring of the grasshoppers, the whistle of the crickets, and the interrupted chatter of the frogs. Now and then a flittermouse shuddered across my eyes, and gradually the strong scent of the trees asked for recognition too.

I thought of Francis lying awake in the forest. Night

is the best teacher of mystery, because day curtains mystery with a veil of light. There would bear in upon him a sense of urgent life, independent of man, moving everywhere around him. It soared upward in the boles of the trees, it beat in the hearts of a million small creatures, it lifted the heads of the grass. The whole earth was pregnant with it. And he would feel the same life pulsing in his own body, and in his head alight with thought; and he would know that it drew from the same source, and that therefore he was one with the trees and the small busy animals and the grass. His merging and continuity with them in one great whole would come in flashes of recognition that were ecstatic in their happiness.

Ecstasy is a large word, but the only true one. The literature describing this cognition, or re-cognition, of one's unity with the universe is almost as wide as the world and as old as a pen. Buddha, Christ, Paul, Plotinus, Mohammed, Dante, Boehme, Pascal, Blake—all speak or write of it, and all who have tried to put the experience upon paper have stated that the flash of knowledge is inseparable from a sense of brilliant light and ineffable bliss. I like to think that, just as the brightness of *self*-consciousness must have visited the animal world in flashes at first, so these flashes of *cosmic* consciousness (as Bucke called it) are tentative visitations of the yet larger and clearer consciousness that all men will possess one day. Do you know the secret document that was found sewn into the clothes of Pascal after his death? Some overwhelming experience must have forced these unrestrained, underlined, excited jottings from Pascal which he desired always to carry about with him but no man ever to see. No modesty of utterance here! He was not minding what critics might say, but caring solely to immesh a memory in words before it escaped him.

> The year of grace, 1654, Monday, 23 Nov. . . . from about half past ten in the evening to about half past twelve midnight, FIRE. . . . Assurance, joy, assurance, feeling, joy, peace. . . . *The sublimity of the human soul.* . . . Joy, joy, joy, tears of joy. . . . I do not separate myself from Thee. . . .

And that Francis was already experiencing such flashes I do not doubt. From now onwards he begins to call all things his brothers and sisters, and not the animals only, but the sun and the soil and the water.

Next I thought of him asleep in the forest. When a man or an animal sleeps in the forest he is indeed one with the life of trees and grass, because, like them, he has no consciousness, but is just a dumb vehicle of life. He may have a faint consciousness of well-being. Is it possible that the trees and the grass have the same?

Then I thought of Francis awaking to the first of the light, as sleepers in the open do. He opens his eyes—and the young body which has been a merely animate and unconscious thing is lit with human consciousness, and with the memory, perhaps, of the flashings of a more splendid consciousness yet to be. The sudden human consciousness will separate him from the purely vegetative unity with all; the other, flashing consciousness will rejoin him to it. We have to ascend, I suggest, from animal consciousness, which is unity without knowledge; through human self-consciousness, which seems a loss of unity but is a preliminary to knowledge; to cosmic consciousness, which is knowledge attained with joy.

And if Francis is our precursor in the attainment of this

75

knowledge, it is fitting that we should see him up with the dawn.

3

One morning he awoke to a vague memory that something pleasant was to happen. That morning Mass was to be said in the chapel of the Portiuncula. Perhaps it was a Mass arranged by himself to celebrate the completion of the building: we do not know. But though, as History now sees, it was a pretty important Mass, no one came near it, except the visiting priest and Francis to serve him as his acolyte. I chose a moment to kneel in that chapel when it was empty, the walls that Francis had built shutting out the encompassing basilica, so that, for all I knew, the forest was back there outside; and I waited till my imagination showed me a young man on the altar steps serving a vested priest who had always been nameless and was now seven hundred years dead.

It was part of Francis' persistent youthfulness that when in doubt he always adopted a method that we used to adopt in our childhood: he would open the Bible at random, or go into a church and listen to the words of a service, in the hope of some private explanation from God. And he nearly always found what he looked for, as indeed we would quite often do. This was St. Matthias' Day, and the priest turned from the altar and read to the single worshipper: "As ye go, preach, saying, The Kingdom of Heaven is at hand. Heal the sick, raise the dead, cleanse the lepers, cast out devils; freely ye received, freely give. Get you no gold, nor silver, nor brass in your purses; no wallet for your journey, neither two coats, nor shoes, nor staff, for the labourer is worthy of his meat. . . ."

Well, we have travelled far enough into the mind of

76

Francis—a mind uncritical and deeply unlearned, and yet despite this, or, rather, partly because of such excellent unencumbered freshness, quite startlingly original and individual—to perceive that every word of this must have sounded as if especially addressed to him. Every bent and bias in his nature turned to it as to a marching order. Joy filled him as it had done when the crucifix instructed him at San Damiano. Mass over, he poured his excitement over the priest, and the priest interpreted the words as best he could, and Francis exclaimed, "This is what I want! To preach and heal and minister, owning nothing but the clothes I stand in, and trusting in the Lord's table to feed me; just as the first disciples did while our Lord was still alive. This is what, with all my soul, I want to do throughout my life."

And there and then, without reservation, modification, or compromise, he kicked off his sandals and cast aside his belt and wallet. He was wearing a long, full smock of undyed serge, which must be girdled somehow, so he picked up a length of rope, possibly the rope he had used for haulage or plumb-line, and tied it loosely about his waist. And so the white cord of the Franciscans, their characteristic garment, came into the world at the door of the Portiuncula chapel. Thus robed and girt, he went out to obey his Master to the last letter of His words. And the old gods trembled.

CHAPTER VII

I

As was natural and naïve, he walked first into Assisi to preach. And probably no one was more surprised than he when, almost from the start, his preaching enjoyed a popular success. He must have felt like some sincere but diffident writer when his first book booms as a best-seller. As with a book, so with his preaching, success beat around it because of its novelty, freshness, passion, and charm. It was novel because it burst at a crack the hard husk of formality which imprisoned the discourses in the churches; it was fresh because, knowing nothing of dogma, it set forth only the love, the gentleness, and the brotherhood of Christ, which the world seemed to have forgotten, and because, unlike the tirades of the lay prophets, it held nothing of wrath for sinners or controversy with the priests, but only companionship and loyalty; it was passionate because the most inveterate scoffer could not doubt the sincerity that rang in that voice or the love that radiated from those eyes; and it had charm because, all unwittingly, Francis was actor, poet, and humorist born, and had, moreover, in his voice, the perfect instrument for his art.

People had never heard anything quite like it. Soon he could move nowhere without a crowd pressing about him as to-day it will press about a film-star. If, as sometimes happened in the beginning, an urchin threw a stone at the barefoot figure, Francis defeated the attack at once with his technique of non-resistance—or, to phrase it more accurately and sufficiently, his immensely potent technique of purely passive resistance: he only smiled on the boy and waited for more; and the crowd, ashamed, yelled their indignation at the little beast, and, in so doing, decided that they were really much nicer than they had supposed; and the boy slunk away, wondering if he had been clever after all; and Francis went on at the point at which he had left off; more certain than ever that his Master was right.

Of course he delighted in his success. What is more, I see signs that, for most of his life, he had to fight the temptations that lurk in popular applause; else what is the meaning of his opening words to the people of Poggio Bustone—surely the pleasantest opening in the whole range of religious oratory: "Dearly beloved, you think I am a very great saint, but I beg leave to tell you that all this Lent I have eaten cakes fried in lard." I repeat, people had not heard this fashion in oratory before.

And then, in addition to all these best-selling qualities, it had the power of words spoken with authority and knowledge. Probably he did not know that his sermons rang with authority. But, rightly or wrongly, the mystic believes, no longer that he accepts God by faith, but that he knows Reality by immediate knowledge; and therefore, let him be never so humble, he cannot argue with you so much as *tell* you; and this knowledge give such force to his words and such power to his personality that, instead of being a vague and ineffectual dreamer (as the hard-headed imagine), he nearly always becomes a man capable of turning his own little world upside down. Consider Paul, Augustine, Francis, Catherine of Siena, Catherine of Genoa, Teresa, Ignatius, George Fox, and Mahatma Gandhi. It is fascinating to study how the best of the mystics contrive, when they are seeing farther than their myopic churches, to harmonise obedience to a well-loved church with the certainty that they are

79

right. On the whole the simplest solution was St. Teresa's: she went on changing her father-confessor, like a housewife changing cooks, till she found one who agreed with her in all things and directed her to do what she wanted.

Francis, all too soon, would have this difficulty to resolve; and its resolution would be his tragedy; but in the meanwhile his path was bright with popular response, and his success was providing a new sensation for Assisi. He was discussed in street and workshop, in booth and bailey and cloister, in the bowers of the ladies and the banqueting-rooms of the rich. No doubt the successful merchants abused him hotly, since his acted challenge made foolish their grammar of money-getting. It was no stuff at all for men who were proud of their financial astuteness, their skill in outwitting their rivals, and their increasing authority in the world. And they must prove that it was stuff and nonsense, for their own peace.

But one of them kept silence. He found that the young preacher's words touched something deep in him: some hunger to give rather than to get, some longing to be done with the pursuit of praise and to be free. The words and the life of old Bernardone's boy were aiming straight at that homesickness for holiness which was in him as in them all, but he, unlike the others, was putting up no shield to keep them out: he let them wound him. His name was Bernard of Quintavalle.

Look at him well, for here, in a sense, is the real founder of the Franciscan Order. A quiet, sober man, who keeps his thoughts to himself; but they are honest thoughts. He has always been honest with his clients, and now he intends to be honest with himself. He allows these new thoughts to mingle most disturbingly with his arithmetic over his ledgers. He has a friend, Peter Cataneo, a doctor of laws and lay canon of the cathedral, and, with the caution of a good business man, he talks the matter over with him, who should be an expert. And, to his surprise and pleasure, Peter confesses to similar emotions within himself, and thereupon, for nearly the whole night (Bernard enjoyed these all-night sittings), they discussed young Bernardone and the faint, lovely, beckoning light he had raised before them.

"But is he genuine? Is he saint or charlatan?" That was the recurring question. And at last this shrewd and circumspect trader resolved to put the young man to the test. On Francis' genuineness what a world of consequences will turn! How crucial always is this question of the leader's sincerity! He invited Francis to come into his house and stay the night so that he could tell him all his ideas, and Francis, inevitably touched by this encouragement from so prominent a burgess, accepted with joy. (In my picture you can see at the bottom of the street facing you, behind the white oxen, the wall of Bernard of Quintavalle's house. Just to the right, out of your view, is the door of the house.) Francis went through the door of Bernard's mansion, and the door closed behind them.

And behind that door they had one of Bernard's all-night sittings, or nearly so; and when at last they retired to sleep, the host, of set purpose, showed his guest to a bed in his own room. Once in their beds they carried on the friendly argument, as good friends will. And then Bernard pretended to fall asleep. And Francis waited till he was sure Bernard was asleep (he wasn't), and then got out of his bed and knelt down and prayed. He was both uplifted and humiliated that God should have used him to quicken the soul of this good man. In gratitude, in humility, in passionate affirmation that he would try to be a worthy tool in God's hand, he said only—and he said it over and over again—"My God and my All." And Bernard was watching. And when Francis, in his earnestness, let the words leave his lips aloud, Bernard heard them. "My God and my All."

Then, I suppose, both slept. And in the morning Bernard said to him, "I have come to a decision. I want to join you if you will let me, and to live exactly the life you are living."

What? Francis stared at his host. What, live the life of a wandering and penniless preacher?

"Yes," said Bernard simply.

But it would mean dispensing all his wealth: selling all his property and giving the proceeds to the poor.

"Well, why not?" said Bernard.

Was he really ready to do this?

"Yes."

Surely this moment, the first in which a man accepted the truth of his message and offered himself without stint, was one of the sweetest of Francis' life. He must have known an exultation like that which came with the leper's kiss.

And this was not all. While Francis stayed silent and staring, Bernard told him that Dr. Peter Cataneo, the lay canon at the cathedral, was only waiting to hear Bernard's decision before throwing up all and joining Francis too.

Peter Cataneo! A man of learning! Another man of importance in his native city! To follow *him*! It is good to see that the young man was a little frightened.

"This is too big a thing for me to decide," he said.

"I tell you what we will do. To-morrow morning you and Peter and I will go into a church and ask God to direct us, and then we will open the Bible and see what it says."

"Very good," agreed Bernard. "Let us go and find Peter and tell him."

Peter agreed to the plan; and early the next morning these three went up the narrow road of my picture, which leads from Bernard's house to the great piazza, crossed the corner of the piazza to the nearest church of San Niccolo, and went in. It was empty, and they knelt and prayed for guidance. Then Francis, leaving the two on their knees, approached the altar and opened the Gospel book. It was the first time he had acted as a leader. He opened it at a venture and dropped his eyes on the page for the first words that should meet them. He read:

> If thou wilt be perfect, go sell what thou hast, and give to the poor, and thou shalt have treasure in heaven.

Only coincidence, perhaps; let him try again. With trembling hand he opened a second time and read:

> If any man will come after me, let him deny himself and take up his cross and follow me.

Yet a third time. If a third time he met such fitness, then certainly God was speaking. He opened the book a third time and read:

> And he commanded them that they should take nothing for the way.

Radiant with conviction, he turned towards Bernard and Peter and said, "Brothers, this is our life and Rule, for ourselves and for all others who may join our company. Will you then go out and sell all, and we will give the proceeds to the poor?"

Bernard and Peter rose to obey the first order ever issued in the Franciscan brotherhood.

The Franciscan brotherhood was born. Up till yesterday Francis had desired no more than to be a lonely knight-errant of Christ, going about and doing good. But Bernard of Quintavalle, by asking if he might come too, had set afire in his romantic head the conception of a whole Order of Knights who would be sworn to do the same.

2

A report flying through the streets of Assisi: "Young Francis has summoned the poor into the Piazza San Giorgio and he is giving them money. Bernard of Quintavalle and Dr. Peter Cataneo have sold all their property and they are helping to distribute the proceeds. Come and see."

What a crowd in the piazza! A crowd of snatching recipients and astounded watchers. Bernard of Quintavalle! Peter Cataneo! Francis rejoicing to give away their property! Was madness abroad?

Yes, Francis was enjoying the day. We catch his gaiety from the records, for they tell how a priest named Sylvester came up to him and said, "If you've all that money to give away, young man, you might have given me a better price for those stones I sold you for your building"; and how Francis, immediately bringing into play his passive resistance, picked up handfuls of coins and thrust them on the unprepared priest, saying, "There you are, Messer Priest! Are you satisfied now?" Much surprised, somewhat shaken, Sylvester went away with the money in his sack and some strange thoughts in his head.

Those stones of the Piazza San Giorgio that watched all

84

this jostle and clamour, under the morning sun!. They have seen so much of the life of Francis. They saw him as a boy coming across the square to learn his letters with the good fathers of San Giorgio. They saw him ride out with the young knights to join Walter of Brienne. They saw him preaching and distributing to the poor. One evening they saw a multitude of Assisans in procession, coming towards the church of San Giorgio with candles and trumpets and olive branches, mourning yet triumphant, as they brought the body of their own saint to lay it here till a greater home should be built. Two years after, they saw a larger multitude: people massed on the square, people packed on coronation stands hung with coloured cloths, people crowding at the windows and in the loggias and on the roofs, and all to watch the Pope on his throne in the square, with cardinals, bishops, and abbots around him, as he pronounced the canonisation of their father Francis in heaven. Did the wise old stones know something of this as they watched Francis so blithely dispensing the property of his friends? Or, simpler and yet grander, did they think that just round the corner dwelt a daughter of the Scefi, now fifteen years old, and did they perhaps observe her in the crowd, watching the scene too? Did they know that she too would be brought with procession and pomp to rest for ever in a new church on the site of San Giorgio, and to give to their square its new name of Piazza Santa Chiara? Clare, the sister and partner of Francis! The bodies of these two guard their native city between them, Clare sleeping in her huge church on its eastern bastion, and Francis in a fane like a fortress against its western gate.

Their last penny handed out, Francis, Bernard, and Peter, these three rich men, walked down the hill. No longer could they be possessed by their possessions; they were free to possess the world. Free to be simple and original, to escape from mediocrity and achieve individuality. Happiness and well-being put a spring into their stride as they went down through the fields to the Portiuncula.

At the Portiuncula they made themselves a temporary shelter; only temporary because, though they might think of the Portiuncula as their headquarters, they had no intention of delaying there: their idea was to roam the world preaching, and either to earn their night's lodging by manual labour or to beg it—or in summer nights to sleep in caves or beneath the sky. Scholars dispute whether they made this shelter by restoring one of the old Benedictine ruins or by building a new home of boughs and branches daubed with mud; but whichever it was, what fun they must have had!

And while they bivouacked here for a while, since their apostolate must begin in their home county, a sturdy young fellow came through the trees, asking to see Francis. His coarse tunic and rough *chausses* showed that he was of lower rank than Bernard, Peter, or Francis: he was, in fact, the son of a struggling farmer, and his daily labour was in the fields. But the flying story of these three rich men had come to him in his fields, and he had meditated on it as he plied his spade or his fork, or chewed a grass in his time of repose. And now, coming to Francis, he expressed the issue of his thoughts in an action as simple as his daily work: he dropped to his knees before him and said, "Brother Francis, I have been thinking over all that you and the other gentlemen are doing, and I want, if you will have me, to be one of you."

86

ROAD FROM BERNARD OF QUINTAVALLE'S HOUSE

HOUSE AND GARDEN OF ANGELO TANCREDI

I question if Francis had a better moment than this. Can we doubt that tears brimmed his eyes as he lifted the young fellow up and said gently, "My brother, this is a wonderful thing that has happened to you. You ought to be very proud. If the Emperor had come to Assisi and chosen you out of all its citizens to be his knight and chamberlain, how the others would have envied you! How much more thrilling it is that God has wanted you!" (Ever in that romantic head stalked the knights!) "Now, come along." And leading him to Bernard, he said, "See, Bernard, what a good brother the Lord has sent us."

Such was the coming of Giles, the ploughboy, who was to be one of the raciest and most famous of all Franciscans.

The next to come through the trees, doing violence to enter the kingdom, was a shock to them all. But a shock of pleasure. Francis opened his eyes wide. Bernard and Peter stared. Giles wondered. It was Sylvester, the priest: Sylvester who had never stopped thinking since Francis with a laugh had poured all that money into his sack. Humbly he asked if he might be one of their company.

Sylvester, and he a priest! To Francis' playboy mind what a thrill to think that his order might now have its own priest! I imagine that he expressed a hope that he hadn't hurt Sylvester by his laughing rebuke in the piazza, and that he was at once delighted and embarrassed when Sylvester said, No, it was that action, and that scene in the piazza, which had made him ashamed of his covetousness and started him on the road to this great and final decision. Francis heard the sincerity in his voice, and accepted him joyously. And Sylvester went back to liquidate his small property and resign his position in

Assisi—and one almost wishes that that attractive little town might be spared any more sensations for a time.

Francis had now a squadron of four good knights; and mark what a variety of professions had yielded them up to him. A merchant, a doctor of laws, a ploughboy, and a parson. Intimation, is it not, that in men of every type there is a sediment of sanctity which only waits for its disturber. To Francis, filled with this conviction, what boundless hopes must have come now! One had but to show Christ properly, and the people came running. Let them hurry out to the work, then. Let them press farther afield and see what would happen.

They organised their first considerable mission; Francis going one way with the ploughboy, who was now very dear to him; and the great men, the learned men, going the other. So, barefoot and singing lustily, he and Giles went along the white, dusty roads and over the stony mountain tracks into the Marches of Ancona—but it is not on this journey that I want you to follow him. I want you to see him next in the Vale of Rieti.

CHAPTER VIII

I

IN my search for illumination I visited Florence and Rome, but it is little of these beautiful, purse-proud, imperious cities that you will get from me, for they have really (let us be frank) little use for Francis except as a statue; and it is a parable that all I could find of Francis in Florence was his threadbare habit in the pompous baroque church of the Ognissanti. But the Vale of Rieti! On this lofty tableland, and on the mountains that encircle it, the spirit of Francis walks still. The people there nurse his memory, because they remember how he loved them.

Like the Vale of Spoleto, the Vale of Rieti was once a lake-floor: it is the next lake-floor in the mountains as you go south towards Rome; but it is much higher up and much smaller, so that its mountains seem to close it round in an oval ring. Its one big town is Rieti, at its southern end, and Rieti is small and individual enough to be lovable. Round the town of Rieti, high on the mountain slopes, guarding it as if they were outposts, stand the hermitages that Francis founded, each holding its legends proudly: Greccio, Fonte Colombo, La Foresta, and Poggio Bustone.

I went and lived a little in Rieti, since it and its valley meant so much to Francis; and soon I knew why he loved these highland people. I felt the smiling courtesy, the simple fidelity, and the virile authenticity of them. I found it easy to believe that Rieti had produced Angelo Tancredi, who, of all the first followers of Francis, was most renowned for his courtesy, and the inferior of none in his loyalty.

Angelo will appear often in our tale, because he became

one of a group of four who stayed about their master like a bodyguard. They were at his side in every sorrow; they supported him with their unbreakable faith when his Order fell away from him; they were with him when the terrible thing happened on La Verna; they sang to him "by request" when he was dying; they fought his battle after he was dead; and they sleep now around his tomb, one at each corner, guarding him still. Leo, Angelo, Rufino, and Masseo; and the first three of them were the Three Companions who wrote his "legend" that the world might know him as they had known him.

Angelo Tancredi, when Francis found him, was a knight of some position and wealth, one of those enthusiastic young men whom Francis could always win. He met him in a street in Rieti. I do not know which spoke first, but soon these two young men, while the traffic went by, were discussing their ideals; and Francis began to chaff him. "Don't you think," said he, "that you have worn that belt and sword, and those fine spurs long enough? What about changing the belt for this rope, the sword for the Cross, and the spurs for the dust and stones of the road?" Oh, like Garibaldi, Francis knew how to appeal to heroic youth. "I do not offer you comfort and glory," said Garibaldi. "I offer you danger, starvation, disease, and death. Who follows?" Such a call is irresistible to young spirits of Angelo Tancredi's temper. Angelo followed.

His house, they told me, was still in Rieti, but it was now the house of an enclosed order of Franciscan nuns, and it was hidden from access and sight by the long, blank wall of an outer building facing the street. No man was allowed past the door of that outer building, and Angelo Tancredi's house within was the most secluded place in the town. This sharpened my desire to see it, and to make a picture of it, and I asked them if they thought it at all possible that a stranger, by guile or privilege, might penetrate that outer bulwark. The only possible way, they said, would be to get a special licence from the Bishop of Rieti himself.

Well, one could but try, so I sent word into the Bishop's palace that a pilgrim lover of Francis, English and alas Protestant, but anxious none the less to stand wherever the saint was known to have stood, begged permission to visit the house of Angelo Tancredi. And that, I feared, would be the end of the matter. But within an hour an answer came to my lodging that, if I would come into the palace, the Bishop would be pleased to take me there himself. Kind, simple courtesy of Rieti! I hurried to the palace and, while waiting in a large, bare room, remembered that I was in the very house, though it was much changed now, where a previous Bishop of Rieti, no less hospitable, had sheltered and tended Francis in his last sickness.

The Bishop, a short, swart, Southern man, in cassock, cape, and pectoral cross, came in to me; and after a brief exchange of explanations, in which he was much more fluent that I, he led me out into the street. We walked at a high speed, for the Bishop was an active little man; and the women and children dropped on one knee to kiss his hand as it blew by; just as they did to Francis when he walked among them in these streets. We came to the long, blank windowless building that hid the house of Angelo, and to tall, stout doors in its midst, forbidding as the doors of a prison. The Bishop pulled the bell-handle, and the bell sounded in an echoing emptiness behind. No one answered. He pulled a second and a third time, mumbling under his breath a continuous commentary which I could not hear and translate; and at last a portress drew back the doors and, seeing the Bishop, kissed his hand. We passed into a vestibule, and went and stood opposite an interior window which might have been the window of a station booking-office if it hadn't been guarded by a double grille. A blind shot up behind the grating, and the sweet face of a nun looked out. At sight of the Bishop she dropped on one knee; at sight of the less holy man with him she dropped her veil. The Bishop explained me to her, whereupon she summoned two other sisters (for further protection, I presumed) and, unhooking her keys, turned the lock of a door and let us in.

Now began a procession through the whole of Angelo's house and garden. It is the procession I want to describe, and not the house, which looked much like any other large Italian mansion and, to tell the truth, very little like the Giottesque houses of the thirteenth century. First went one sister, with her veil down and a little bell in her hand. Next went another sister, with her hands folded beneath her scapular. Next came the sister who had opened to us, with the Bishop at her side, and both chatting volubly; and lastly, climax and justification of it all, came the heretic, something shyly. At every corner the sister in front rang a pretty little tinkle on her hand-bell, and, as we turned the corners, we would see one young sister, or perhaps two, in the corridor who immediately dropped their veils, picked up their heavy brown skirts, and ran— ran breathlessly to cover like small brown rabbits. We went upstairs and downstairs and out into the pleasant garden; and, at every tactical point, the leading sister rang her warning tinkle; and the frivolous, unconsecrated man, if he was lucky, saw some little sister in the path of danger drop her veil, pick up her skirts, and scuttle in panic. After the bell had sounded three or four times the large house took on the silence of a mausoleum. One felt that nothing was to be heard anywhere except the beating of hearts which knew that a threat walked abroad.

I have never felt so important in my life. But I still do not understand it. They could not have supposed that I, so carefully guarded, and in the presence of the Bishop, would have attempted any light behaviour; and it could not be, surely, that I was desirable.

But thank you, dear sisters, and bless you: you gave me a vision of your sacredness, and you have a big place among the things that made me love your Rietan vale. Lord Bishop, my gratitude and my deep respect.

Greccio and Fonte Colombo loom larger in the later years of Francis, and we shall come in due time to them and their stories. It is the village of Poggio Bustone that stands high in the year 1209—as high as it stands upon its mountain spur above the pleasant vale. Stands, did I say? The verb should better be hangs, or adheres, or slips, or scrambles. Like Assisi, it scrambles on the knee of a mountain, but the knee in this case seems very near the chin, and the little white town seems much less securely fixed. At night, when the mountain behind is absorbed into the dark sky, the lights of Poggio Bustone look like stars. The road winds up to it in an unending spiral, and, when you reach its walls, if you turn and look below, it may be that you will not see the feet of the mountain, because they are under the blue mist.

Up this winding road, in the year 1209, came Francis in his grey-brown habit and cord. And as he passed through the walls into the village the people came running out to

93

learn what this portent might be. And with a smile he gave them the greeting, "Good morning, good people."

They have never forgotten that first salute. To-day near the centre of the village you can see a white stone in a wall and read:

BUON GIORNO, BUONA GENTE
Saluto rivolto da San Francesco
entrando a Poggio Bustone
nel 1209

And if you are in Poggio Bustone on the 4th of October, which is observed throughout Italy as the anniversary of his death, and if you are in the street early enough, you will see a man with a tambourine going from house to house and knocking at each door, and calling to the people within, " Buon giorno, buona gente."

"Good morning, good people." Had this book not been one of a series, with its title prescribed, I should certainly have called it by these words. They haunt me as the meaning of it all.

Manifestly here were people after Francis' own heart. It is said that they were lost in sin as the time, but that would only have made them more after his heart. And, whatever their weaknesses, they were affectionate as children and quite ready to be improved. Like their Rietan brothers in Greccio across the vale, they begged Francis to stay with them and see if he could rid them of their beastliness and make them good. (True history this: no novelist's trimmings. And at this point let me state that every incident in this book is culled from the early biographies, from Thomas of Celano, The Three Companions, Bonaventura, the *Speculum Perfectionis*, and

94

the Chronicle of the Twenty-Four Generals. And that every incident enjoys the warranty of many of the scholars. All the dialogue except in the few places where I have confessed to some guesswork, comes from the recorded conversations of Francis and his friends. Only the interpretation and the "imagining" of the scenes are mine; the work of a novelist, perhaps, but more, I hope, the work of a lover.)

These Rietan, or Sabine, peasants asked him to stay and make them good. The desire for goodness was in them as it was in Bernard and Peter and Giles. And Francis, lifting his gaze to the mountain above them, knew that here was a solitude where he would be happy to dwell. The call of the mountain to the mystic is universal: if Francis saw a mountain close to his work, he climbed as near as possible to its peak so that he might escape for a while from the vineyards and the orchards and the earthbound occupations of men. Think of Poggio Bustone, Greccio, Fonte Colombo, and, greatest of all, La Verna. If it is fair to say of Francis, who loved the whole secular world, that there were two things in it that he loved more than all others, then those two things were mountains and music.

He clambered up Poggio Bustone's mountain to the highest point he could reach, and there found a recess or grotto where he could live and be alone. And seven hundred and twenty-eight years after him I climbed the same way behind a figure in the same brown habit and cord. The friar in front of me was Padre Augusto de Carolis, *parroco* of Poggio Bustone, who, with Rietan courtesy, had insisted on leaving his house in the village to guide me up the steep path to the grotto. This stony track twisted and turned between the brush of hornbeam that

95

mantled the lower slope of the mountain. It swung round boulders of grey stone, pearl-grey as Quaker girls, and sagged under the branches of dwarf sycamores, ashes, and oaks. Sun-bleached mountain flowers bordered it everywhere. After every fifteen minutes of climb we came upon a tiny shrine which commemorated some miracle of Francis on this spot; but acceptance of these legends is obligatory upon none, and to most of us the miracle will lie in the love which marks the path of goodness with shrines.

As we got higher we looked down into the deep, dry gorge beneath the village, and heard the wind rushing down it like the ghost of last year's water. And Poggio Bustone, which from the plain had seemed so high up, now looked almost level with the floor. We toiled on, and at length, almost at the line where the brushwood met the naked peaks, we came upon the little Santuario which walls in the grotto of Francis.

Because of something that happened to Francis here, it is important that you should turn as I did and observe the view. The whole vale lay outspread beneath us: a flat, oval floor, ringed round with mountains. There across the vale was the little hermitage of Greccio, high up above a tilted amphitheatre in the hills. A little to the south of it was Fonte Colombo, hidden in a thick mountain grove. Everything in the large view—the infinitesimal villages below, the luxuriant plenty covering the earth, the darkness in the gorges, the spread of the lakes, the sweep of the birds, and the glow beyond the mountains—everything, for a man like Francis, newly alight with loyalty to God, was such as to overawe him with the greatness of his Master and the littleness of himself.

And here, accordingly, after a period of contemplating

God, and while men were busy in the village far below, Francis, poised as it were between both, was overwhelmed by a feeling of inadequacy, futility, and despair. He sickened as he remembered his past life: its sins of selfishness and disunion seemed dark indeed against the pure wholeness of Love. And he knew that the old selfish urges were within him still. Vanity and ambition were only a little way below the surface. Were they not, perhaps, defiling the springs of his obedience now? How could he ever be what he wanted to be? Against the perfection of God, against the perfection of holiness he longed for in himself, how skimped and inadequate, how weak and unshapely, was the pattern he had created so far! It hurt, repelled, the artist in him, the lover, and the saint. Imperfection, hopeless imperfection. . . . Here is the same boy who stood by the gate of Assisi.

Do not be so dull-sighted as to call him morbid. When you have seen the goodness of God, you may judge him: not before. Beware lest by morbidity you mean only something stranger than mediocrity; and by normality something less than daring. He flung himself upon his knees and prayed. "O God, be merciful to me, a sinner. . . . Purify me, purify me, purify me that I may handle Thy work. My dearest Lord, I want to love Thee. My Lord and my God, I give Thee my heart and my body, and would wish, if I knew how, to do still more for the love of Thee."

And, suddenly, the whole experience turned right over. Diffidence turned into confidence, despair into elation, guiltiness into the rushing certainty that his sins were forgiven. He knew that God was within him and that therefore he must win. Catholics and Protestants alike will recognise the experience and call it *justification*. Jumping up, he stood looking rather breathlessly at the wide prospect of the world. Assurance of success abounded in him like the exhilaration after wine: he felt—but let us have it in his own words, as he told it to his brothers.

My most beloved [he said], be comforted, rejoice, and do not be sad because you seem so few. And do not let my imperfections, nor yours, frighten you any more, because the Lord has shewn me that He will increase us into a great multitude and spread us over the earth. It is because I want you to be encouraged that I am compelled to tell you what I have seen. I had rather be silent, but my love compels me to speak. I have seen a great multitude of men coming to us and desiring to put on our habit, and their sound is in my ears as they come and go under the orders of holy obedience. I have seen the roads from all the nations full of men coming into these parts: the French are coming, the Spaniards are hastening, and the English run. . . .

The English run. To Francis in 1209 the year 1937 must have seemed as remote as the year 2660 to me, and yet in that year I, having come from England, stood upon the very spot where he filled with the assurance that I should be there—and you, too, for in reading this you have run in the spirit to the same place.

I think that Francis in his joy stretched out his arms to the wide, rolling world before him.

2

It is no infrequent experience to find, on returning from one's travels, that trouble is waiting for one at home. Francis returned to find hostility rampant around the Portiuncula.

The vested interests of Assisi, from laughing contemptuously, had now got very angry about this mad business in the forest. To have men of rank and substance giving all their property to the poor, instead of to their families; to have young men refusing their inheritance and defying their parents (for more had joined Francis now); to have them going about in peasant costume and either begging for their food or earning it by menial labour—all this was becoming too serious altogether. It was a threat to every institution they held dear. It was subversive; and something must be done about it. Bishop Guido must be approached and told to keep these amateur evangelists in order.

The appeal to Guido plunged him into perplexity. It threw the various parts of his character into uncomfortable conflict. We have called him kind, affectionate, commonplace, and litigious. Well, kind and affectionate, he loved Francis, who would come and pour out his ambitions to him; practical and of commonplace mind, he did really think the young man was going too far; litigious, he didn't fancy these old fools teaching him his business or trying to curtail the activities of the Church; but legalist, he suddenly remembered that Francis, an unauthorised layman, had no right to preach at all! Yes, he must have the young man up to the palace and explain *that* to him.

So, hearing that Francis had returned from Rieti, he sent an invitation to him to come to the palace. Francis came readily. And in some room in that palace there occurred an interview between Guido and Francis which is noteworthy, since it differentiates so well the characters of these two.

Tenderly the Bishop pointed out to the youthful enthusiast that some of his activities were illegitimate. And Francis was amazed. As ignorant of canon law as of theology, he had never supposed that by going about and

99

copying Christ in every detail he had been behaving most irregularly. And he was most anxious to be an obedient son of the Church. He was perfectly ready to be good. What must he do to put himself in order? Get the consent of Rome? If that were all, he'd go to Rome to-morrow. He and his brothers would all go. He'd seek an audience of the Holy Father himself——

The Bishop arrested the impetuous flow. A worrying assault upon the Pope seemed as unwise and impracticable to Guido as it seemed simple to Francis. Here was the opportunity to begin reasoning with the lad. Didn't Francis think, he asked, that his ideal of living without any property at all was a little extravagant? Surely one must have some sort of security against to-morrow. What if people ceased to give in charity? What if he and his brothers fell sick and couldn't earn their supper or bed? The thing wasn't practicable; it wasn't common sense. Nobody admired more than he the ardour that was inspiring the brothers, but surely they could find a vent for it in one of the ancient monastic orders. Why not seek admission into the Benedictine Order? He would use all his influence——

"My lord Bishop," said Francis—and if you understand his fine answer, I need say little more to justify his emphasis on poverty, "if we had possessions we should need weapons to defend them. Possessions produce quarrels and law-suits, and these are the opposite of the love of God and our neighbour. For this reason I and my brothers, who desire to live only in love, are resolved to own no property whatever in this world. We are going to trust completely in God to provide us with a roof at night and food by day."

And the Bishop, listening, remembered that at that very

time he was engaged in litigation with the Crucigeri of San Salvatore and with the Benedictines of Monte Subasio. And that both these were fellow-workers with him in a gospel of love. He could answer nothing.

Francis went back to his brothers. He was full of a plan for a March on Rome. The whole brotherhood, now twelve in number, would march to the capital and lay their policy before the Holy Father. Twelve of them! Was there not a good omen here? With no clear idea, probably, as to whether he was playing at apostles or at soldiers, the Captain gave the order to march.

No baggage-train was needed for this company on the march: no tents or stores or mess-float. It was the lightest expedition that ever advanced on Rome. With bare heads and bare feet, in their grey-brown frocks and cords, laughing and chaffing, they took the road that countless armies had taken before them, in the course of two thousand years. They were men in a new uniform, bringing a new idea.

One can hear them talking as they go. One can hear Francis, because he was the real creative mind, talking more than any of the others.

Now, then, what is our Rule going to be? What is it we are asking the Pope to sanction? Eh, Lord Bernard, what do you say? In what way are we different from the old Orders? Peter, you're the only lawyer among us; Sylvester, you're the only holy man; tell us. As I see it, it's this: first and foremost, we want to imitate the life of Christ and to carry out His commands exactly, abating none of them and explaining none of them away. We want to see what will happen if a few brothers really get together and do this. Secondly, we desire to be equal with the lowest, and this means that we want no property beyond our

tunic and our cord, since anything more we must regard
only as a loan till we find someone poorer than ourselves.
What's more, as I said to the Bishop, property would
almost certainly entangle us in quarrels, and that would
separate us from our brothers and destroy our teaching.
And in any case we probably couldn't keep it if we had it,
since Christ has commanded us, if a man take half of it,
to give him the other half; which we should most certainly
do. So, you see, as I've always said, for us poverty is
cardinal. The Lady Poverty is our guardian angel.
Which reminds me, what are we going to call ourselves?
The Poor Men of Assisi. No, that's been done before.
There were the Poor Men of Lyons who seceded into
heresy and opposition to the Church; we mustn't get
likened to them, because we're going to be the most loyal
sons the Church ever had. The Brothers of the Poor?
The Brothers of the Lowest? Wait! I believe I have it!
In the lawyer's documents the big men of the cities are
called *majores*—that's so, isn't it, Dr. Peter?—and the
humble men whose business is to serve are called *minores*.
The Lesser Brothers. *Fratres Minores*. Friars Minor. That
is our title—how will that do, my lord knight, Angelo?

And all agreed that it would do.

Throughout the journey we detect this note of laughter
covering seriousness. They are twelve men. Such a host
should have a leader: which is it going to be? Why, you,
Francis, of course. No, I am among you as he that
serveth. Bernard—Brother Bernard is the man. He is a
great man, a steady man, and the first of us all. Bernard,
we elect you our leader and Vicar of Christ: where you
tell us to go, there, by holy obedience, we go; and where
you tell us to stop, there, by holy obedience, we lie down
and sleep.

POGGIO BUSTONE

HERMITAGE OF THE CARCERI

And all acclaimed Bernard as their leader, and forced him into the captaincy, and went on their way, singing.

And so by Spello, Clitumnus, Spoleto, Terni, and the friendly Vale of Rieti, to Rome.

But if Bernard had been their leader on the march, there could be no question, once in Rome, who was to represent them before the Pope. Francis was their creator and prophet: he must be their spokesman. And so Francis, leaving them in the broad piazza before the Lateran Palace, approached the door.

Within the palace the Pope was walking up and down a corridor. Let us consider him, Pope Innocent III, in this last minute before the little spare man in his habit and cord contrives an entrance and comes along the corridor.

Here is the great Duce who has arisen within the Church to lead it to its largest empire. Pope at thirty-seven, so resplendent was his early career, he is even now only forty-nine. The son of a German noble and a high-born Roman lady, he hides within his cassock the heart of a German warrior and beneath his cap the mind of a Roman statesman. A student of Bologna and Paris, he is lawyer, theologian, and schoolman. Handsome, elegant, courtly, and imperious, he does not forget that, before they called him Innocent, his old German name was Lothair.

A little while past we looked at Charlemagne. I dare assert that we are now looking at the greatest power in the world since that golden-haired, seven-foot emperor. "Perhaps no man," says Father Cuthbert, "has ever been the ruler of the world as Innocent was." By force and guile he has subdued those mutinous burghers of Rome and captured the mastery of the papal city. By organising the Guelph party into a powerful tool of the papacy he has driven the German overlords from their

castles in Central Italy or reduced them to vassalage. As
we have seen, he has sent his armies south to capture the
Two Sicilies. In his character of guardian he will put the
young Emperor, Frederick, into his pocket. All the other
kings, or nearly all of them, he has tamed or is about to
tame. The king of Aragon has admitted his vassalage.
The kings of Portugal, Leon, Castile, and Hungary have
been, or are to be, rebuked and disciplined. To-morrow
our own John of England will be compelled to write, "To
our lord Pope Innocent and his successors we yield up all
our kingdom of England and all our kingdom of Ireland
to be held as a fief of the Holy See." He has put the
Eastern Empire into his pocket too. A few years ago he
preached a crusade against the Holy Land, and when the
quarrelsome crusaders turned north and attacked Constantinople, a Christian city, he reprimanded them, of
course, but a statesmanlike preoccupation with other
things hindered him from more drastic steps till they had
captured and sacked the city. Good could be wrought
out of evil, and, taking a long view, surely it was good that
Latin and Catholic warriors should be capturing the
heretical Empire of the East. The conquest achieved,
he suddenly recovered from his abstraction, accepted the
fait accompli, and with a sigh at the vindictiveness of men
bestowed the imperial purple upon a Count of Flanders.

He is overthrowing the spiritual enemies of the Church
as energetically as the temporal. In Provence, land of the
troubadours, home of the most elegant civilisation since
Athens, where intellect has brightened and claimed its
freedom, and criticism stalks abroad, his armies are
delivering, with flame and pillage and slaughter, the
chastisement of his fatherly love. There is a damnable
heresy in those parts—the Albigensian heresy—which

dares to say that Good and Evil split the world between them, that the God of the Old Testament is not the good God, and, worse yet, that the priestcraft of the Roman Church is witchcraft and its sacraments a mockery. Innocent has not spared it : he has mobilised all the power of the Church for a Holy War. It is going well. The heretics who have resisted hotly, like the traitorous poison they are, are being exterminated—liquidated, as we now call it. The lust for liquidation is exuberant in the Provençal clergy themselves. The Abbot Arnold at the sacking of Beziers, when asked by the papal infantry how they are to distinguish Catholics from heretics, cries, " Slay all! Slay all! God will know His own." This, be it noted, is in the same year in which, many hundred miles away, a youth in a tumbledown chapel hears a voice say, "Repair my church, which, as you see, is falling into ruin." In a few years the crusade will have triumphed, the gay, laughing culture of the troubadours will lie beneath the ruins of Provence, freedom of faith and criticism will lie dead with it, and the Inquisition will sit upon the ashes to consolidate the power of Innocent.

Such is the man who paces the corridor in thought, Innocent III, greatest and strongest of the popes, as the world measures greatness and strength.

And now there is someone at the door. Steps are coming along the corridor. The handsome and still-youthful Pope lifts his head from his large cares, and sees approaching him a little smocked and barefoot figure, eager but frail. And for a second they look each other in the face, these two ; and the great contrast stands before us again : the man who would command all, and the man who would serve all ; the one who desires to be the greatest of the *majores*, and the one who asks to be the least of the *minores* ; the man who believes with all his heart in holy force, and the man who knows it to be the weakest weapon in the world. The storm, and the still, small voice.

Innocent stares at his visitor. In his surprise he listens for a half-minute. He hears something about a new order of Brothers Minor who would like his blessing. By the Mass and the Madonna! To him, who has forced the loyalty of all the kings of the world, comes this pitiful and preposterous figure offering his loyalty! Is it to be wondered at—nay, can we who are often unpardonably peevish when disturbed at important work, blame a great Pope that he told his interrupter to "go and roll in the mire with his pigs."

Which, of course, was an unfortunate phrase, since, had he but understood, this was exactly what Francis was asking his permission to do.

But clearly the moment was inopportune: the Holy Father was vexed. Francis turned round and went back along the corridor.

3

But this first encounter had expressed neither the whole of Innocent nor the whole of Francis. Innocent, though spiritually blind compared with Francis, was a much finer and cleverer man than such incivility suggests. And as for Francis, if his technique was one of "no resistance," it was equally certainly one of "no retreat." Once when he asked the Bishop of Imola's permission to preach in his diocese, his lordship answered crossly, "Thank you, but I can do my own business without any help from you." (How constant is human nature!) Without a word of argument Francis drew his cowl over his head and, walking out, left the Bishop an hour in which to cool. Then he returned, and the Bishop cried angrily, "What's this? Why have you returned?" "Because," said Francis, "if a father sends his son out by one door, there is nothing left for him but to return by another." And the Bishop took him and embraced him and told him that he could preach wherever he liked.

So Francis, when he left the Pope's presence, had no intention of giving in. He looked about him. And who should he stumble upon in the Lateran Palace but the good Bishop of Assisi; a meeting which we can be sure he regarded as personally arranged by God. Guido, as we are expressly told, thought differently. His first feeling was one of annoyance that the rash young fool should really have arrived to worry the Pope. Who on earth did he think he was? Besides, he belonged to his own jurisdiction of Assisi, and he wanted his work, which was undeniably successful (let the bigwigs of his city say what they liked) reserved for his own diocese. But Francis could always twist Guido round his fingers, and when he poured out to him, as to his one father and counsellor, the tale of his rebuff, the Bishop's heart was touched, and he decided to use his influence with the Curia. Good man of affairs that he was, he acted ably. He picked upon the one Cardinal who would be most likely to understand Francis: Cardinal John of St. Paul.

Cardinal John of St. Paul was a saint. The Church of Rome, even in its most worldly periods, has always been a magnificent instrument for producing saints: let us remember that, if it produced Innocent, it also produced Francis; and Cardinal John was one of those Christlike characters that are its glory and justification down the ages. Guido brought Francis and the brothers to him. And the Cardinal, after talking long with Francis and

107

Bernard and Angelo and the rest, took knowledge of them (in the rare phrase of Luke) that they had been with Jesus. Like called to like, deep to deep. But if he was a saint, he was no genius, and his first suggestion was the same as Guido's, that they should enter some old-established order. Surely what had been good enough for Benedict should be good enough for them. But Francis would not hear of this: he persisted in his conviction that he was called to something new. And the Cardinal in the end bowed before the impassioned conviction. His kind, understanding eyes saw that this young man would never, like the Patarini, Albigenses, and other heretics, combine love of Gospel poverty with hatred of the Church and its priests. This man was all love. He might be critical of abuses in the Church, as was the Cardinal himself, but his love and forgiveness would extend, not only to individual sinners, but to the Church as a whole.

And in this the Cardinal saw much better into the heart of Francis than some of those who have called him "a morning star of the Reformation." He saw, because he was like Francis. Love is unity, not apartness; and Cardinal John and Francis would no more have lost their love of their ancient mother Church and gone outside it than an Englishman, however critical of much that is obtuse and bull-headed about England, would lose his love for a dear, ancient land and seek naturalisation as a Swede or a Swiss.

More than satisfied, thankful to God for the gift of a good man, the Cardinal promised to bring the petition of Francis before the Curia. And he did so. "He and his Brothers," he explained to the Cardinals, "are simply asking permission to do what Christ did, and the Apostles after Him, and that is to go about preaching and ministering, while they support themselves with the work of their hands or by the alms of the faithful."

What! The faces of the Cardinals puckered with incredulity. Did he mean that they proposed to live without property at all?

Certainly.

To have no permanent roof of any kind—no corridor nor cloister?

None at all. Nothing but what the day might yield.

What, *really* to have no thought for the morrow, as to what they should eat and drink, and wherewithal they should be clothed?

Yes. They desired to throw themselves completely upon the promises of God.

The Cardinals were amazed. Amazed that anyone should really take Christ at His word. Some laughed cynically; others shook their heads, admiringly, but doubtingly; others suggested that they must be directed towards one of the ancient orders: what was good enough for Benedict should be good enough for them.

And Cardinal John routed them all with the simplicity of his goodness. "But these men only want to put into practice the orders that Christ undoubtedly issued to some of His disciples, and if we say they are impossible of fulfilment, are we not insulting Him?"

To this no answer was possible, and it was decided to summon these strange men who took the words of Christ so seriously.

So presently Francis and his brothers were brought in and stood before the Pope and Cardinals. The Pope, kind and courteous now, welcomed them and invited Francis to lay bare his purpose. And he watched narrowly as the young man stuttered out his ideas and his hopes, his past

experiences and his future plans. Innocent was more that
a little impressed. This is shown by the fact that,
according to all the chronicles, he dreamed that night
about the young petitioner. It is proved also by his
subsequent action. Innocent was far too intelligent, far
too wide-minded in his interests, to be a man of force
and violence only. He was a man who might have had
vision, had he had time.

His answer now was gentle. Looking at the group of
Brothers, he said, "My little children, this life of yours
seems to us too hard and rough, for though we do not
doubt your fervour, we must think nevertheless of those
who will follow after you, lest this way should be too
harsh for them. Now, my son, I want you to go and pray
to God that He will make clear to you whether what you
seek comes from His will; and we will pray too. Then perhaps if we feel surer, we shall be able to grant you your
request."

Which words closed the audience. Francis, with his
quaint, new-model army had undoubtedly made a breach
in the wall of Rome. He had halted for a little the man
of iron and compelled him to sue for time.

It must have been exasperating to him, however, to
be told to seek further instructions from God as to whether
his vocation was a true one, when he had known it to be
this, with final conviction, for a year past. But, desiring
always to be humble and obedient, he betook himself to
prayer. He prayed, we may suspect, less that God would
convince him than that He would convince His Vicar upon
earth.

And in the morning he was brought again before the
Curia. Again the Pope went to the chair among the
Cardinals, and Francis, with his brothers, stood before

him. And the Pope asked him if he had anything to say.

He had a good deal to say. He astonished these great and important men by telling them a little story. It was a story which had come to him during his night of meditation, and which he believed to be the answer of God to his prayer for persuasive words.

"My lord," he began, "a very poor woman lived in the wilderness, and a great king, passing by, saw her and loved her, and desired to have sons like her."

One sees the eyes of the Cardinals fixed upon him, partly because this was a strange way to speak to the Holy Father, and partly because all men are children and like a story. And Francis continued:

"The King deigned to wed the poor woman; and sons were born to her, but all the time she lived in the wilderness, and her sons lived with her. And when they were grown up, she sent them to the King, saying, 'Don't be afraid, for the King is your father, and will know you and provide for you.' So the sons came to the King, and when he saw them he wondered at their beauty, and asked, 'Whose sons are you?' And when they answered, 'The sons of the poor woman in the wilderness,' he embraced them with great joy, and said, 'Fear not, for if I feed strangers at my table, shall I not feed you, my own true sons?'

"My lord, God is that great King, and I am that poor woman by whom he desires to have true sons after His own likeness."

The Lord Pope (say the Three Companions) was amazed beyond measure. Well he might be. Francis had insinuated with disarming delicacy that since the Church entertained many who were strangers to the Gospel, she might recognise, when she saw them, her own true sons. With all the unconscious authority of a mystic, he had affirmed to the head of an authoritarian Church, "*I* have the truth."

It is high credit to Innocent that he allowed himself to be impressed rather than offended. I think he was gazing intently, curiously, at the young man from Umbria, as he remembered that vivid dream last night. He had dreamed that he saw him propping up the church of St. John Lateran as it tottered to fall. A most singular dream. Did it mean anything? Had it come from God? Shrewd general that he was, with a genius for picking the right man—sincere lover of his faith, with a readiness to try any tactic that would strengthen or advance it—he decided to give the youth a chance to prove what he could do.

"My son," he said, "we have decided to give our approval to your way of life, and our authority to you to preach. Go with the Lord, and as the Lord shall inspire you, preach penitence to all. And if He shall multiply you into a greater fellowship, then you will come to us again, and we will accord you more than this. We shall then commit to you larger powers with more assurance."

In great joy Francis fell on his knees before the Pope, and promised him obedience and reverence. He had got what he wanted. A licence to preach penitence meant that he must not touch on any questions of dogma, but he was not interested in questions of dogma. The Pope, ever an organiser with a belief in discipline, instructed the other brothers to kneel down and, in his hearing, promise their obedience and reverence to Francis as their leader. This they did with the best of hearts. Then Innocent, turning to Cardinal John, their counsel, instructed him that they were to be given the lesser tonsure so that the world might know them for clerics under the protection of the Church.

And with that the business was at an end. The Franciscan Brotherhood, which had begun so happily and irregularly, was now constituted an Order within the Church. Francis had won the Pope, but that asute politician had also captured Francis. This regularising of the Order was an indispensable step, and the Franciscans, so far from regretting it, were always proud of it; but they were to learn later, the best of them, and Francis in particular, that by it they had inevitably lost something. The tonsure round their heads was, to a certain extent, a band constricting their freedom to see new things. Now begins for Francis the tragic difficulty of cramping his new vision within the ligaments of a Church which could not as yet see as much as he. He will accept the difficulty, and take it up bravely, because his is to be the way of peace and persuasion, not of combat; but it will be his cross, and on it, like an unflinching servant of his Master, he will be crucified.

As for Innocent, how surprised he would have been if someone could have told him that morning that History would see in his acceptance of this queer, ardent young man, not only the noblest and gentlest of all his strategies, but also the cleverest and most successful. For just as it was a noble thing for a man of force to say to a man of love, "Go out and see what *you* can do," so it proved to be a very wise one, since it was Francis mainly, and by love only, who rebuilt the Church.

CHAPTER IX

I

ALL are agreed that on their return from Rome the
Brothers lived in an "anbandoned hovel," and ministered
to lepers, at a place called Rivo-Torto, or Twisted Stream,
on the plain near Assisi. Not all are agreed where this
Rivo-Torto was. A large, cold, lonely church on the high
road to Foligno claims that it covers the actual "hovel";
and as you go into it, you certainly see, down in a kind
of bear-pit, a neat stone shed like a cow-byre. But, for
my part, I had no sooner visited the church than I felt
that everything about it was too good to be true. It protested too much. The twisting stream against the church
wall twisted too obviously; one felt that it had been aided
in its twist for the strengthening of the faithful. The
hovel—may God and the good priests forgive me—was too
much like a film-set. Its walls were hung with quotations
from Wadding, Bartoli, and the Twenty-Four Generals,
which were meant to prove that it was the original
"first place" of the Friars Minor; and they proved
nothing. Of all the Franciscan shrines that I visited
this was the only one that seemed empty of the *feel* of
truth.

Most scholars, Catholics and Protestants both, carry the
site of Rivo-Torto a kilometre's distance along the road;
and my desire, if not my knowledge, goes with them. They
place it where two ancient field-chapels lose themselves
among some farm cottages fringed round with oaks, figs,
and limes. The first chapel is called Santa Maria Maddalena, and the second San Rufino d'Arce; and it is known
that in Francis' day a leper village stood between the
chapels, where the hens now strut and the old horse pilfers

from the haystack. Like Assisi up on the hill, the settlement was divided according to the social status of the lepers, the *majores* living near Santa Maria Maddalena, and the *minores* near San Rufino. Wherefore it is well to look for the home and office of Francis near San Rufino.

I left the road, then, and, passing through the trees, walked straight to this little chapel. It caught the heart to look at it. A woman from the neighbouring farmhouse ran in to get the key, and returned, and unlocked the chapel door. I walked in, and a hen and some chickens walked in too. We saw, they and I, a dusty little oblong room, with a stone altar still on its daïs. Did the lepers kneel here, and the Brothers among them? A very different congregation now. Potatoes and tomatoes shared the floor with barrels of flour and casks of wine; and onions stood neatly brigaded on the altar step. San Rufino was now a cottager's outhouse and store. Well, why not? Why not God's abundance spread upon His floor? Were not these roots and fruits, this flour and wine, of the same family as the devotion of men? Did not one Father beget them both? Yes, it was no pretty conceit, but a simple statement of a simple fact, to say that this universal abundance was the same thing, on a lower level of creation, as the *abandon* and the lavish self-offering of a Francis. Perhaps this was why God was so ready to sit, as we were told, in the uplifted bread and wine.

I left San Rufino rather quietly, and went on to Santa Maria Maddalena. A small, staring boy unlocked it for me, and I stepped into its half-darkness. What here? Only the empty apse and the altar's step to remind me of scenes that these walls must once have watched. They sheltered to-day nothing but a pool of maize on the floor and a wine-press against the wall. The abundance—and the press. The fruit—and the crushing it must undergo, if its virtue was to be given to men.

I came out into the sunlight, and here found an audience waiting for me: two black-eyed girls from the cottages, and two smiling gossoons who seemed to be their current admirers. The girls, less bashful than the boys, asked me with laughter, "Where did I come from? England? What was England like? Did they know San Francesco there? Would I take their pictures?" and I answered them as I loved them, and I took their pictures and their names and addresses; and then they all strolled away into the vines— these blithe heirs of the lepers—while I sauntered up and down between the haystacks, and tried to see the past.

Some kind of cottage or cow-byre it must have been. Derelict when Francis came to it, but quickly restored by that irrepressible builder. And it stood somewhere near here; perhaps within a yard of where I was standing. Perhaps it was much the same as that cow-shed yonder. And within it at night-time slept all the brothers, except those who were afield on preaching tours. So huddled were they, sometimes, that Francis would make chalk marks on the walls to show where each was to sleep and pray.

And yet, ever after, they looked back upon their life at Rivo-Torto as a springtime of unclouded joy. Perhaps never again were they quite such an intimate and happy family. Here were the first of Francis' company, a happy few, a band of brothers. Here were Bernard, Peter, Sylvester, and Giles. Here within the walls were all those who stood by him when his Order deserted him. Here were Leo, Angelo, and Rufino. Here were those who, when writing about him after his death, to protect his teaching from its betrayers, called themselves always, and a hundred

116

times, *nos qui cum eo fuimus*—we who were with him—we *know*.

We must meet Leo and shake his hand. Leo was the tenderest figure of them all. The love of Francis for Leo, and of Leo for Francis, is one of the most fragrant things in this old Italian romance. A diffident little priest, he was Francis' chosen confessor and director—Francis himself refusing always to be anything more than a deacon; and if one may whisper a thought that flits through the mind, what a testimony it is to Francis that the man who knew his every temptation and fall worshipped him! Worshipped him so completely that he sometimes wondered, as we shall see, if he were not unworthy of such a man's notice and affection. He was also Francis' amanuensis, because he was an exquisite penman, and Francis an atrocious one; and when we look at the breviary which he so laboriously made for Sister Clare, we may suspect that, if there was a weakness in this quiet soul, it was a pride in in his penmanship. It was he who inspired the others to sit down and write when men were trying to alter or obliterate the features of his master into those of a conventional stained-glass saint. He was the chief of the writers, the leader of the *nos qui cum eo fuimus*, the first of the Three Companions. The Pecorello di Dio was Francis' nickname for him, the Little Sheep of God; but love made the little sheep a lion when they began to belie his master. Then the Pecorello became Leo indeed! And in the end the pen of this little secretary, scribbling away in retirement, proved mightier than the power of the Popes and of the whole recalcitrant Order. It is to Leo almost entirely that we owe the Francis whom the world has been unable to forget. He saved the message of his master.

Then there was Rufino, so different, a young nobleman

of the Scefi house, melancholy in temper, timid and lonely in soul, and yet so passionate in his pursuit of perfection, that Francis nicknamed him Saint Rufino. I have no record of it, but I am bold to maintain that Francis was sometimes facetious in his presence about the neighbouring chapel of San Rufino.

And Masseo. Masseo, the tall, the handsome, and the eloquent. Choosing this burly fellow for his companion on many a preaching tour, how Francis loved to tease him! Once as they came to a place where four ways met, so that they could turn towards Arezzo, Siena, or Florence, "Which way, Father?" asked Masseo; and Francis answered, "The way God wills, Masseo. Which else?" "But how shall we know God's will?" protested Masseo. "Quite simply," replied Francis. "By holy obedience you will spin round and round till I order you to stop."

The words " by holy obedience " precluded argument, so Masseo spun round and round at the cross-roads; and it is to be hoped that no one passed by. Francis kept his eyes shut, and at a given moment, cried, "Stop! Which way are you facing now?"

"Towards Siena," gasped Masseo.

"Then," explained Francis, "it is clearly God's will that we go to Siena."

Or if they came to a town where they were not known and, after the preaching, went from door to door begging their food, Francis, who was small and, to a casual glance, insignificant, got only crusts and such like, while Masseo, on a different circuit, collected splendid dishes from the women, either because they thought him so handsome, or because they felt that a body so big must need a deal of keeping up. And Francis would chaff him about this success on the way home. Sometimes Masseo was ready with his badinage too. He witnessed Francis' bewildering success as a preacher, and that was text enough for anyone who wanted to be impudent. Francis may have lived cramped in a hovel, but the picturesque news of him had shot over Umbria, Tuscany, and the Marches, so that he and Masseo had only to be seen approaching a village for the church bells to ring, the children to rush out, the women to leave their work, and the labourers to toss down their tools in the fields, and all to crowd around some flat stone on to which he had stepped as a rostrum. Masseo would keep the crowd within bounds, and enjoin them to listen to him, for he was a very fine preacher; but on one occasion at least, as they walked home, he rallied Francis, "Why after you? Why after you? You are not fair to look upon; you are not a man of parts; you are not of noble birth; why, pray, does all the world run after you?"

"Would you know why?" answered Francis. "Because in all the world God has not been able to perceive a viler creature, and so He has chosen me to confound the nobility, the might, and the wisdom of the world, that people may know that all things come from Him, and not from the creature."

Well, that may have been the reason, but I am not satisfied about it, and I don't think Masseo was either.

Then there were two brothers for whom Francis had a special reverence because they were touched of God, and simple. Brother Juniper, hero of a hundred deeds as soft-headed as they were large-hearted; whom Francis has summed up for ever in the words, "Would God I had a forest of such Junipers!" And John the Simple, who, after being told that his business was to copy Brother Francis in all things, knelt when he knelt, stood when he

stood, and coughed when he coughed. I think Francis'
smile for John the Simple was full of affection.

But Francis has limned his brothers for us with his usual
grace and humour. "The perfect Friar Minor," he wrote
in one of his exhortations, "must be as true to Poverty as
Bernard of Quintavalle, as simple and pure as Leo, as
chaste as Angelo, as intelligent and eloquent as Masseo;
he must have a mind fixed on high like Giles; his prayer
must be like that of Rufino, and he must be as patient as
Brother Juniper. . . ."

He had his nicknames for them all. Bernard was the
Founder; Peter was Lord Peter because he was so learned;
Giles, late farmer and so often his squire, was the Knight
of my Round Table; another was the Florentine Pugilist
because sometimes he wanted to discipline the others;
another was the Gonfaloniere; himself was the Poverello,
the Little Poor Man; and his body, as all the world knows,
was Brother Ass. Nay, he was not above giving a title to
the Holy Spirit Himself, who was the Minister General of
the Order.

And of course there was the angel of that house, she
whom he called My Lady Poverty, the widow of the
world.

"They were addicted to joke and song," say the Three
Companions; and we may read how, after begging, they
would spread out their collections to see who was the best
beggar, and how sometimes, when they fell to singing,
Francis would saw one stick across another and pretend
to be accompanying them on a viol. The lad who clowned
in the prison at Perugia was here in the hut at Rivo-
Torto.

And, as at Perugia, he would hurry to the service of
the unhappy. One night that crowded dormitory was

disturbed by frightened cries, "I am dying! I am dying!" All rose; and Francis, bidding them light the lamp, asked, "Who was it that cried out?"

"It was I," wept a young brother. "I am dying."

"Dying! But how?"

"I am dying of hunger."

Now, there is no doubt that Francis, like every specialist in religion, preached a strict asceticism to his brothers that, by disciplining the old greedy, grasping, separatist self, the Body, they might free the Spirit for the richer enjoyment of unity—his end being, not the killing of joy, but its heightening. And there is no doubt that, eager always to lead them from in front, he practised the sternest austerities himself. Nevertheless, he had hardly heard the words of the young sufferer before he told the brothers to spread the table with all the food in the place. And when this was done, he sat down and began to eat, saying to the frightened boy, "Come and eat with me." And he intimated to all the others that they too were to sit down and eat.

After the meal, as a kind of grace, he preached them a small homily on temperance in all things including temperance itself.

"Dearest," he said, "I order each of you to consider his own nature and, if you feel you need more food than some stronger brother, to take it. Beware of too great abstinence, and remember always that our Lord prefers mercy to sacrifice. Besides, we must look after Brother Body, or it will turn melancholy and become a drag on us. After all, if we want it to serve us in work and prayer, we must give it no reasonable cause to murmur. But by all means, if it starts grumbling after receiving a fair ration, let us make the lazy beast feel the spur."

In the same spirit he got up early one morning because he was worried about an old brother who seemed too infirm to fast. Awakening the brother, he said, "Come out with me." And he led the way into the vineyard (perhaps the same way as my merry-eyed girls went) and there looked around for the vine which carried the best grapes. Choosing one, he pulled down cluster after cluster, and, sitting down under the tree, began to eat the grapes joyously, instructing the old brother, by holy obedience, to sit down and aid him in this employment. And that brother, to the end of his life (says the narrative), could never tell this story without tears.

Francis was stern (if that is the word) about one thing only: loyalty to Poverty; and even then he would soften the sternness with humour. At Rivo-Torto there was a novice who "did hardly pray at all, and worked little, but did eat bravely"—God forgive me, but surely he is my brother. Francis considered him well, and decided that he was a carnal man; as I fear he was. And one day, after contemplating him at a hearty meal, he surprised him with the words, "Go your way, Brother Fly, for you eat the labour of your brothers, and are idle in the work of God, like some lazy and barren drone." It was the order of expulsion. Brother Fly recognised it as such, and went at once: in fact, had not the light young persons of to-day spoiled a good phrase, I should have written that he buzzed off quickly.

2

But you will not understand the *luogo* or "place" of Rivo-Torto unless you hear something of the *eremo* or "hermitage" of the Carceri a few miles away. Francis instituted two kinds of resting-places for his brothers, *luoghi* and *eremi*. In his hatred of possessions and ties, he seems to have shied from the word "house." The *luogo* was the centre for the preaching and working friars; the *eremo* their place of retreat into prayer. And the latter, to Francis' eye, was the more important. First things first: meditation was the spring of all spiritual force; the *eremo* was the arsenal from which to draw new love, new power, and new words about the Spirit. "Preaching," as he said, "soils the feet of the soul with dust." The *eremo* was Mary, and the *luogo* Martha.

This figure, that his Order was Mary and Martha both, is not mine but his. We possess a Rule which he drew up for brothers living in a hermitage, and a delightful document it is.

"Those who wish to live in a hermitage must be three or at most four brothers. And two of them shall be mothers and have the care of the other two. But the mothers shall lead the life of Martha, and the others the life of Mary. The two sons shall have each his own cell where they may pray and sleep. And as soon as the sun has set they shall pray the Compline, and try to maintain silence. (That 'try' holds the true touch of Francis.) And . . . after the Trines they can break the silence and go to their mothers, and, if they wish, can beg alms of food from them for the sake of God, like other poor people. And the brothers who are mothers shall guard their sons from all men. . . ."

With the kindly consent of the ground-landlords, the Benedictines of Subasio, the Carceri became the *eremo* balancing the *luogo* of Rivo-Torto. By following the bed of the Twisted Stream the brothers came at length to the foothills of Monte Subasio and a dark, steep gorge that seemed to climb right into the heart of the mountain. A dense wood of ilex, oak, and walnut filled this steep ravine; and flowers peeped about its pathways: cyclamen, hawkweed, orchid, and violet. The place was a haunt of birds; but below their flutter and chirp the indigo ilex grove seemed to hold a section of the everlasting dark and its accompanying silence.

Near the top was a little shrine, possibly erected long ago by the heathen Umbrians to the god of the glen, but now converted by the Benedictine owners into a Christian chapel; and beneath the shrine, curtained by the trees, were some natural caves.

The dark, silent grove is there still, but the shrine and some of the cells are enclosed in the white hermitage of the Carceri which, like so many Franciscan hermitages, hangs over the wooded ravine like a martin's nest on a wall.

Here was everything that Francis loved: a mountain height, trees, birds, clear spring-water, a shrine to pray at, grottoes to sleep in, and loneliness. He made the grottoes into an *eremo* for the family, and nicknamed them their *carceri* or "prisons." He himself went often to one of the cells, and it was at its door that he took part in his endurance contest with the nightingale. Delighted by its prolonged concert, he begged Leo, who was with him, to come out and join in. But Leo, that shy, quiet soul, refused, declaring that he had no voice; so Francis (who, we remember, was as pleased with his voice as Leo with his penmanship) went out and explained to the nightingale that he too would sing his Lauds to God, and they would see which could sing the longest. But after an hour or two he gave in, pronouncing the nightingale an easy victor.

Such was the Carceri, the hidden power behind the house at Rivo-Torto.

Well, I may leave Rivo-Torto now, because I feel I have realised something of the life lived in this place, where now the hens strut and the old horse browses on the haystack. Here dwelt one of the few associations of perfectly free men that the world has seen: free of everything that makes for limitation; free to go where they pleased—cramped in a nutshell, but kings of infinite space; quit of everything that bred care and envy and grasping, for though, as you may be thinking, poverty is often a cause of anxiety and grab, it cannot be so when men are pursuing it for its own sake; when, so far from wanting to keep up a position, they desire the lowest position of all; and when they have a complete trust that God, Who cares for the sparrows, will supply their daily need—a gamble on God which He honoured, for it is historic fact that the Lord's table never failed them. Here Francis staged his challenge to the vulgar, quantitative measurements of the world. Trade and the towns were creating the new, modern age, and this challenge, still valid and still unaccepted, was staged by a tradesman's son, a child of the town. Hardly aware of what he was doing, he challenged all preachers and priests who held then, or hold now, a tithe of self-interest and ambition; and he challenged all of us laity who, though we must have some property, I suppose, in any social order, cannot sit loosely to our possessions and travel light through the rich world. He challenged our self-pushing, our purse-pride, and our snobbery, and simply by creating before our eyes a club of really independent gentlemen.

CHAPTER X

I

AT that time in the Spoletan vale there was an ass with a destiny. We know nothing about the animal, neither its name nor its character nor its features; nor its master's business in the valley. We know only that one day it was coming along the road towards Rivo-Torto, with this master, a curmudgeonly fellow, goading it behind. At Rivo-Torto he desired to stable it; and it seems likely that, having been accustomed to stable it in the ruined hovel, he had long resented the friars' possession of the place, and that this morning his temper would brook no control. He drove the ass right into the midst of the brothers, saying, "Get you in, long ears. There's no reason why you shouldn't be comfortable here too." The brothers, who were at prayer, looked round, and lo, here was a new brother, complete with grey habit and cord. The peasant deliberately tied up the beast, and Francis, true to his principle of purely pacific resistance, said, "Come, brothers. God has called us to preach the Gospel, and not to keep a hospice for asses. Let us go elsewhere."

And they all went out—but where to ? Possibly to the Carceri, while Francis went house-hunting. As always during his early days, he took his difficulty to Bishop Guido, and asked the loan of some old priest-house or chapel, but Guido, though sympathetic, could offer him nothing. He went to the canons of the cathedral, but they could not help him either. He climbed the mountain and visited the Benedictines of Subasio, and at once the friendly abbot—it was almost too good to be true—suggested the Portiuncula. Yes, he could have the Portiuncula and its chapel. And if his conscience insisted on paying rent so that it might be a loan and no more, they would accept in quittance an annual basket of fish. One request only the Abbot made—a pleasantly sentimental request: that if, as now seemed probable, the Franciscans grew into a big fraternity, the little chapel was to be always the *caput et mater* of the Order.

Nothing could have pleased Francis better, and he blessed the ass that had driven his family into the Port-iuncula. Not only had it a charm for him above all other places in the valley, but its situation was ideal, almost equidistant from the lepers of San Salvatore and those of Rivo-Torto. The brothers trooped in enthusiastically and built themselves huts in a rectangle around the chapel. Each made a house by interweaving branches cut down from the forest trees, much as the bedouin to-day will make a bivouac of palm-branches in an oasis of the desert, for though the chapel might be the permanent head of the order, they themselves were but "strangers and pilgrims passing by." Around the huts they planted a hedge, and this was the only convent wall. Within the enclosure they staked out a garden, and appointed a gardener: Giles very likely, who had been a farmer yesterday, and remained a devoted gardener till his death in old age.

Was their happiness complete now that they lived in a garden with their own chapel in the midst of them, and with the forest trees all round? Not quite, because happiness is only perfected when masculine and feminine meet. They did not know this, but completion would come with a sister.

And the sister came. We agreed above that Assisi might well be spared any more excitements for a time, but it was not to be. All previous sensations were outdone by the scandal which shook it now. To the conservative fathers of the town it must have seemed to threaten the foundations of society. And even the radicals and libertarians must have shaken their heads over the extremes of liberty in which Francis dealt.

Not without cunning we have intruded here and there mention of a girl-child in a nobleman's palace; and she has been growing up while we have been on our travels. The Lady Clare was now eighteen. There are many descriptions of her, and all unite in providing a perfect romantic heroine. Sometimes, studying the life of Francis in a purely romantic mood, one feels as if the Author had resolved that beauty should drift about the tale from its opening to its high tragic close; and that the Lady Clare in the freshness of eighteen is a good symbol of that beauty. She had an oval face, delicate skin, chiselled features, and fine golden hair. Her father bore the fine name of Count Favorino Scefi, Lord of Sasso Rosso, and he was a scion of ancient Roman stock. Her mother was the Lady Ortolana, of the noble family of the Fiumi. The children were five: Boso, Penenda, Clare, Agnes, and Beatrice; and the whole handsome family had a palazzo within the city and a castle perched dizzily on a crag of Subasio. It is almost as if, in consideration of a common human weakness, the Author had provided a princess out of a castle.

But let us see her more realistically. Her childhood was natural enough. After reading the Lives of the Saints, she wanted to wear a hair shirt. She played at rosaries on the floor, with pebbles for beads. There in a private corner, with tight-shut eyes, she gabbled her *Ave Maria* and her *Pater noster qui es in cælis*, and contemplated the Five Joyful Mysteries. Remembering our own sisters who at thirteen or fourteen fell in love with holiness, we may be certain that she argued hotly with father and brother about her saintly ambitions and the pieties generally, and then went off and wept alone in her room—though not displeased to be a martyr. We may be certain that she fiercely took the side of old Bernardone's boy in that sensational row with his father, and that if, as we have suggested, she stood watching, with fingers at her mouth, the scene in the Piazza San Giorgio when Francis was helping to distribute Bernard and Peter's goods to the poor, she wished pitifully that she could distribute some of her father's property too. Then Sylvester, the priest, who is believed to have been her kinsman, and Rufino, who almost certainly was, both caught the infection and left all to join Francis; and the arguments must have flared up again and flashed across the dining-board of Count Favorino and his family. Both father and elder brother would hold it their fine male business to put the hot-cheeked girl in her place. The Lady Ortolana, on the other hand, would keep silence. She herself was of a devout complexion. It is recorded that she used to set off on a quiet pilgrimage, as soon as she had got the Count off on one of his punitive forays. The Lady Ortolana, we think, would listen far more sympathetically to her daughter in some feminine room upstairs. And then there was an aunt, Bianca Guelfucci, also of a pious mind, who loved the child and secretly took her part. What "ever so thrilling" talks must have passed between niece and dear, understanding aunt! Here, in short, was an eternal family arrangement: the men horsy, clumsy, vain, and dictatorial, and the women humouring the stupid creatures, but quietly going their own more sensitive way.

And the unstable compound produced the usual explosion. The Count, seeing with pride the beauty of his daughter, determined that she must marry into the loftiest circles. A determination well justified, because soon a young man, wealthy, noble, and attractive in every way, offered himself as suitor for the Lady Clare. Favorino was delighted; and so was Ortolana; and they put his offer before Clare. What must have been the Count's bewilderment and wrath, and Ortolana's discomfiture, when Clare answered furiously that she had consecrated herself to God and didn't want to marry anybody ever! Favorino, throwing back his head, hid his pain behind a loud laugh, and swore that she'd do as she was ordered; Clare wept and ran to Bianca for comfort; and, in a sentence, there were *diverses croix chez M. son père*.

Her resistance was not likely to be softened by the fact that Francis was now preaching a course of sermons in the Cathedral. It says much for the Church of his day that churchmen, from the beginning, were much less hostile to him than the business men and the noblemen, and when he returned from Rome with the Pope's approval upon him, and when praise of his preaching was bruited everywhere, the canons of Assisi invited him to preach at San Giorgio, Santa Maria Maggiore, and the Cathedral. And was it not characteristic of three devout women, the Lady Ortolana, the Lady Bianca, and the young Lady Clare, that they should be seated among the crowds who listened to the most-talked-of preacher of the district?

And the more Clare gazed up at the young deacon, his eyes alight with the ardour of his conviction, and heard him proclaim the joy of complete self-giving, the more her whole being throbbed its answer, "Yes!" Having seen this truth, she must go out in pursuit of it. Never could she be content with anything less. Her young vital body trembled with the delight of being in love with sanctity.

A study of the writings of Francis, and of his recorded

sayings, enables us to conceive the kind of sermon to which she was listening. It would have appealed to the spirit of adventure. He would have cried to the people to be free. He would have told the meaning of his little band in the forest. "You cannot all abandon your possessions, as we have done, but at least you can change your attitude to them. At least you can see that there is a taint in all *getting*. All getting separates you from other men; all giving unites you to them. Oh, believe me, that, once you have seen this, all getting, over and above your simplest needs, will be tainted with distress, and all giving will be a source of joy. I tell you, you do not know the joy, the liberation, and the fulness of living, that will come to you if you will make this simple change of heart. The whole face of the world will change for you, taking on a new graciousness, and the face of every brother will be beautiful. It is because we of the Brothers Minor see all this, because we know it by the great joy that has come into our own lives, and because we desire to prove it to the world by our lives, that we are resolved to 'get' nothing. For our barest needs we will accept what is given us in charity, and that is all. We desire to strive no more, nor quarrel any more, that we may help forward the day when people shall know their oneness in God, and they shall not hurt nor destroy in all His holy mountain."

Some such his words: of his manner let Thomas of Spalato, who heard him preach, tell us.

I was a young student at Bologna when I saw Francis preaching on the piazza before almost every man in the city. He spoke with such skill and eloquence that many of the wisest scholars there were filled with admiration at the words of so simple a man. Yet he had not the manner of a preacher, his ways being rather those of conversation . . . but God gave such efficacy to his words that they brought to reconciliation many noble families who before had been shedding each other's blood. And such devotion did all men and women feel for him that they would crowd around him and try to tear off bits of his habit, or merely touch the hem of his garment.

Staring up at this vehement young orator, who had become since his self-liberation a natural leader, a power and impulse to bring to birth the new things with which the world was astir, Clare, a vehement young woman, decided that he was the most wonderful person in the world. Let the mediæval hagiographers burke the issue as they will, I must believe that, whether she knew it or not, she loved him then, loved him always, and never loved anyone else. Loved him, however, with no thought of ever being anything but his adoring servant in spiritual things.

As the congregation crowded out into the sunlit piazza, one can hear Ortolana and Bianca discussing the sermon, but one does not hear Clare speak.

Now she was possessed by the desire of meeting Francis and talking with him. Could she not see him—oh, why could she not see him? Thus she pleaded with Bianca in their confidential talks. He was a minister of God, and he only could understand all she wanted to tell. No, none of the old parish priests would do. They wouldn't understand.

"But what will your father think?" asked Bianca. "He gets so hot at the mere mention of the young man."

"I don't know—I can't help that," answered Clare. "I want to obey him in all things, except when he forbids me to do things which I know I ought to do."

And the girl, whose ardour was as irresistible as Francis', ended by compelling Bianca to take her down to the Portiuncula.

And so, in her turn, Clare came through the trees, like Giles and Sylvester before her.

Of the feelings of Francis, as he looked down upon this golden girl, and heard her ask if it would be at all possible for a woman to live somewhere the same life as his brothers, I dare not speak. I dare not, lest a moment of such bloom should fall in dust at my touch. I suggest only that when that first meeting had ended, and Clare had gone, he was on his knees before God.

The action that he recommended, the plan that he and Clare and Bianca drew up together, is easier to handle. To understand it, we must realise that Francis moved in his own clear atmosphere, unfogged for the most part by the conventions that frighten us. The larger part of him was like a new, free creature in the world. And the curious thing is that he never knew it. Humble as the humblest, it was unawares that throughout his life he acted with a princely air, as of one above the popes. Happily ignorant, he supposed that his own inspiration and authority were enough to start an Order, to draw up a Rule for it, to enrol the brothers without any novitiate, to abolish penance for all his sons, to address encyclicals to "All Christians throughout the World," and to soar over the heads of royal generals and papal legates and try by a personal visit to the Sultan to end the crusades in his own way. And now, when he had satisfied himself, after many meetings, that Clare's call was the same as his own, and that there was danger in delay, he did not hesitate. Mere deacon though he was, he promised to accept her as a sister, to "clothe" her in his own chapel, and to place her in a convent till he could decide how best to arrange her life. So far from worrying, he was immensely thrilled at the idea of starting an Order of Sisters.

But how was the high, tough, prickly fence of Count Favorino to be overleapt? Remembering his own father with his locks and his chains and his bastinado, he wasted little time in wondering if they could come to terms with the Count. Bianca assured him that it would be impossible, Favorino was so set on Clare marrying the young nobleman. "Oh, but she can't do that," said Francis, and simply and straightway arranged for her abduction. If it was a crime, it was the crime of Sylvester Bonnard.

One may recall his boyhood's longing to be a knight-errant. Here was the business of a knight-errant waiting to be done.

Palm Sunday, 1212. The first day of Holy Week, the day of Christ's triumphal entry, the day when the children cried Hosanna! to welcome Him within the walls, this was the day that Francis chose for Clare's flight to him— and oh God, what were her thoughts when for the last time she went with her family to High Mass in the Cathedral! The people crowded the church because this Palm Sunday Mass was one of the most popular services in the year. And among them knelt Clare, dressed, so her Life tells us, in the brilliant clothes of a child of the nobility: scarlet robe, jewelled belt, high, stiff head-dress of white lawn, and embroidered shoes. But what were her thoughts, what were her thoughts, as she knelt with her face in her hands, and heard the care-free singing of her mother and of her sister Agnes, who so adored her (or did little Agnes know?), or when she turned a side-long glance at the tall figure of her father, whom she loved well, because he loved her in his own clumsy way? Now came the great popular moment of the service: the choir burst into the anthem, "The children of the Hebrews, bearing branches of the olive trees, went to meet the Lord," and

SANT' ANGELO IN PANSO

CLARE'S GARDEN

the people, leaving their places, crowded in slow procession towards the altar to take from the hands of Bishop Guido their consecrated boughs. *"Obviaverunt Domino, clamantes et dicentes, Hosanna in excelsis!"* Well may we believe the story that Clare, overpowered by emotion, stayed kneeling in her place, her face buried in her hands.

And then a strange, tender thing happened: something which must always suggest that Bishop Guido, Francis' confidant and counsellor, knew what was toward, and had approved it—for, remember, these were violent days, and if it were a question of violence outwitting the Church, then Guido would be on the side of the Church. Perceiving that Clare had not moved at all, he left the altar, came down to where she knelt, and put her olive branch in her hand.

Just before midnight that night Clare ran to the backdoor of her house, tore away some stones that blocked it, and passed out into the street. They will show you the traditional door to-day, just as at Haddon Hall they will show you the door through which Dorothy Vernon eloped to her lover. In the street Bianca awaited her; and the woman and the girl went out of the Porta Moiano and down through the darkness to the forest around the Portiuncula. Trembling at their business, they trod their way through the undergrowth and the trees, but as they drew near the Portiuncula, they saw that Francis had staged a welcome for Clare that she might be comforted and happy. See, all the brothers were coming out in procession to meet her, carrying torches and candles, and singing their gratitude to God! *Obviaverunt Domino, clamantes et dicentes, Hosanna in excelsis!* Bernard was there, and Peter and Giles; Leo, the little priest, and Angelo, the knight of Rieti; and Sylvester and Rufino, her cousins.

The procession gathered her to itself and, turning about, took her into the little chapel. There they sang the first Mass of the morning, and at the right moment Francis robed her in the coarse tunic of his Order and tied his white cord around her. And there before the altar at which he had heard the Gospel that determined his life Clare heard the Gospel for Monday in Holy Week, and the long Gospel for Holy Monday contains these words:

"And being in Bethany, in the house of Simon the leper, as he sat at meat, there came a woman having an alabaster box of ointment of spikenard, very precious, and she brake the box and poured it on his head. And there were some that had indignation among themselves, and said, Why was this waste of the ointment made? . . . And Jesus said, Let her alone. . . . She hath done what she could."

CHAPTER XI

To the right of Assisi's hill, in the heart of the plain, and at the point where the rivers Chiagio and Tescio meet, there is a little Campo Santo with its white cloisters framing it and its dark cypresses guarding it. It stands alone in the fields, a half-mile from the village of Bastia, whose dead it keeps. On a Sunday afternoon you may see the Bastians in their best black clothes straggling towards it with flowers in their hands. One Sunday I joined in their long, broken procession. Like them I was walking to find the buried past, but a past buried deeper than any they were remembering. As I walked up the cypress avenue, I hardly saw the white colonnades, because I was seeing this place as it had been seven hundred years ago. In those days the meeting of the two streams made a marshland, so that this low eminence rose like an island out of the mists; and for that reason they called it Isola Romanica. It must have been a very quiet place, with the forest coming down to it, and the two streams enfolding it, and the marsh-water around. A perfect place for a settlement of Benedictine nuns; and here they were, in their convent of San Paolo.

Now, the first thing to strike you, as you enter the Campo Santo, is the contrast between the modern, pinnacled, rather garish cloisters which frame the garden and the ancient chapel, oddly long in shape and very primitive in construction, which stands in its midst. That chapel is all that remains of the convent of San Paolo. It stood here before Francis was born; in the stormy years after him which put the nuns to flight, it was turned into a fortress, as you may see from some windows like gun-slits; and now it is a chapel again, surrounded by peace. The marsh-waters have withdrawn, and the forest has become fields, but in a sense it is an island still, enclosed by the sacredness of death.

I walked into the chapel, which was all I had come to see. And the first sight of its old dusty altar, recessed into a crumbling apse, held me in a spell, for it was to the altar in this apse that Clare ran and clung for sanctuary, when Count Favorino, Madonna Ortolana, and their indignant kinsmen came to seize her and take her home.

Francis, early that morning of Holy Monday, had delivered her into the care of the sisters of San Paolo; but as soon as the sun was up, revealing all to her family, they had come raging down the hill from Assisi to fetch her back. And there on that altar step, clinging to the altar as might a child poised between terror and grief, Clare passionately defied her family, vowing that neither threat nor force nor supplication could make her abandon the life she had chosen.

Not a very important struggle for which that old apse kept the ring—just a girl of the Middle Ages fighting for her freedom against her father and his few followers—or was it more? Was it the impact of the Eternal upon Time, a decisive battle between the Spirit and the World? Why is it that that old chapel which has seen so many battles in its fortress days, and watched the retreat of many discomfited assailants, remembers to-day only this victory when Clare's kinsmen withdrew? A tablet on its wall tells the visitor the story. When I was there, the whole place was dusty and dirty, and the altar steps were soiled with the grease of night-lights which the pious Bastians kindle in the name of their dead; two were burning fitfully as I gazed. Because of the smallness of the gun-slit windows, not to mention their grime, the walls enclosed a twilight. The place made me think of some very old man who had become slovenly and forgetful with the years, but who remembered one thing vividly and liked to talk of it.

2

To the left of Assisi's hill, high up on the slope, where the olive orchards are thinning, there is a range of farm buildings remarkable for lifting a tiny belfry into the sky and for having chapel-like arches built into its walls. It is Sant' Angelo in Panso, and incorporates within its walls all that is left of the old Benedictine convent of that name, to which Francis, with Bernard and Philip the Long, brought Clare after the broil in San Paolo.

My first journey up to it was lazy and foolish enough. One early evening I went to Natale, my excellent Assisan driver who was always ready, for a reasonable fee, to take me anywhere in Italy, and I asked him if he could get the car up the track to Sant' Angelo.

"Sissignore" was the whole of his answer as he opened the car door.

I had little doubt that he would say "Yes, sir," because he had already offered, with seriousness and, indeed, urgency, to drive me to the very summits of Subasio. I got in, and soon we were driving rapidly out of the Porta Nuova.

What kind of road we were on, after a mile of going, I do not know: a mule-track, perhaps, or merely a goat-track, or no track at all. When I asked Natale what it was, he replied simply, "A road for pigs." And over it we bumped and leapt and swerved, sometimes within inches of an overturn into the olives; and the journey was not made less exciting by Natale's custom (for he is a devout lad) of lifting high his right arm in salute to every wayside shrine we passed. A bumping, roaring journey, but a slow one, because Natale, who is undefeatable, would get out with mutterings, every now and then, to rebuild the road in front of him, and secondly because, whenever I asked him a question, he would stop the car for a friendly discussion, one arm leaning on the wheel. Thus our following of little mountain boys was able to keep up with us in their eagerness to see the end.

And yet it must have been—since Natale knows every inch of the country—the natural way up from Assisi to Sant' Angelo. Did Count Favorino, then, and Monaldo, his brother, and Boso, his son, and their friends and men-at-arms, come galloping up here in their final, unbearable fury, riding for vengeance, when they learned, eighteen days after the flight of Clare, that Agnes too had run to join her sister? I asked Natale what he thought about it, but either he knew nothing of the story, though he stands his car daily under the church of Santa Chiara, or he did not catch the nature of my question, for he only shouted, as the car leap-frogged over a hummock, "Coraggio!"

The story goes on that Favorino and his men (some authorities say that Monaldo led the expedition, in the absence of his brother) dragged Agnes from the convent and a little way down the road, but that, in answer to Clare's prayers, she became too heavy for strong men to carry; which legend may spring from the truth that the girl put up such a fight that strong men, not unchivalrous, decided to struggle with her no more. (And yet in the church of Santa Chiara they show you the skull of Agnes, and it is so small!) The armed company gave up the fight, leaving the girl to go her own way. And she went, running back to the sister she adored.

I spent an hour wandering about the buildings of Sant' Angelo, amid the smell of hay, manure, and wine. The walls were like a palimpsest, one age having written its story over the faded traces of another. And the life of the present day played all around them: children romped in the hay, a woman gathered faggots down the slope, a man unlimbered his oxen by a door, and everywhere the stony, labouring earth, as forgetful of the past as the mercy of God, produced what it could, some maize and clover between the gnarled old olives, valerian and fennel and orchis in the grass, and some vines and figs against the wall. Butterflies danced in the last of the sun: red admirals and marbled whites; and beehawks and greylings and brown fritillaries.

When I came away the sun had dropped behind the mountains, and the great plain was filled with sunset. I thought of another sunset, the one that illuminated the vale after the men-at-arms had ridden away, and of Clare and Agnes looking at it alone.

I called Natale, and got back into the car; and as he tumbled it down the steep path, I saw riding slowly ahead of it a troop of men in knightly array, but sullen and quiet, as they returned to town defeated.

3

On the lowest slope of Assisi's hill, perched on a shelf amid a crowd of trees, is San Damiano. Dull indeed the man who can look upon it without emotion and wonder.

I remember climbing a field-path towards it one evening and thinking, "Within those walls, if anywhere in the world, men and women brought the Spirit to birth." It is difficult to doubt the soundless movement of the divine among men, as one looks at San Damiano. To its door a worried and straining youth was led; within its walls he seemed to hear a voice directing him; something moved him to rebuild the place for a purpose not yet seen; there, when at his wits' end to know what to do with a girl who wanted to fight at his side, he placed her at last; and here for forty years she defended his cause, refusing to die till the victory was in her hands.

For that is what happened. The friendly Benedictines, hearing that Clare and Agnes were without a home, promptly offered to Francis, for their permanent use, the chapel and priest-house of San Damiano. Once again, something almost too good to be true! How could he doubt that God was working on his side? San Damiano! Think of him running up the track to tell Clare! Imagine her thrilled and sparkling response! Think of Agnes listening! And other women, said he, were only waiting to join them. Her action had inspired them. A sisterhood was already begun, the Sisters of Clare! "Come and I'll show you San Damiano."

Then think of Clare and Agnes setting their tiny new home in order. The furnishings would be of the simplest and barest, but Francis always allowed to his brothers and sisters the luxury of a garden. And Clare made herself a garden near her cell, though it was hardly a garden in the full meaning of the word. It was on a terrace no broader than a cell floor, and walled in on three sides, but here she encouraged the creepers to twine, and planted violets and roses and lilies; and from its parapet she could look over the vale towards the Portiuncula and, on a happy day, see Francis coming up the hill.

Other sisters came to her, and Francis drew up for them a Rule as simple as that of his brothers. The brothers would do all their begging for them, since women could not wander alone in those turbulent and licentious times, and the sisters in return would do all the sewing for the brothers, and weave the cloth for their habits and embroider altar linen and vestments which they would use in their own little chapels or give to the poorest churches. And the brothers would seek out the sick poor and send them to San Damiano, where the sisters would nurse them. It should be a hospital and convalescent home for the poorest, and an infirmary, sometimes, for the brothers.

In fact, San Damiano was married to the Portiuncula.

Like the First Order of Friars Minor, the Second Order of Poor Clares had just happened around Francis. These things happened around him because he was what he was. A woman had raised the standard of Poverty at the side of Francis, and thousands of wistful and tired women responded. The sisters multiplied almost as fast as the brothers. It is a happy thing to tell that Bianca Guelfucci was one of the earliest to join her favourite niece; happier still that Madonna Ortolana and the youngest sister Beatrice came down the hill to join her after the death of Favorino. Like the *luoghi* of the First Order, branches of San Damiano sprang up all over Italy, to house those who were coming in. And among the postulants were princesses and queens.

Which points to a significant thing. Francis has been called the Patriarch of the Poor, and rightly, because they worshipped then, and worship still, the young man who emptied himself of his riches to be one of them. He set wide the doors of their hearts when he deliberately called himself the Poverello, the little poor man. You should see the old beggar-women shuffling on their knees to the spot where he died, at midnight on the anniversary of his passing. You should see the old crippled men swinging up on their crutches, to gaze upon the statue with the kind eyes. But the strange thing is that the inmost meaning of his call was best understood by spirits of an aristocratic temper.

Though is this so strange, after all? As M. Abel Bonnard has well shown, the peasant spirit craves always for possessions; the aristocratic spirit, if of the highest quality, learns soon that they imprison it. Francis was, or thought himself, an aristocrat, but he had the genius to transfigure a tradesman's desire to excel into something really noble. His Franciscanism is really the sublimation of the aristocratic idea. Scorning the vulgarity of scratching for wealth and rank, and competing to be superior to others, it achieves the fine courtesy of being equal with the lowest. "Courtesy," said Francis, "is one of the properties of God," and if he saw a beggar less worthily clad than himself, he promptly handed him his cloak and thanked him for the temporary loan of it. As a youth he was fastidious about things that offended the senses; he raised this into the higher fastidiousness which shudders from things which soil the spirit.

And what happened? His first disciples were Bernard of Quintavalle, a wealthy magistrate, Peter Cataneo, a learned jurisconsult, Angelo Tancredi, a knight, Leo and Sylvester, priests, Rufino, a son of the noble Scefi, and Clare, a daughter of the same proud house. And presently we shall meet among his Tertiaries, the Lady Giacoma, a Roman patrician, Orlando, lord of Chiusi, Giovanni da

Vellita, lord of Greccio, and the Lady Colomba, mistress of
Monte Rainero. Behind them come Louis, King of France,
John, King of Jerusalem, Aiton II, King of Armenia, Roger
Bacon, our own scholar and philosopher, and yes—who
is this with the aquiline face where intellect broods,
so consciously enthroned? Dante. Clare counted among
her followers, besides her own aristocratic family, Agnes,
daughter of the King of Bohemia, Elizabeth, daughter of
the King of Hungary, and another Elizabeth, Queen of
Portugal and daughter of the King of England. Francis,
with Clare at his side, created a new and nobler aristocracy
across the world.

Francis, with Clare at his side. A last word about the
troubled question of their love. The orthodox biographers,
even Father Cuthbert, are plainly frightened by it. For
myself, though I speak as a sinner, I can feel little doubt
about the simplicity of it all. Francis could have loved
her as a man loves a woman, if his call, which was to a
love of God and the whole universe in God, had suffered
him to do so. Clare, a woman, and therefore less con-
science-tormented by these fine distinctions, loved him
quite simply all her life. But it was a love that had lifted
itself high above the normal earthly plane.

I draw these rash affirmations from my reading of the
following facts. Francis' attitude to Clare was subtly
different from his attitude to other women. Always when
he had composed a poem, he wanted to send it to Clare.
Once, when faced by a critical decision, he chose Clare
out of all the world to choose for him. When he was sick
and dying, he turned in to her to nurse him. Some of his
last thoughts before death were of her. And, more
touching still, he would sometimes avoid her, as if a little
afraid.

145

And Clare? Clare never took her spiritual eyes off him. She, though as forceful a woman as most, rested always on him as her lord. A true woman, never understanding his avoidance of her, she would beg to be allowed to come and eat with him, and beg him to come and talk to them. However the feminists—and I am one—may dislike the Miltonic phrase, it was very nearly true of Clare: "He for God, and she for God in him." Faintly steals into memory, as one thinks of this lifelong allegiance, the shadow of a little obstinate queen who knew that her late Consort had been infallible. As I said in the beginning, if the infallibility of the Popes clashed with the infallibility of Francis, there was no question, even to this loyal daughter of Rome, whose infallibility was right. Pope after Pope, revering the Abbess of San Damiano, came to her for counsel and comfort, but when one of them offered to absolve her from her vow to uphold the rigorous poverty of Francis, her only answer was, "My Lord, absolve me from my sins, but not from following Christ." When the same Pope forbade the brothers to minister to the sisters, except to take them alms, Clare promptly countered by refusing every ounce of food they brought, saying, "If we may not receive the spiritual food our good brothers bring us, neither will we take any earthly food from them"; a retort which surely makes Clare the patron saint of the hunger strike. The Popes tried to force her Order into the old Benedictine system with its convents, lands, and financial security, but Clare saw that this would have smothered all the bright new shoots created by Francis, and her gentle, indomitable, monotonous reply was, "Soon after his own conversion I and my sisters promised him obedience." And in the Rule for which she contended throughout the years she styled herself, "Clare

146

the unworthy handmaid of Christ and small plant of our blessed father Francis." She gave the Popes no rest till they granted to her and her children throughout the world what in her fine aristocratic way she called " the privilege of most high poverty." And twenty-seven years after Francis' death, lying on her couch with the kind old hands of Leo, Angelo, and Juniper to smooth her passing, she received and opened the Papal Bull. And she read, "The sisters shall own neither house, nor convent, nor anything, but as strangers and pilgrims shall wander through the world, serving the Lord in poverty and humility." A few hours after, grasping within her fingers this permission to be a true daughter of Francis, she died too.

CHAPTER XII

SOMEWHERE about this time Francis went to preach in
the district around Lake Trasimene. To arrive at Trasimene from Perugia the road climbs the shoulder of
Monte Colognola, and then dips down towards the lake-
basin. At the top of the shoulder one sees the first ribbon
of water, still and blue at the feet of the mountains. A
little farther down and one commands the whole great
sheet and the mountains round it. My first thought, as
the panorama broke upon me, was that the Vale of Rieti
must have looked like this when its oval floor was a width
of water. Castled villages on their mountain spurs hung
upside down in that clean mirror. Two towns of Passignano hung suspended in front of me, one the right way
up and perfectly focused in the sun, the other upside down
in the lake, and just a hair's breadth out of focus. Two
islands lifted their wooded slopes out of the mirror and at
the same time inverted them in it. Beyond the Passignano
headland I saw—and this is the important point—that
the mountains drew back a little way to leave a crescent
of plain between themselves and the reeds. Over this
enclosed segment the olive trees shimmered in a silver
mist.

Trasimene. The name rolled up twenty-one centuries
like a strip of cloth, and I was looking at the year 217 B.C.

The shape of the land was no different in this morning
of 217 B.C. The mountains were more densely wooded,
but there were olives in the narrow plain, and reeds by
the water, and a road running near to the reeds. But there
was a low mist about the road. And in the mist—slaughter.

It was a great and very famous slaughter. Early this

morning Hannibal had hidden his horse and foot on the mountains around that crescent of land: his Africans and Spaniards had blocked its exit at Passignano, and his Gauls had waited on Colognola. And into this ambush the Roman army had come marching in column of route. Before they could deploy, the warriors of Hannibal swarmed down from the heights, and there was little for them to do but slaughter Rome in the reeds. In their panic the Romans rushed into the lake.

> They advanced as far as they could [writes Livy], till only their heads and shoulders were above the water. Many tried to swim away. But they had to abandon the attempt to swim so great a sheet of water; their strength failed them and they either sank in the mud or, trying to reach the shore, were met by the enemy who waded in and massacred them one by one.

Fifteen thousand died, and mingled their decay with the bed of Trasimene.

Having considered Hannibal's work on the bank of Trasimene, I dismissed fourteen intervening centuries and saw another figure moving along that road by the rushes: a single figure in a homespun habit and cord. It was another conqueror of Italy, so let us look into his strategy.

Francis cast his glance over the lake and saw the wooded island out there, rising above the water. Isola Maggiore, it was called, and it held his eyes. Here was beauty in an ample solitude. Here was a supreme quiet in which a man, by prayer and fasting, might link himself with the stillness of Eternity. Here, that is, was something which must lure Francis like the peak of a mountain. It was spring as he stood gazing at the island, just as it was spring when Hannibal slaughtered the Romans. Lent was at hand. Modelling himself always on his Master, he determined to spend the forty days in the solitude of that island. He persuaded a disciple to row him out; the boat drifted against the rocks of a tiny natural harbour, and he stepped, or waded, ashore. The legend states that he took with him two loaves, and that when his disciple came to fetch him away, forty days after, he saw that there were still a loaf and a half left.

Merely a legend, you say. More than likely; but—it is just possible that it is not so. Let us tread carefully in regions of experience about which we know nothing. We just do not know—we coarse, material men—what happens to a human spirit when it is able to link up and become one with the—what shall I call it?—the Life of the Whole. And the greater our ignorance the shriller our dogmatism. Let us remember that it is firm fact, and not legend, that the two Catherines—of Siena and Genoa— lived for longer periods than this on nothing but the wafer that came to them in the Mass. And that they discharged immense tasks all the while. And that, like sensible women, they tried hard to eat, but could not. Let us remember that St. Peter Claver, the Jesuit, lived his full span of seventy years on a meagre diet of dried maize, and that he had the muscular energy most of the time to carry on his back the exhausted slaves from the hulks. Or in a smaller way, but one more acceptable to moderns, let us remember the extraordinary eating, or non-eating, of Lawrence in Arabia. Francis was something of a Lawrence, an independent, wandering enigma, only he chose a land of the spirit for his Arabia.

These phenomena may be all pathological; or, again, they may not be. For my part, I will make no pronouncement on this "miracle" of Isola Maggiore, nor, standing

WHERE FRANCIS LANDED ON ISOLA MAGGIORE

WHERE FRANCIS PREACHED TO THE BIRDS

in my mist of ignorance, will I presume to judge the extremes of asceticism it implies. Am I, who can hardly struggle out of a warm, comforting bath when others are waiting for it, going to turn a silly, superior grin on a man far greater than I because he practised heroic austerities in the hope of adventuring far and discovering nobler countries of consciousness for me and others of his well-loved brothers to dwell in? A part of him lagged always in the Middle Ages, true; but it may be that in this matter the mystics of every faith, clime, and age, Eastern, Western, Greek, Christian, Moslem, Hindu, Catholic, and Protestant, have known what they were talking about when they affirmed that a man must submit to the severest athletic training if he would fit himself for the adventure into Knowledge.

Anyhow, Francis lived forty days on the uninhabited Isola Maggiore, trying to make himself worthy. To Christ, when fasting in the wilderness, angels came and ministered; to Francis a rabbit. A rabbit was his comforter on the island. And now, since we have made acquaintance with many of Francis' human brothers, let this small creature lead in, as in a child's picture-book, the famous procession of his animal friends: animals of a Noah's-Ark variety who beyond question loved and obeyed him in a way that would seem miraculous if we had not met mere carnal men with a good portion of his power.

At the Portiuncula a lamb would follow him like a dog, even into the chapel; and a cicala, which lived in a fig tree near his cell, would come at his call and sit on his hand. In the darkest and grandest hours of his life above the clefts and abysses of La Verna, a falcon watched with him. At Siena in his last sickness a pheasant was given him, and "Our Creator be praised, Brother Pheasant," Francis

151

would say to the handsome fellow as it followed him about. Near the same town a flock of sheep came bleating all around him. In one of the few pages of Thomas of Celano's *Life* that ring simple and true (for Thomas strained too hard to prove two things: first, that Francis conformed to the conventional idea of a saint; and secondly, that Thomas of Celano was a fine writer) we read:

> It is certainly wonderful how even the irrational creatures recognised his affection towards them . . . for once when he was staying at Greccio, one of the brethren brought him a live leveret that had been caught in a snare; and when the blessed man saw it, he was moved with compassion and said, 'Brother Leveret, come to me. Why did you let yourself be so deceived?' And forthwith the leveret, on being released by the brother, fled to the holy man and, without being driven thither by anyone, lay down in his breast as being the safest place. When he had rested there a little while, the holy father, caressing him, let him go, so that he might freely return to the woodland. At last, after the leveret had been put down to the ground many times, and had every time returned to the holy man's bosom, he bade the brethren carry it into a wood which was hard by.

He built nests for the doves, and put out honey and wine for the bees in winter. He wanted to petition the Emperor for a decree that everyone must feed the birds on Christmas Day. Cowper sang,

> I would not count among the number of my friends
> A man who needlessly sets foot upon a worm;

and Francis, as indifferent to the gibe about "sloppy sentimentality" (if it existed in those more demonstrative and honestly emotional days) as he was indifferent to anything else that contravened his vision, would lift the worms off the road and set them in the safety of the bank. At Alviano, as he began to preach before a crowd, a number of swallows, building their nests, made such a chattering that he could not be heard. So he paused in the sermon, and, turning to them, said, "My sisters, the swallows, it is now time for me to speak, because you have been saying enough all this time. Listen to the word of God and be in silence." And lastly, though this is more legendary, the far-famed wolf of Gubbio. The legend states that the wolf, after eating many of the citizens of that town, was completely tamed by Francis, who, in the course of a long chat, pointed out to him the discourtesy and unneighbourliness of such behaviour. The wolf accepted the rebuke, and thereafter became a pattern of courtesy and the pet and pride of all Gubbio. And who shall say that there is not a substratum of truth in this very early story?

2

I put out from Passignano in an extraordinary home-made craft that must have been a contemporary of Francis' boat, if indeed it wasn't the actual one. It had a flat floor of nailed rafters, and its sides were two planks bent to meet at bow and stern; and why the lake of Trasimene didn't come up between the cracks I don't know. Some of it did. Three fishermen of Passignano propelled it with oars that were merely long poles with planks nailed on to them for blades. Amidships two of them, old men, pulled with their backs to me in the bow; while in the stern (not that the stern differed from the bow; it was just the part that entered the water last) stood a splendid young Italian giant, whom I took to be the captain, facing me with laughing eyes and ready chatter as he pushed hard to keep the boat going true.

And so we went for an hour over the placid water towards Isola Maggiore.

I found the little bay of Francis' landing; and sent my fishermen off to drink wine with their brothers of the little fishing community that now lives on the other side of the island. I wanted to stand alone where Francis stood alone. His landing-place was a spot of much beauty, with trees stooping down to meet the rushes, and the rocks stretching out to form a natural quay. The air was so still that the water moved no more than the rocks. Only the frogs leapt in the reeds, and the lizards ran for safety as my footsteps broke the silence. The piety of the island had marked the site with a little shrine, and planted a winding avenue of ilex and cypress up to the grotto where Francis slept.

What Francis saw when the eastward sun awoke him in the morning my picture will tell you.

But feeling that I knew something of Francis now, I did not halt here. I climbed through thistle and thorn and bramble to the low crown of the island. Here, without doubt, he was wont to stand. Here on a summit in the midst of a lake he found what the mountains gave him: a wide prospect of the world, and all the sky. "Sister Water" stretched all around him to the blue mountains and grey, castled hills. "Monsignor Brother Sun" traced for him the whole of his arc from rim to rim. Sometimes the clouds heaped up to veil the divinity on which his thoughts rested. And except for the hum of insects, nothing but silence, as I can vouch, hung between him and the distant mountains.

And at night! What a canopy of stars to instruct his soul! By day the sky was a picture of that white, still, empty radiance which is the mystics' One; night, lowering a dark glass that he might see through it, showed him that the same still, empty Unity held all the worlds.

Upon this spot, then, a man kept company with God. Like Moses, he was "there with the Lord forty days and forty nights." And the Lord said, "Behold, there is a place by me, and thou shalt stand upon a rock; and it shall come to pass, while my glory passeth by, that I will put thee in a clift of the rock, and will cover thee with my hand while I pass by. And I will take away my hand, and thou shalt see my back parts; but my face shall not be seen."

Here, among the thistles and the stones, were moments of communion, illumination, and knowledge that are of greater importance to our race than the most heralded discoveries of science. Or so it sometimes seems to me.

3

After this period of rearmament he returned to the mainland and opened his campaign.

High above Lake Trasimene, higher than Perugia above the vale of Spoleto, so high that, as they say, its children seldom meet the plain, throned on a mountain's steep, and buttressed by Etruscan walls, sits the town of Cortona. Francis toiled up to it, and began to preach. How many were his converts we do not know; but, anyway, this form of conquest is not measured by numbers, but by depth. One only, perhaps; but one who fills a gracious niche in the temple of Francis.

Guy was a rich youth bearing a noble name and—what he appreciated more—a wide fame for courtesy; and Francis won him at a throw. It was Angelo Tancredi over again. Guy begged him and the companion who had joined him to make his house their home during their stay in Cortona; and, overjoyed at their ready consent, sped off to make himself the perfect host. He himself bathed their feet when they came in from the dusty occupations of the day, and allowed no one else to wait upon them at table. He insisted that all he had was at their service, and that if they needed anything which he hadn't got, he'd be hurt if they didn't enable him to procure it for them. The Lord's table indeed, well spread in high Cortona!

Even at this distance we can scent that rich produce of youth: hero-worship. Francis too must have smiled tenderly at the so palpable thing. Like Christ with the young man who had great possessions, Francis "looking upon him, loved him." When alone with his companion he said, "My dear brother, this youth is so kind and courteous that he would do well for our company." And from that moment, without saying anything to Guy, he prayed that he might be given to him. And before he left the house, Guy dropped on his knees before him and asked if there was any chance that he too might become one of the Brothers.

What, sell all he had and give it to the poor? Was he equal to that?

Yes, yes . . .

But had he really counted the cost? Would it not perhaps be better for him to remain as he was, being good and kind to all? It was not for all to become homeless knights of Poverty. Some must stay and have homes and families——

But no. Guy wanted nothing less than the whole offering. This young man with great possessions did not turn away. And in a few days Cortona saw what Assisi had seen: one of its wealthiest and best-known citizens distributing the whole of his goods to the poor. Cortona saw him receive from Francis himself, in a public ceremony, the coarse grey smock and white cord.

And then Francis and he went out of the city to find him a new home. They went out of the western gate and, dropping and twisting down the slope, came to a thickly wooded gorge. It is a gorge to remind one of the Carceri gorge, though it is less steep and less narrow, and therefore less majestically dark in its bottoms. On either side of a tumbling and sliding stream (they say that the Carceri stream runs only when disaster is near to the world) are dense groves of ilex, oak, chestnut, and lime. And if you skirt the upper end, as Guy and Francis did, you come upon caves. But to-day the caves are enclosed within the white, rambling walls of the Celle, or Cells; and the earliest parts of that lovely hermitage are the parts that Guy built. For here he lived for most of his life. He became a priest, and climbed often to preach and minister to his old friends the Cortonese, but, as Father Cuthbert has well said, it was mostly by his life of contemplation, poverty, and selflessness that he challenged the proud city above.

According to the annalist, Wadding, Francis made another convert in Cortona at this time: Brother Elias. To all who know the full story, mention of that name is drama enough. Brother Elias—a dark name, look at it how you will; a name as shadowed as Guy's is radiant. By the least forgiving of Francis' lovers it is reckoned an evil name: I prefer to call it a tragic one. Brother Elias, according to many, is the villain of the last acts, the Judas in the passion of Francis, but, like Pietro Bernardone before him—aye, and like Judas himself—he was not wholly evil, and one's pity can run out to him. His tragedy was simply this, that though deeply religious in his way, he was the natural opposite of Francis, and yet, attracted maybe by the fame of Guy's adhesion, he became a Franciscan.

But let Brother Elias wait : he will be with us soon.

4

Next, to find a place of much picturesqueness in the life of Francis, I left Central Italy for the Adriatic coast. I went to Rimini. And very early one morning I motored out from Rimini to hunt for a certain hamlet straddled on a ridge of the Apennines.

We soon left the flat lands by the sea and began our climb into the hills. The lower hills were tossed and rounded like an eiderdown quilt after a restless night. The mountains behind were a disorder of ridges and crests like a wind-whipped sea. And the highest of all, like a wave rearing up and about to break, was Monte Titano, which holds the toy republic of San Marino on its back.

I see I am likely to forget Francis in the joy of describing the Apennines under the morning; but doubtless it was a morning just like this when he came this way, tramping barefoot to Montefeltro. So, having found an excuse for the description, I shall proceed with it; and you must put up with it, consoled by the promise that it will not be long, and that it will be very pretty.

Soon we were right in the folds of the higher Apennines, and the sun was still so low that it lit every white building into bold relief, threw blue shadows everywhere, and chiselled deep groves in the mountains whose feet were yet in last night's dark. Everything green was the superb blue-green of early morning, larks soared and sang, and

158

the blue smoke of new-lit fires went up from little cottages. Pumpkins lay on the roofs to ripen, and the *granturco* hung on the trees to dry. We topped ridge after ridge, till at last we saw what we wanted to see: the torrent of the Conca tossing its silver rope down the steep valley floor.

(That is all.)

We were in sight of our goal. My driver, an intelligent citizen of Rimini, stopped time and again to ask the peasants the road to Sasso Feltrio, but the mountains had shut them in with their language for so long that he was hard put to understand them.

"Romagnola," he shrugged. "They speak Romagnola."

However, one of them pointed at last to a cluster of habitations on a sky-line, and to a white road twisting up to them. That was Sasso Feltrio, he said; and we engaged our gears, and roared slowly up to it.

Once in the village, I left the car and walked along the street (with all the children of the place behind me) till I came to the foot of a green, rounded knoll. This, they all assured me, was the site of the old castle; and up it we went clambering. There was nothing on its summit now— nothing but the tall grasses, some outcrops of rock, the small shack of a peasant, and a cutting wind. And a view, of course, of the whole storm-tossed mountain world and the far-off littoral and the sea.

But the peasant brought out his bright Italian smile (is there a welcome anywhere like the Italian peasant's, and have they no law of trespass at all?) and took me to where, deep in the ground, were the ruins of an arched doorway, and then down the slope to where, lonely in a cottage wall, was a stone engraved with the proud Malatesta arms.

With the children in train I left him and returned to the

159

crown of the knoll where the grass and the scabious washed against the recumbent rocks and over the dust of an old castle. Was this, then, the site of the castle of Montefeltro? Was it somewhere here that Francis first clasped hands with the young Duke Orlando of Chiusi? But here is the story.

In the spring of 1213 he was preaching in the Romagna when word came to him of a fine congregation up at the castle of Montefeltro. Montefeltro, he learned, was beflagged for a festival. Its lord had invited all his noble friends, and others less noble, to come and celebrate with a tournament the knighting of one of his family. It would be a scene of chivalry resplendent on the mountains, and it was not likely that Francis would keep away from it. He came quickly. Standing on my knoll, I picked out his quickest route and saw him coming along it with an impatient step. There along that ridge, with the deep vale of the Conca on one side and the vast quilted waterways of the Marano on the other, he would come, till he paused in the dip below me to look up at the scene. The scene has been described by Johannes Jörgensen in a way with which I will not compete.

> Francis came to this city on a May morning just as the banners flying from the towers and the blare of trumpets announced the festival. Gaily dressed pages and men-at-arms hastened over the drawbridge, knights on powerful chargers brightly caparisoned, thronged under the gateway, swinging carriages bore ladies young and old, with laced bodices and high head-dresses, up the steep road to the castle. . . . He stood there a little while and looked at the banner that waved over the gate with the bearings of the barons of Montefeltro.

A moment to enjoy the spectacle, and then the grey-brown smock mingled with the many-coloured doublets and the rich mantles, and pushed through the gateway into the bailey. His was the poorest garment there, and yet in that press of haughty people it clad the only name that the world has remembered. A young lord to whom he spoke, and because he spoke to him, catches a little of the memory, but not much. For the rest,

> The knights are dust.
> And their good swords are rust;
> Their souls are with the saints, we trust.

It is probable that he was recognised and acclaimed even then. It is possible that of all the proud names assembled within those battlemented walls the name of Francis of Assisi was best known. His friars, dedicated to joy and jesting, kindness and song, were now popular figures on all the roads of Italy. And one divines from the chronicles that when some of the happy visitors recognised this particular friar as none other than Francis himself, the rumour of it swayed the whole throng like a sudden wind in the barley. One divines that the young people, with their bright clothes and flushed cheeks, delighted him with the mediæval version of "Speech! Speech!" and that Francis, lifted by popular acclamation on to the castle stairs, "looking upon them, loved them," and burned with a desire to win them all. It may be that the thought rushed across him that now, for once, he was the troubadour of his childhood dreams, since he had come wondering into a baron's castle, bringing a tale of love to the assembled knights and dames. I suspect it did, because, with his usual quick wit and freedom from convention, he surprised the silence by declaiming some words from a troubadour's song:

> So great the good that I foresee
> That every pain is joy to me.

This was his text; and, speaking to it, he told these rich, proud people why he had chosen the way of poverty as the road to a nobler wealth.

That he was heard in a deepening silence, and that his words were not wholly lost, is shown by something that happened immediately he stepped down from the stairs. One of the noblest guests, Duke Orlando dei Cattani, Lord of Chiusi in the Casentino, made his way through the crowd towards him and, telling him how much his address had meant, asked if he might speak with him in private.

"Why, of course," agreed Francis, "but go first and do all that your hospitable host expects of you. When the festival is over, we will talk together as much as you like."

La cortesia è una delle proprietà di Dio.

And so, the jousting and the junketing done, Francis and the young Duke had a long and absorbing talk together. Orlando was another of those knightly and courteous young men in whom Francis could always awake the sleeping saint. And as they talked, Orlando's enthusiasm, and his eagerness to help, burst forth in an impulsive and extraordinary offer.

"Father," he said, "I so want to do something to help you and your Order, and I've been wondering what it shall be. But listen, and don't say no, till you've heard all. I own a mountain just above my castle of Chiusi. It is really a wonderful place: its peak dominates all the country for miles around, and the curious thing is that while the peak is covered to its very point with pines and beeches, its sides are rent into clefts and chasms. In our parts we believe that the mountain was split like that by the earthquake that marked the passing of our Lord. Well, it seems to me that it would be the perfect place for you and your brothers when you are in need of solitude; and I want to give it to you. It is called Alvernia."

Alvernia was the old name for La Verna.

Moved by the young man's offer, but doubtful for the present what to say, Francis temporised by promising to send some brothers to look at Alvernia.

When did Christ first hear the name of Golgotha, and did it seem to Him only the name of a hill?

CHAPTER XIII

Now, in everything that befell Francis he saw—super-stitiously, we may think—the finger of God pointing his way. And it chanced that this offer of the high solitudes of La Verna followed soon after his first, and abortive, attempt to reach the Saracens. I have not told you about this because it was a frustrated effort of which little is known. Whenever Francis sails from the port of Ancona, he sails into mist; and it will be only along the margins of Egypt and Palestine that we shall be able to follow him with any certainty. This first attempt to get to Syria met with shipwreck. And this shipwreck must have been a bewildering, discouraging experience, because it introduced doubt into a new, consuming idea.

The idea had been the result of the victory of the Christian armies at Las Navas in Spain. In July, 1212, at Las Navas, they had overthrown the Moorish power with such a roar of collapse as resounded through the Catholic world. To Francis this reverberating victory must have meant, first, a thrill of delight, and then an outrush of pity for the fallen foe. And so the new idea leapt up in him. Why not try, for a change, to win the infidels by love? You could do nothing—nothing at all—by all this hate. And nothing—nothing in the end—by force. All his sight, and all his experience, told him that this was true of individual men: it must be true also of peoples. Force and violence and vindictive punishment only hardened their recalcitrance. Forgiveness, and the refusal to punish or hurt them, and the persistent returning of good for evil, broke their hostility down—slowly but very surely. In the long run force failed as certainly as love conquered. One day, perhaps, the Church would really believe that its Founder had been right; and in the meantime it was for him to act out His teaching before the world, and prove it true. *He* would go on his own crusade. *He* would send *his* army. An army in grey frocks carrying nothing but the weapons of the Master, which were love, persuasion, patience, and faith in the goodness of men. He would go into the camps of the Saracens and call them brothers. "Good morning, good people." He would go to Syria or Egypt, where their great men were to be found. If they martyred him, no matter: that would be the beginning of something. Something that would *work*.

As impatiently, and as alight with the glamour of it all as when he started for the Two Sicilies, he gathered a few brothers together and set sail for the East.

And they were shipwrecked. Shipwrecked on the coast of Slavonia! What did it mean? And not only shipwrecked, but shanghaied on that wild shore by the autumn storms. And so much was waiting to be done, if not in Syria, why, then, in the still-unvisited parts of Italy! Francis paced the shore, or brooded on the mountains, looking across the Adriatic towards Italy. And at last the same impatience, and the same spirit of adventure, drove him to stow away with his companions on the first boat bound for Ancona. As when he took his father's best cloth for the service of the Lord, he seems to have been strangely unaware that this was a form of robbery. The incident, to tell the truth, defeats me. It is difficult to see how a body of men could have hidden themselves in a trading bottom of those days; and it is difficult (and diverting) to imagine the emotions of the sailors when they overturned a covey of friars in the hold. Still, Francis was able to pay something for their keep. A friendly Slavonian had equipped the brothers with a supply of food, and he shared this with the crew, and, as additional payment, preached to them sometimes under the stars. And I am sure the brothers, on whom manual labour was incumbent, worked hard at the ropes and swabbed the decks lustily.

Ancona is no great distance along the flat seaboard from Rimini, so it was probably after his arrival there that he came preaching in the hills around Montefeltro. And at Montefeltro, into which he had turned by chance, Duke Orlando offered him La Verna. At first, so tentative his acceptance, the coincidence of Slavonia and La Verna does not seem to have struck him, but gradually he began to wonder if here were God's signal. Was God urging him towards a life of contemplation rather than action? Was He discouraging him from further preaching and inviting him into the solitude with Himself?

As you read this, perhaps you recoil from it. And in truth, to our commonplace spiritual understanding, it does seem, at first shock, a foolish idea.

> I cannot praise a fugitive and cloistered virtue that never sallies out and sees her adversary, but slinks out of the race, where that immortal garland is to be run for, not without dust and heat.

So Milton: so a million others equally God-fearing and self-confident.

But this attitude forgets several things. It forgets that there can be heroes in the duty towards God as well as in the duty towards man. It forgets that the contemplative does his duty towards man no less than the explorer or the scientist. What higher service than to explore deeper and deeper into the divine, to bring within the compass of human consciousness the experience of unity with the One, and to manifest it to the struggling and suffering people. Francis knew that his discoveries of God up in the mountain could be a fount of inspiration for his brothers labouring below. And, rightly or wrongly, he believed in the efficacy of prayer. Most blindly of all it forgets that, for the mystic, God is not only a God above the clouds, but a God immanent in, and penetrating, all existences; a God that becomes almost visible when love looks out of any creature's eyes. For the mystic He passes by in every pedlar on the road and every bird on the wing. And therefore to penetrate deeper and deeper into the love and service of God takes one farther into the love and service of one's fellow-creatures. It was because Francis was a contemplative that he fought for the birds. It was because he was a contemplative that in Brother Robber at Monte Casale he recognised Brother God, though, to be sure, somewhat crusted over. And because of that recognition he knew how to treat him and to save him. Milton would have mishandled him gloriously.

Francis had experiences of Reality, or God, which are above our understanding: let that be clear. We are following in his footsteps, but, alas, we can follow, in the main, only his outer life. Of that long companionship with God which was his inner life, and which supported and enriched his indefatigable labours in the world, we shall not find the footmarks, because they are in the skies.

But I hope we can believe in them enough to understand why the offer of La Verna induced a period of indecision and crisis. He came back to the Portiuncula, where he had heard his first call, in the hope that that faithful altar might speak to him again. But no answer came. There was only silence without, and the worrying irresolution within.

I am willing to admit that his weaker as well as his

nobler parts were at work. He was tired and discouraged: a man who put such strains upon himself could not escape the lassitudes that visit even us who watch carefully that we do not work too hard. And in this weariness the feeling that he was no good whatever at managing the huge organisation his Order was becoming, and the longing for peace and solitude and blissful communion with God, would meet to form a strong stream of argument in favour of the contemplative life. He knew no psychology: he had never heard of rationalisation, that interesting mechanism by which we reason out a laudable motive for doing what we want to do. But it was possibly operating.

As an artist he had great gifts for creation and inspiration, and hardly any at all for business and affairs; and the smallest artist among us will know something of his experience—"Oh that someone would take on all the management of my life, and leave me free to think and create!" And preaching sometimes seemed like hackwork, compared with the perfect thing he wanted to create. Using his life as his medium, he wanted to create a perfect spiritual "form," which would be understood, perhaps, only by the few and by the future. He didn't want to "write down to his public." Any artist will understand.

And any lover. We shall not understand the first thing about Francis unless we allow that he was in love—strange as it may sound—with the Absolute. In love with the Absolute in Its character of absolute love. And we must accept humbly, unless, cocksure with ignorance, we prefer to spurn haughtily, the statement which every mystic has left us, that union with the Beloved, as they always call It, yields ecstasies that the most perfect human love can never know. We are permitted to think these ecstasies illusory, as we may think a lad's ecstatic adoration for his common little girl illusory: the point is solely that they are facts of experience. And Francis, untroubled like all lovers by the grinning of the world, longed in these days to be alone with the Beloved, because he was hurt and depressed.

But, besides being artist and lover, he was also saint, and no struggling saint is going to elude self-torment. The sweeter the idea of living with the Beloved, the more it would look like self-indulgence, and the more he would wonder if the devil were not in it somewhere. And at last Francis, whose powers of pure thinking, as he well knew, were weak, admitted that he was defeated by the problem.

Someone else must solve it for him. And, as usual, he adopted a method like tossing a coin and trusting that God would direct its fall. And the method he adopted is interesting, because it reveals in a single flash his faith in the priesthood and his faith in a woman's sense. Up among the dark woods of the Carceri, living alone in a cave for a period of retreat, was Sylvester, his first priest; behind the white wall of San Damiano was Clare, quietly going about her business of worship and ministration. A priest of marked contemplative gifts; and a loving woman, with a soul saner, simpler, and less self-tormented than his.

He came out of his wattle hut and called, "Masseo." And soon Masseo's burly figure was coming towards him. To this trusty and understanding friend, who had the gift of words, he told everything, and then bade him go first to Clare and ask her to pray to God and then to say what solution came to her. And after that he was to go on up to the Carceri, find Sylvester, and put to him the same· request.

And Masseo left the Portiuncula and took the path which led first to San Damiano on its hill, and then high up into the dark Carceri gorge.

And Francis waited, either pacing the clearing around the chapel or walking out into the forest. Everything shows his suspense: his fear of what he would hear, and his impatience to hear it. It would decide his course, and he would be at peace. But in these long hours while Masseo was away he could settle to nothing. He paced up and down and, as the time passed, began to peer through the trunks for a glimpse of Masseo, or to strain his ears for the sound of his feet.

And now someone was coming. The undergrowth rustled, and the twigs on the pathway cracked. Yes, there was the tall figure and well-favoured countenance of Masseo. Francis hung the moment with Italian gestures. Telling Masseo to say nothing till he was asked, he took him and washed his feet, as one might to a guest of distinction; he prepared him a meal, as for one who had been on a journey: he served him with his own hands; and when he was refreshed, he asked him to walk out with him into the wood. And when they were well away from the sight of all, there in the bird-broken silence, he knelt down before Masseo and, drawing back his cowl, asked, "What does my Lord Jesus Christ tell me to do?"

Masseo answered that both Clare and Sylvester had said that he must go out and preach, "for he was sent into the world for the salvation of souls."

Francis rose immediately and said, "Then let us go forth in the name of God."

CHAPTER XIV

I

AND, taking Masseo and Angelo Tancredi with him, he went out to preach.

In the relief of a problem solved he was happy again. Conflict drains away energy; its solution releases it. It is not to be wondered at, therefore, that of the sermons we can apparently place immediately after this, the first should be his most successful revivalist effort and the second the most famous sermon in the world.

He passed through the little walled town of Cannara, and at sight of him the whole population streamed after him to hear him preach. In a field outside the town he turned and spoke to them, and such was his fervour and force that the whole congregation, swept up in some sort of herd movement, wanted to make their vows straightaway. But even the unpractical and outrageous Francis felt that it would be unwise to empty a village of its people and lead them away behind him like a Pied Piper. So, smiling on them, he told them to go back to their labours for the present, while he thought out some scheme which would enable those who were sincere to stay where they were and be his followers too.

And thus it was that the Third Order, like the First and the Second, just happened around him. You can believe that my interest was high as I walked through Cannara and, when beyond the walls, stood wondering which was the homely field that gave us the Tertiaries of Francis. For just as from the preaching of William Booth on Mile End Waste there sprang an Army that carried its red-and-blue flag into every country of the world, so somewhere here in the grass began an Order that marched across

Europe and (thanks to the dissolving conditions of the time) proved far more powerful than the infantry of William Booth to remould the shape of Society.

The members of the Third Order, as Francis conceived them, were to stay in the world but not be of it. They were to eschew wealth and pomp and place. They were to keep only enough property for simple living, and devote all their surplus to the poor. Whatever they felt they had amassed by unjust means or undue profits they were to give back or away—which must have meant the ruin of half the tradesmen members. They were to refuse to swear any oaths unsanctioned by the Pope. They were to refuse to carry arms or to fight against their brothers in Christ. And in the same spirit they were to forswear all litigation among themselves. " The Third Order," wrote Bernard of Bessa, " is equally for clerics and lay folks: maidens, widows, and married people. The intention of these Brothers and Sisters is to live honourably in their residences and to busy themselves with pious actions and to flee from the vanities of the world. And among them thou seest noble knights and others of the great ones of the world in humble costume acting so beautifully with the poor and rich that thou canst well see that they are truly God-fearing." It is easy to see how such an Order, which quickly caught within its net kings and princes, queens and princesses, sages, scientists, painters, and poets, hastened the collapse of a feudal Society already in decay.

I know little of the Oxford Group Movement of our own time, but mention of it here may give us some small understanding of the Franciscan Tertiaries.

Some great movements have begun in a tennis-court, or in a train, or in a beer-hall, or in a college common-room.

It seemed to me fitting that Francis' Order should have begun by the wayside and in the grass.

And as I stood there thinking this, the fancy came to me that there cleaves always to Francis, whether he approves or not, a Fourth Order. It is the Order of those who do not abjure their fighting and their oaths, who cannot abandon their comfort or their fame, who still like the top table at the feasts and are not in the least eager to return their excess profits, but who, in spite of all this weakness, love Francis of Assisi and wish they were more like him. Perhaps they even, in a small way, limp after him, loose fellows though they are. They look wistfully after his disappearing figure, and wish they were not so like Brother Fly, in that they do not pray too much nor work too hard, but do eat bravely. The Limping Quaternaries, shall we call them? I have been a member of the Order for a long time, limping on as well as I may; and I suspect that most of my readers are members too, or I should have lost them long before this. God bless them all, and lead them on to better things.

Leaving Cannara in the plain, and taking a road that goes in the low hills towards Bevagna, one sees after a time, a row of houses along the highway. Cantalupo. The road here is straight and carries the eye to its end, where it begins to climb up to the walls and towers of Bevagna. All is open country to left and right of the road, and above you is a great view of the sky, from out of which you might expect at any moment the birds to come.

And Francis, trudging this way from Cannara, either on the day of the mass-conversion or on another, was arrested by a fluttering and a chattering and a general argument in a group of trees before him. He stood still and looked. The trees were as heavy with birds as the apple trees with blossom in spring. And, like the blossom, a spattering of birds was on the ground. Stepping nearer to them, he gave them that greeting which, so he tells us, the Lord had revealed to him as the proper greeting between Christians, "Il Signore vi dia pace" ("The Lord give you peace.") And, turning to Masseo and his other companion, he said, "Wait for me a minute, because I must preach to my sisters the birds."

And forthwith he began a sermon.

It is difficult to suppose that it was other than an acted poem by a man who liked to call his troupe the Jesters of the Lord, but, none the less, one may search history for a sermon quite as efficacious. It was preached to the birds, but the world heard it. The world heard it, fell in love with it, and was a little different after it. Having assumed the unfamiliar dignity of a historian, I am sternly pursuing moderation of statement, so I will withdraw my assertion that it was the most famous sermon in the world (though it was) and say only that it was the most popular. That it slew Byzantinism at a blow. That it sent Art back to Nature. That it turned the eyes of the artists from the stiff and formal Byzantine patterns and directed them towards birds and trees and the men on the highroad. That it ushered in Giotto and the Renaissance. That, by sending Art to Nature, it helped to send science there. That it humanised religion. That it played its part in humanising literature, because very soon everyone began to write about Francis (they are still doing it), and the most sensitive among them found that it couldn't be done without letting in the fresh air and the song of birds, and without writing simply in the language of the common people. That thus it prepared the way for Dante and the *dolce stil nuovo*. That, in brief, it opened eyes and thawed hearts; and the world changed. I do hope I have not exaggerated.

Somewhere in these fields, two thousand, two hundred and more years ago, when Bevagna was called Mevania, the whole power of Umbria and Etruria went down before the Roman armies under Fabius; and Umbria, as a free people, ceased to be. But the fields, like that ancient chapel at Bastia, have forgotten all this; to-day its broad view holds nothing remarkable except a little gabled shrine with a narrow garden planted around it. The garden covers the place where a son of Umbria met and exchanged courtesies with some birds. It is planted with ilex and oak, with box and juniper, and with roses; but the wilder growths have asserted their right to room, and you can see cow-parsley and yarrow and shamrock and valerian. Which is exactly as it should be, since the Umbrian preferred the *minores*. A farm-track borders one side of the narrow rectangle, the highroad another, and the open fields the remaining two. And in the hazy distance Assisi lies on its mountain slope like a litter of white stones.

If you walk to the shrine and study its inscription, you will read, "In this place St. Francis taught the praises of God the Creator to his sisters the birds"; and then a pleasant portion of his sermon.

Here is the sermon, as the Fioretti give it to us.

"My little sisters the birds, you are much beholden to God your Creator, and you ought to praise Him because He has given you liberty to fly about in all places, and has given you double and triple raiment. And again you are beholden to Him for the element of air which He has appointed for you; and for this also, that you neither sow nor reap, but God feeds you and gives you the brooks and the fountains for your drink, the mountains and valleys for your refuge, and the tall trees wherein to make your nests. And since you know neither how to spin nor to stitch, He clothes you and your young ones. Wherefore your Creator loves you much, since He has bestowed on you so many benefits. And therefore take care, my little sisters, of the sin of ingratitude, and study always to please God."

And, as the inscription on the pedestal concludes, poetically, but, as it happens, not at all inaccurately, "And the birds departed from him to announce to the world the word of life."

2

The modern psychologists say—and one's own introspection lends colour to their view—that the lines of a man's character are set forever in the first years of childhood. What he was as a child of five he will be, inescapably, as a man. That is not to say that if he dissected flies in his nursery he will later dissect the cat in his business office. These early energies and drives may be, and very often are, "sublimated" into power that he uses for good social ends. Thus his tendency to dissection in the nursery may mean that he will become a kind and skilful surgeon in the operating-theatre. If this is a sound theory, then no man illustrated it better than Francis.

As a child listening to his Provençal mother, he had wanted to be a troubadour, or, alternatively, a knight-errant; he became both in the spiritual field. He had wanted to be a poet; he ended by writing the poems on fleshly tables of the heart, his Brotherhood one, and his life another. He had wanted to be admired and liked, and he secured the love of the ages. He had wanted to be a

great prince and soldier, and in the Chapter General of
1217 we see him as a young Commander parcelling out
among his satraps the provinces of a conquered Italy and
issuing a General Order for his armies to march forward
into Germany, Hungary, France, and Spain.

In other words, a Chapter General assembled at the
Portiuncula under the presidency of Francis, and organised the "counties" of Italy—Umbria, the Marches, Tuscany, and the rest—into provinces of the Minorite
Brotherhood, and deputed bands of missionaries to cross
the Alps for the further expansion of the Minorite idea.

This Council of War shows, in a kind of Grand Finale
to Act I, the early triumph of Franciscanism. Through the
leafy avenues of the forest to the Portiuncula hedge-wall
(which must have grown quite high now) came brothers
from every corner of Italy, many of them old friends
happy to meet their Founder again, and others of them
new converts eager to look upon the face of so celebrated
a man.

However, we will hold back our descriptions of a
Franciscan Chapter for the still more picturesque "Chapter of Mats" two years later. But lest I have given you a
wrong impression of what Francis meant by conquest, I
will report to you his words, first, on those who were
appointed Provincial Ministers, and then on the missionaries. The first he addressed to the assembled Chapter,
and you can hear in them the doubt, the misgiving, with
which this strange captain of spiritual war viewed all
authority and organisation. It was a misgiving registered
on one of the most sensitive spiritual instruments that
humanity has produced, and it was all too abundantly
justified in the end.

"You are to be minister-*servants*," he pleaded, "not

177

masters. Guardians (*custodes*), and not sergeants. You must tend the brethren as a shepherd his sheep. Let all the minister-servants remember what the Lord says: 'I came not to be ministered unto, but to minister.' Let them remember that to them is committed the care of the souls of the brethren, and that if any soul is lost through the minister's harshness or bad example, that minister will have to render an account before our Lord."

I expand the haunting misgiving from a letter he wrote long after to Elias, the Minister-general. "As sure as you love the Lord and me, His servant and your servant, see to it that no brother in the whole world, let him have sinned as he may, in any way, is permitted to go from you without forgiveness, if he asks for it. And if he does not ask for forgiveness, then ask him if he does not want forgiveness. And if he comes a thousand times before you with his sin, then love him altogether more than you love me, that you may draw him back into well-doing."

The business of the ministers settled, the Chapter passed on to its most stirring moment, the appeal for volunteers to cross the Alps and preach in the savage lands of Germany, Hungary, Normandy, and Spain. These were Christian lands, certainly, but their inhabitants, so many of whom had come ravaging over the Alps, had the worst reputation among the simple peasants of Italy. Not a man in that Chapter who did not look upon those who stepped forward to volunteer as men marked for great hardship and possibly for martyrdom. They gazed at them in silence. It is good to see standing among them the reverend figure of Bernard of Quintavalle, and we can imagine Francis' gratitude to his first follower, so quiet and safe and solid, as he charged him with the leadership of the mission to Spain. ("If I could have had a thousand

178

lives," said Bernard, many years after, as he lay, a very old man now, and dying with a smile for all around, "I would have chosen to serve no other master than Christ. Hear my prayer, that ye love one another." And with the smile still about his lips, as if he were remembering the early heroic days when Francis was still alive, he died.)

When the Chapter had broken up into talkative groups, there came a yet greater sensation: Francis quietly announced to one of the groups that he was going too. "Yes," he said, "it behoves me to be a form and example to the others. If I have sent them to distant lands, to bear labour and shame and hunger, it is only right that I should go likewise to some distant province, so that the friars may sustain adversity more patiently by remembering that I am doing the same. Will you go and pray to God that He will show me in which land I can best serve Him and you all?"

The brothers, surprised and not a little disturbed, went away to pray. And in time they returned, but before they could speak, Francis exclaimed, "In the name of our Lord Jesus Christ and the Blessed Virgin and all Saints, I choose the province of France, in which is a Catholic folk, and especially because they are known above all Catholics for the reverence they show to the Body of Christ."

I know nothing that illustrates better than this our opening thesis that the child was father to the man. Here is Francis persuading himself that it was because the French revered the Blessed Sacrament that he must go over the Alps into Provence, when anyone can see that he had selected Provence because it had been the dream-country of his childhood. That this old childish fantasy was present in his mind is confirmed by his choice of a partner. He chose Brother Pacifico, who had not only been a troubadour himself at the Court of Frederick in Sicily, but had been crowned by that most cultivated patron a "king of verse." It is as though he said to this real, professional poet, "Come; you and I must go to Provence. You'll be the troubadour, and I'll be your jongleur. And we'll see how many of the troubadours and jongleurs there we can enrol among our *jongleurs de Dieu*."

The Chapter dispersed, and the missionaries departed into the hazards that waited beyond the mountains, and the ministers into the dangers of office.

It was a central moment. One Act had closed, and the bell was sounding for the next. Though they did not know it, it was that point of time at which Franciscanism passed from its joyous and triumphant youth into the conflicts and disillusionments of manhood. Now would come the real clash between the Spirit that was in it and the Body of our limitations. Now the Franciscan idea would really meet its Adversary in the outer world and in the inner heart of the Brotherhood itself where the world still lingered. Now its first rushing self-assurance was to find the rocks and be broken into swirls and spray, or split into troubled and diverging streams.

The missionaries, crossing the Alps, met the Germans; the ministers, dressed in their new authority, met the devil in themselves; and Francis, going north for Provence, met Cardinal Ugolino.

CHAPTER XV

SEEN in other than a Franciscan light, Ugolino, Cardinal Bishop of Ostia, makes a fine figure. And a singularly attractive one. To begin with, he was tall and handsome, and, at the time of his entry on to the Franciscan stage, his face, naturally noble, had been embellished by the delicate handiwork of seventy comfortable and princely years. And there was sweetness in his face, because he added to an affectionate nature the benevolence of a big man who had never known anything but comfort, admiration, and authority. Or, shall we say, the benevolence of a big man who, by quickly crushing all who opposed him, did not allow them further to disturb his benevolence. His noble appearance, his rank in the world, and his position in the Church, were such as to turn all eyes towards him when he entered a room. In the world he was Count of Agnani, and one of the family of the Conti, who were such quintessential counts that they took their family name from the title—*The* Counts, as we might say. That he was also nephew of the reigning Pope, Innocent III, was another shining decoration. And in the Church, which considereth not the rank of men, he occupied as Cardinal Bishop of Ostia and Velletri, and Papal Legate of Central and Northern Italy, a position second only to that of the Pontiff himself. And in addition to his fine presence, in addition to all these worldly and unworldly dignities suspended around it, he possessed a native eloquence, a gracious scholarship acquired at Bologna and Paris, and, so far as his spiritual lamps would allow, a very real piety. No whisper of scandal ever sullied his reputation for austerity, and, indeed, there is no doubt that, somewhere within his magnificent robes of office, languished a small, smothered mystic and saint—a saint who half understood, and wistfully admired, both Francis and Clare.

But unfortunately he was a practical man. That is the only weakness we can disclose in him, but it is a weakness which in an ordinary Christian is a danger, and in a Franciscan a disaster. As a practical man he believed firmly in the rod and the sword. He quite honestly believed that severe punishment was a kindness to the wrong-doer as well as to the righteous who witnessed it. Which was a happy condition for him, because it meant that no amount of browbeating and bullying by Cardinal Ugolino need unseat his benevolence. He quite honestly believed that inquisitions and frightfulness were the best way of extirpating the heretics—unless, peradventure, a better way would be to extirpate the heretics themselves. His later career as Pope Gregory IX, wherein he combined a humble love and reverence for Clare of San Damiano with the most frightful savagery against the Albigenses and other unbelievers, shows that nothing of this is unfair description. The pity of it is that he preferred the sagacious, practical, "strong" man in Cardinal Ugolino to the poor, small, wondering saint. Yes, very accurate is a pope's description of him as "a cedar of Lebanon in the garden of the Church."

Like all such men, he loved organising. And that was a very great disaster. He worshipped discipline, which, to be sure, is a thing well worthy of worship if it is self-discipline, but unfortunately these practical men always understand by "discipline" an obedience enforced by external penalties, which is not a worshipful thing at all, because it is a cowed, tamed thing. It may be a necessary evil sometimes, but it is an evil all the same, because its other name is fear. Let us put it bluntly: like Innocent III, Cardinal Ugolino, scholar, statesman, and controller of mighty forces, was a far stronger and cleverer man than Francis—as the world measures strength and cleverness—but he was a spiritual ignoramus compared with him.

And Ugolino now decided that it was time somebody organised the Brothers Minor. That young man, Francis, was a perfect saint, of course; but, like all saints, he had no organising ability. It was really time that someone with an organising genius—himself, say—took a hand in the business. The creation of these knight-errants of Christ and Poverty was a lovely idea, no doubt—most poetical—but a bit dreamy; still, sublime in its way, and if someone could lick the Order into shape, it might be made into a great power for Holy Church.

"I see great things in it—immense things, if it is properly handled. It wants tightening up; yes, it certainly wants tightening up. Such an enormous body of men needs discipline. That Francis, bless his heart—he's a far greater man than I am, but he couldn't discipline a rabbit; and nothing can be done without discipline. Of that I am confident. That Cardinal John of St. Paul, who has been their Protector, was just such another: a perfect saint, but with his head in the clouds. A couple of nice dreamers together, they were. But now that he is dead I feel the perfect Cardinal Protector would be somebody—well, somebody like myself. I feel that Francis and I would make a good team, because I should bring in all that he lacks. I could convert into a fine fighting army what looks like becoming, I must confess, an undisciplined rabble. I very much like the idea of an Order of missionaries who will show forth to the world the humble, the gentle, the more self-sacrificing side of Christianity. It is really time that side was emphasised. Then we shouldn't hear so much of these heretics attacking the worldliness of the clergy. If, as everyone seems to think, I shall be the next Pope, I should like to have such an Order to my hand: they could be of great use to *me*, and *I* could simply *make* them. I should like to put these humble, saintly friars into the very highest positions of the Church. That would teach some of these pompous and carnal ecclesiastics a thing or two." (Scholars will aver that every word of this imagined soliloquy is warranted by the relations of Pope Gregory IX with the Franciscan Order.)

And now, by good fortune, just as Ugolino chanced to be in Florence, Francis appeared there; filled, it was said, with some crazy idea of leaving his Order to run to seed while he risked danger and death in France. Ugolino immediately summoned him to a meeting. I am sure that it was an enthusiastic meeting. The big, generous, affectionate man welcomed the famous little friar with a warm cordiality—not empty of patronage. I seem to catch his greeting across the centuries: "My dear man, come in, come in! I've been thinking about you a lot, and longing to talk to you. It's simply wonderful what you're doing. Wonderful! I am only wondering in what way I can be of help."

And Francis, because he too liked affection, and because he was a little raddled just now by doubts of his Order and distrust of himself, felt grateful for the goodwill of this powerful man. It was one of Francis' failures, who was usually shrewd enough in reading character, that at first he saw nothing else in Ugolino but his affection, interest, and real piety. As he had sought counsel and direction from Bishop Guido, so now he longed to submit himself to the wisdom of Ugolino. It was genius asking help from mediocrity; a lamp trying to read by the candle. Later he saw everything; but by then an affectionate friendship existed between the two men which it would have been unthinkable to break; and Francis could always forgive.

We have some records of the conversation at this meeting, and I interpret them thus:

"My dear man," said Ugolino, "what's all this about your going off to France? You're needed here in Italy. Don't you realise that many of the bishops are as critical of your Order as I, personally, admire it? Your Order, if you only knew it, is threatened on many sides. The place of its leader is in Italy."

"My lord, the place of a leader is in front of his army. I am satisfied that I cannot send my brothers into hardship, and not go myself."

"Oh, quite so, quite so! I think that's an excellent sentiment. I agree with you entirely, but I would go further and ask, why, for the present, send the brothers at all? Surely there's quite enough for them to do in Italy. When you've consolidated your position in Italy——"

"My lord, forgive me, but I do not quite know what you mean by consolidation. We have organised ourselves into provinces, and I know no more that we can do except trust that God will care for His own. It is not as if we were going to fight or quarrel or resist anyone. We, thank God, have nothing to defend. Why, then, should we not go on? We believe that we have been raised for the salvation of souls, not in Italy only, but throughout Christendom. And not in Christendom only. As soon as we can, we are going to the infidels too——"

"Oh, quite so, quite so! And don't think for a moment

185

that I want to hinder you in the pursuit of your vision. My sole desire is to help you—to help you all I can. But, you see, I look over a far wider country than you, and I think (I *must* say) that it would be most unwise if, at this juncture, you disappeared somewhere where we couldn't find you, and that it would be quite fatal to your Order if unhappily you died or were killed. You see: you do not realise your own importance, but we outsiders have no two views about it! Surely I am only talking practical common sense. For the sake of your Order, until we have established it on a firmer basis, I hold that you should be at the centre of things. That is my view, and I put it before you with all the earnestness I can command."

And Francis, desiring to be always humble and obedient, and possibly misdoubting lest there were some self-indulgence in his journey to France, agreed. Brother Pacifico went on alone; to found the Franciscan Order in the land of his brother troubadours.

Ugolino had turned Francis back. He may have been right on this occasion, but it stands as a symbol. From beginning to end the work of Ugolino, though done from the highest motives, was to dull the temper of Francis' sword.

2

This repulse of Francis was followed by the failure of all the missions except that which Bernard of Quintavalle led into Spain. In Germany, Hungary, Portugal, and France the brothers were mocked, maltreated, and beaten. The serious folk took them for Albigensian heretics who should rightly be expelled, and the ribald took them for rogues and vagabonds who were proper targets for stones and sticks. To the serious they could show no warranty from the Pope; and to the ribald they could speak in no language which did not deserve guffaws. The Catholic world was too old, and too remote from its youth in Christ, to understand apostles who came wandering like their Teacher without scrip or purse or shoes, and with no means of subsistence except the scraps earned by manual labour or the alms offered by those to whom they preached. A thousand years had conditioned all Christian men to expect their apostles in glorious apparel and faintly terrible with the power of Rome. These beggarly vagrants who refused to have any power behind their backs except the power of their faith, they treated as half-wits and drove back over the Alps into Italy.

And the friars came home, defeated and murmuring. All except the best of them murmured against Francis for having set them an impossible task. Too high-flown altogether, this idea that the Gospel must conquer by spiritual means alone, unaided by anything that savoured of material protection and power! On their return they thanked God that Cardinal Ugolino, a man of some common sense, was taking the Order under his protection.

Covert murmuring is so pleasant a pastime that it spreads quickly. The contagion reached the ministers. Unable to rule by grace of personality as Francis did, unable to await the slow processes of love, remote from his refining charm and relapsed into their own denser air, they began to mutter about rules and discipline and the right to punish. Anxious men, unable to trust their God as he did, they began to argue the need of having some property in common. And they too turned their eyes towards the Cardinal.

And if the ministers were asking for discipline and security, the younger converts who had never seen Francis

began to crave for learning. They had seen the Dominicans, who made of learning a primary duty; and they
wanted to imitate them. And how could they get learning
if they observed the extreme poverty that their Founder
desired? How study without convents, cloisters, libraries,
and—money? They could only hope that Cardinal
Ugolino, himself a graduate of Bologna and Paris, would
persuade the Founder to mitigate the rigour of his ideal.

Francis heard of the *débâcle* and the disaffection with a
falling heart. He liked success. As a child he had dreamed
of worldly triumphs, and during these last years he had
been as happy as a boy in the nobler success which had
come to him in his own lively land. But now he was
learning that he would have to ennoble still more his
conception of success: he would have to measure it by its
depth in the heart of a few rather than by its width over
the surface of the world. He saw that the first wide
triumph of his movement, while achieving many good
things, had also swept in the germs that must destroy its
meaning. It had enrolled too many who were not clear in
their sight, and every brother of inadequate vision
brought with him an unseen recruit, Brother Death. And
this ancient adversary would whisper always to his companion the pale word, "Compromise." He learned that
his perfect followers would have to be few, because they
must be his equals in vision. Every true prophet and
every good artist has to learn this. And if they meet no
equals, what then? The loneliness of the greatest, the
loneliness of Christ and of Shakespeare and of Francis, is
a thing to ponder.

For Francis, despite the failure, knew that he was right.
His technique of love and purely pacific resistance might
be slow in its effect—yes, slower than he had thought at

first—but it must win in the end. He knew this with the same clarity as he knew the light of the sun; and even if he hadn't, he would have accepted it humbly as the bright knowledge of his Master.

But while his assurance that he was right only hardened, his confidence in himself as a leader began to crack. He could *see* and *feel*, but could he organise, control, and plan? Were not the malcontents right in hinting that he was all very well as a prophet, but if the Order got much larger, he'd have to be superseded as a general? But even if they were right, where would they find a general who had both the vision to see the complete ideal and the ability to organise it without compromise?

It is a piece of fine insight in Father Cuthbert to place at this moment the episode of "The Perfect Joy." Francis must have been thinking much about joy in these days of despondency. He had always preached the manifestation of joy and laughter as a first duty of his brothers on the road, and was he to fail them in his example now? He must find the joy in all this, and show it forth.

The road from Perugia to the Portiuncula goes up a hill and down again, as it passes the little hill-town of Colles-trada. Or it did this before they re-shaped it for the motorists and ran it round the foot of Collestrada's hill. To-day this steep section of the old road is merely a lane for pedestrians and carts—or for a wandering historian. If you go up it, coming from Perugia, and when you have reached the top, turn round to look the way you have come, you will see on the mountain ridges behind you that proud and stormy city—a very throne of the World Spirit—lifting its towers and campaniles into the lumin-ous sky. And you will see the whole picture framed in the dark, tall cypresses which flank the steep incline. Then, if you turn your back upon Perugia, with a sigh for its beauty and its wickedness, you will immediately descry in the midst of the plain before you the dome of the Portiuncula.

When I stood on the top of the hill, one bright September evening, and turned back to look towards Perugia, I swept the centuries out of the way (such was my business wherever I went) and saw the snow falling heavily between the cypresses, and two figures in corded habits and cowls toiling up through the blizzard, one lagging behind the other. They were Leo and Francis; and Francis was the heavy-footed one behind. He was returning from Perugia, where he had been in conference with the hearty Ugolino; which had helped, perhaps, to put the weight in his feet. Still, there, a little way in front of him, walked Brother Leo. There at least was one who, like Clare at San Damiano, would never question that he was right, though the whole world went from him. And so, each thinking his own thoughts, and their cowled heads bent to avoid the harsh, driving snow, they tramped up the hill towards Collestrada.

The rest must be given in the words of the Fioretti: one cannot paraphrase a lily. I use the beautiful translation of the Franciscan Fathers of Upton, as amended by Thomas Okey, and somewhat by me; and I thank both parties for the loan of it, the more especially because I have not asked their consent.

"As St. Francis went once on a time from Perugia to St. Mary of the Portiuncula with Brother Leo, in the winter, they suffered greatly from the cold, and St. Francis called to Brother Leo who was going on a little in advance, 'O Brother Leo, although the Friars Minor in these parts give a great example of sanctity and good edification, write it down and note it well that this is not the perfect joy.'

"And having gone a little further, he called to him a second time, 'O Brother Leo, even though the Friars Minor should give sight to the blind, and loose the limbs of the paralysed, and though they should give hearing to the deaf and speech to the dumb, and though, what is more, they should raise the four days dead, write that not in this is the perfect joy.'

"And going on a little further, he called, 'O Brother Leo, if the Friars Minor knew all languages, all science, and all scriptures, if they could prophesy and reveal not only the future but the secrets of consciences and souls, write that not in this consists the perfect joy.'

"And going yet a little further, he called again, 'O Brother Leo, little sheep of God, even though the Friars Minor spoke with the tongues of angels and knew the courses of the stars, and the virtues of all things, men and trees and stones and roots and water, write that not in this is the perfect joy.'

"And advancing still a little further on his way, he called aloud, 'O Brother Leo, even though the Friars Minor should preach so well as to convert the infidels, write that herein is not the perfect joy.'

"And Brother Leo, in great astonishment asked him, 'Father, I pray thee, for God's sake, tell me wherein is the perfect joy.'

"And St. Francis replied, 'When we shall have come to St. Mary of the Angels, soaked as we are with rain, and frozen with the cold, and dying with hunger, and shall have knocked, if then the porter comes in a rage and asks angrily, "Who are you?" and we reply, "We are two of your brethren," and he answers, "You lie. You are two lewd fellows who go up and down corrupting the world and stealing alms from the poor. Get you gone from here"; and he will not open to us but leaves us out in the snow and the rain, in cold and hunger—then, if we should bear abuse and cruelty and dismissal patiently, without disturbance and without murmuring, write, O Brother Leo, that this is the perfect joy.' "

CHAPTER XVI

I

THE enemy was within the city: it is important to know the points at which he had entered, and the priming of his guns.

Francis' First Order was "a city set on a hill." In his conception it was a company of men who would enact again before the feudal world that life which had shaken the Roman world from Galilee. He wanted a corporation of Christs, no less; he had no desire to found a new monastic order. His appeal was an heroic appeal, but he addressed it only to heroes. For those who could not go the whole heroic way he had invented the Third Order. But now he saw (though I suspect it was a case of feeling rather than seeing clearly) that the enemy had made three breaches in his wall. These breaches were the demand to hold property in common, the demand to back discipline with force, and the demand for learning.

And all these demands he must resist.

He must hold the place he had made for Poverty. First, because Christ had chosen Poverty: had He not espoused her in the manger among the animals and lived with her all His ministry, so that he had to borrow a coin to teach a lesson, and beg a room for his last meal; and had He not confirmed His loyalty to her by resting at last in a borrowed tomb? Secondly, because, as he had said to Bishop Guido, any possessions whatever, whether held privately or in common, would entangle his Order in quarrels and claims, and so separate it from that perfect unity with men which was Love. Thirdly, because his challenge to an acquisitive and possessive world lost all its force if he clothed its nakedness with property.

Poverty was the essence, the heart, the inmost being of his idea. Without her it was but one more pious movement within the unchallenged order of Society.

And anyhow, he was sworn to her by an oath of chivalry.

And he must hold the little place he had swept clean of force. His wandering preachers must have no weapons of conquest or shields of protection at all, except the truth of their message and the beauty of their lives. Christ had had no power behind Him; He had not asked letters of protection from any pontiff; He had known that if the people martyred Him they would simply put the victory into His hands. He had not sought an authority from the High Priest which would force the lesser clergy to permit Him the use of their pulpits. "O you Brothers Minor," Francis had said one day, hiding a weariness under the mockery, when they suggested that he should get the Pope to coerce the lesser prelates, "you will not allow me to convert the world as God desires. For I wish by perfect humility and reverence first to convert the prelates, who, when they shall see our holy life and reverence towards them, will beseech you to preach and convert the people, and these shall call you to the preaching better than your 'privileges', which would lead you into pride. . . . But as for me, I desire only this privilege from the Lord, that never may I have any privilege from any man, except to do reverence to all, and to convert the world rather by example than by word." And Christ had not controlled His disciples by punishments: when Peter would deny Him, and Judas betray Him, He had said only, "What thou doest, do quickly," and had broken the hearts of both.

These two positions are easy to understand. It is less easy to see why he must resist the demand for learning.

But look more keenly. Note that he saw all round him something like a craze for the possession of learning. The first half of the thirteenth century was marked by a kind of "gold rush" for the ornaments of learning. In that time eight new Italian universities sprang to life in Peggio, Vicenza, Padua, Naples, Vercelli, Rome, Piacenza, and Arezzo. Sixty more sprang up in the other countries of Europe. And in all this excitement the large, wide-open eyes of Francis saw much that was invisible to the old Cardinal and to the enthusiastic youngsters. He saw that learning is not wisdom, because wisdom comes only when the apprehensions of the heart and the spirit are joined to those of the mind. He saw that learning is not even knowledge, because facts have to be experienced to be known. In a dazzling sentence, which every scholar should repeat three times a day, between his hours of labour, he said, "A man's knowledge is as great as his deeds." Learning flatters a man that it is both wisdom and knowledge; and, alone, it is neither.

Then he saw that, however this might be, ninety per cent. of the enthusiasts were pursuing learning for self-decoration, and not for wisdom. With those outside his Order who were earnestly pursuing wisdom, and divorcing it from pride, he had no quarrel. Nor with those who had been scholars before they joined the Brothers Minor: these he accepted and honoured as such—with a little chaff. Two of them, Peter Cataneo and Gregory of Naples, he appointed to high position. Antony of Padua, most learned of all, he would call charmingly, "Brother Antony, my bishop." And in his Will he wrote, "All theologians, and those who serve us with God's word, we should honour and revere." But those who had come to him unlearned he wanted to hold back from the gold rush, because he saw the same dangers in the accumulation of learning as in the accumulation of property: pride, jealousy, and separation. They had not donned his habit and cord for this. They had come to perfect themselves in love, not learning. Love would teach them all they needed for their work. Love alone could know God: "by love He can be gotten and holden, by thought never." Real love taught in a flash what a hundred volumes could never teach a man. "Only those that do the will shall know the doctrine"; and Francis wanted his men to speak with authority, and not as the scribes. And, lastly, love alone could win men. "There is a defence against learning, but there is no defence against love"—such is the gist of one of his sayings. "Not by what a Brother Minor argues will the people be won, but by what he is."

Hear the pitiable disappointment, but hear also the true accents of the seer, in his words to one of the Chapters. "My brothers, my brothers, the Lord said to me that He wished me to be a fool and a simpleton, and that He wished to bring us along another road than learning." Hear how he explained it to Leo and Rufino and Angelo, and those dear few who really needed no explanation because they never doubted that he was right. "My best beloved, there are many friars who place all their study and care in acquiring knowledge, leaving their holy vocation, and wandering out of the way of humility and prayer. But those whom they think they have converted by their knowledge and their preaching, the Lord has really taught by the lives of holy, poor, humble, and simple friars, though these do not know what they have wrought. These are my Knights of the Round Table." And to a young novice who asked if he might possess a psalter for himself, he answered smilingly, "Charlemagne and Roland and

Oliver fought the heathen with much sweat and labour, and died holy martyrs. But now there are many who content themselves with merely telling about the saints and reciting what they did"—(I bow my head)—"and you, after you have got your psalter, will desire a breviary, and say to your brother, 'Bring me my breviary!'"

Which pretty charade Francis immediately acted before the young brother, sitting on a throne and calling, "I! A breviary! I! A breviary!" And then, giving his blessing to the abashed boy, he said, "Brother, I also was tempted to have books, but when I wanted to know the will of God I took up a book in which the Gospel of the Lord was written, and I read, 'Unto you it is given to know the mysteries of the Kingdom, but unto others in parables.'"

But perhaps the whole position is best summed up in an episode at Siena when he lay dying. A very learned Dominican came to his sick-bed and asked, "How am I to understand that threat in Ezekiel which says, 'If thou speakest not to warn the wicked man of his ways, his blood will I require at thy hand'? I fear I know hundreds of wicked men whom I am not for ever warning. Will their souls really be required at my hand?"

Promptly, and with his accustomed smile, Francis answered, "But why ask me, Doctor? I am but a simpleton, and should rather be taught by you than teach so learned a master."

The Dominican, however, would not be put off by chaff. "No, no," he persisted, "I have heard expositions of this text from many wise men, and now I desire yours."

"Very well," agreed Francis, "I understand it thus: that the servant of God should so shine forth with holiness that his life is a brilliant and inextinguishable light rebuking the wicked."

And the Dominican was satisfied. Leaving the sick-room, he said to the friars outside the door, "My brethren, the theology of this man, founded on purity and contemplation, is a flying eagle, while our science crawls on its belly on the earth."

2

But let him see these truths of the spirit with surpassing clarity, he could not see at all how to give them body and form in a world-wide organisation of men. Here he blinked, and frowned, and was disquieted. How organisation without common property and without force? In all his writings and admonitions you can trace this bewilderment: property he rejects till the end; punishment he does not believe in, and concedes only with a hundred safeguards. He would have liked his friars to be only loosely bound together by love as they had been at Rivo-Torto. All chains applied from without he perceived to be a denial of the spirit of love. Men must forge from within the chains that bound them together (this is another of the great ultimate truths which he saw). If they saw the unity, the identity, of all life, the chains would be forged in the act of sight. Such a method of binding men together may seem quite impracticable in our present world, but that is no censure on Francis: it is merely to say that he came a few centuries before the world was ready for him. But the ideal cannot be uplifted too soon.

His weakness lay in his desire to trust Ugolino. His simple, affectionate nature longed to believe that Ugolino was the man to help him now. Ugolino was so genuinely devout, so friendly, and so enthusiastic. And sometimes he said things which showed moments of real mystical perception: had he not once, in a such a moment, inverted their positions of cardinal and deacon, father and son, and himself sought advice of Francis as to whether he should divest himself of his dignities and become one of his humble brothers? Sometimes he felt he would like to, he had said.

But—Francis doubted. Shrewd eyes saw what a trusting heart didn't want to see. Doubting himself, he doubted Ugolino too. "O God, show me how to guide and save these brothers whom Thou hast entrusted to me, that I may be a good shepherd and lose none. . . ."

Did Ugolino doubt? I think not. I think he thanked God that he was there to look after them. He was confident that he could manage the saint tactfully, and give some coherence to his raggle-taggle following. He was now gripped by his idea of using them as a great instrument of reform and of appointing bishops from among them, to teach the world that the Church preferred sanctity to social rank. Of course when he had put this inspiring idea to Francis, the young fanatic had rejected it, saying (rather beautifully, really), "My lord, my brothers are called *minores*"; but with a little tact and patience one could win him round. The idea was too good to let drop. One must go slowly. The first thing to do if he wanted to be a true friend to Francis, as he did, was to overcome the suspicion and hostility of so many of the Cardinals. If only they could know Francis as he knew him, and hear his stirring words, they would quickly see that he was no Peter Waldo, tainted with heresy, but a loyal son of the Church, and a genius too—yes, quite a genius in his way. Another of his inspiring ideas struck him: he must get Francis to preach before the Pope and the College of Cardinals! Of course! He must arrange this for him. Splendid!

The rest is most agreeable reading. Between the lines of the chronicles it is not difficult to detect Ugolino's happy, hearty plans for his protégé's triumph, and his enthusiastic faith in this new—I am half ashamed of the word—this new horse. One sees him button-holing the Cardinals and pouring over them his superlatives: "The man's a perfect saint, my dear fellow. . . ." "The man's a genius if ever there was one. . . ." " His talk is the most wonderful thing I ever heard. . . ." One watches his delighted scheming with Francis. "You must preach the sermon of your life, my boy. A lot hangs on this—yes, I've great hopes of what may come of it. You must prepare your sermon as you have never prepared one before." One even feels that at times he would have liked to write the sermon himself.

But at least he could organise it. He forced him to prepare the sermon word by word and commit it to memory. He meant so well, and he did not see that by doing this he was organising a fresh mountain stream into a neat little conduit. His organisation and enthusiasm quickly reduced Francis to an appalling state of nerves.

Francis wrote out the sermon—he who wrote so atrociously—and learned it off by heart—he who usually trusted to the sight of God's people before him, and the immediate surge of love. And tramping up and down to con it by heart, he felt a sham, as all do who adopt this method. "Preaching soils the feet of the soul with dust." Wonderful word! His nervousness affected the Cardinal, and by the time Ugolino and he were walking into the presence of the Pope and Cardinals, each was as nervous as the other.

I like Ugolino for this anxiety. I like him for wanting his young friend to shine. Thomas of Celano says frankly that he was "in an agony of suspense, praying to God with all his might that the simplicity of the blessed man might not be despised."

And Francis stood in whatever was the preaching place —pulpit, rostrum, or floor—and looked around at the brilliant audience of Pope and Cardinals. All the artists, perceiving the pictorial value of this scene, have seized upon it as a subject, thereby lifting it almost to a level with the Sermon to the Birds. And as I think of that, I am tempted to wonder (remembering that Francis was of a whimsical turn) whether, looking at the high dignitaries on the benches, he recalled the birds on the branches. One has seen high-necked bullfinches with sleek, round bellies who were very like the senior clergy. One has seen pert redbreasts who reminded one of the smaller bishops. I remember a wise old owl, blinking at me from a lonely branch, who might well have been the Pope, if he hadn't been so extraordinarily like the present Lord Chief Justice. Much taken by this idea, which first came upon me in Italy, I opened my Celano to see if he gave any names to the birds of Bevagna. I found that he mentioned only doves and rooks. Well, perhaps that is no unfair analysis of any gathering of clergy. I then walked into the Upper Church of San Francesco at Assisi to see what Giotto had given us in his fresco. I distinguished doves, sparrows, quails, and goldfinches. Some pretty parallels here, if one wanted to be unkind. Next I got Natale to drive me up to Montefalco on its hill, and, going into the church of San Francesco there, studied Benozzo Gozzoli's picture in the apse. Gozzoli gives us pigeons and geese. Well, well.

But enough of this. It is not only disrespectful but, worse, inapt, since Francis was probably much too nervous to feel whimsical. He looked at the Pope, and at the

Cardinals all round, and at the staring, anxious figure of Ugolino, and immediately forgot every word of his sermon. O fellow public speakers, have you never, when rising to address an audience of exceptional distinction, trembled on the brink of this deathly experience? Francis, like you, sent up an ejaculatory prayer to God Who seemed to have forsaken him. But He had not forsaken him. He had merely struck Ugolino's sermon out of his hand that Francis might preach Francis. The old surge of love and eagerness welled up, and out of the fullness of it he poured a stammering, stuttering, gesticulating appeal. He gesticulated so fervently that at times he seemed to be dancing on the floor. Silence settled upon that dignified audience as they watched the slight and threadbare figure throwing dignity to the winds and speaking the matter of his heart.

Reading between the lines of the chronicles, one guesses that the sermon had a mixed reception: the saints were impressed; the kindly souls were amused, but liked him well; the haughty formalists were disturbed and disapproving; the sinners, smelling a challenge, became wordily critical; Ugolino was not quite sure what he thought; and Francis went out from the presence of all, a little sadly, his doubts unhealed.

3

He escaped from worry into action. Casting off doubt, he put on the old trust. All that he could do was to be loyal to his vision. So, giving himself the parting counsel which he always gave to brothers sent on a mission, "Cast your care upon God, and He will provide for you," he sent himself on a new preaching tour.

He was away a long time, and behind his back the dissidence grew. Always the technique of non-violence leaves the field to the enemy, preferring the ultimate to the immediate victory. It has one thing, if one only, in common with the technique of British warfare, in that it loses every battle except the last.

He came back for the Whitsuntide Chapter of 1219. This was the "Chapter of Mats," always a proud story for the Franciscan chroniclers. Five thousand brothers from Italy, France, and Spain came tramping over the hills into the plain of Spoleto. Camps of sun-shelters, for it was late May, sprang up on all the fields and in the wood around the Portiuncula; and because their roofs were woven reeds stretched on poles, the whole forest and nearer plain seemed a garden-city of mats. These bivouacs must have delighted Francis, if he arrived after they were set up, but as he went on towards the Portiuncula clearing, a sudden sight, striking on his eyes, halted him with amazement and pain. During his absence somebody had built an imposing hall of stone and lime near the little chapel. Side by side with St. Mary of the Little Portion stood a very Large Portion indeed. Not a word had been said to him about this building, and it appeared to him as the acted challenge of the enemy. Well might they have carved over its door the name "Betrayal." It meant that the Queen of his Order, Madonna Poverty, had been cast out, to wander in the woods and on the mountains, a widow of the world again. Oh, memories of Rivo-Torto, and the caves of the Carceri, and the wattle huts shared with Bernard and Peter and Giles!

Well, if it came to an acted challenge, Francis was as good an artist as any. He lost his temper completely. This seems undeniable; and may I be absolved for feeling glad that he could sometimes do it. On at least two other occasions, and for precisely the same reason, he lost his temper and his Franciscanism at the same moment and cursed as a son of Pietro Bernardone should. To-day, before the brothers realised what was afoot, he had summoned his loyalists and climbed to the roof of the offending hall. Left and right hurtled the tiles and the laths, each a glove of challenge to any who should insult the Lady Poverty. It is proof of the veneration in which he was held that this house-breaking was watched by the assembling brothers in silent dismay. The crowds of townsmen and hinds who had come to stare at the preparations for the Chapter made a ring round the entertainment, and stood there at gaze. The men-at-arms sent by Assisi to police the multitudes in the plain, getting word of a disturbance, hurried up and saw Francis and his brothers on the roof and the roof flying from under them. They shouted to him to stop, but quite politely, even sympathetically.

"Brother," they called, "you cannot destroy that house because it doesn't belong to you. It has been built by the Commune of Assisi as a place of reception for all these visiting brothers."

Francis heard. And, distressed perhaps at his own impatience, touched by the goodwill of his town, however blind it might be to his purpose, and glad of an argument by which he could persuade himself that his brothers had been good, he answered wearily, "Well, if you say this house is yours, I will touch it no more."

And he came down from the roof, still sadly, as if his words hardly convinced him.

And that sadness of Francis broods over the otherwise immensely successful "Chapter of Mats." So vast an assembly in the plain is like a picture spread before us of his great international Order, and it tells the old tale again that loss of quality is the price of quantitative success. In this great congress beneath Assisi's hill the fresh, clear river of Franciscanism is meeting and mingling with the salt tide of the world. Much of the old freshness and sweetness is there. A guest-roll of five thousand delegates was the greatest strain yet put upon the Lord's table, and many were amazed that Francis had tempted Providence so far as to make no arrangements for their food; but the Lord's table did not fail him. The people of Assisi and Bastia and Cannara loaded up their asses and their mules and brought abundant food to those big, hungry friars in the plain. So overflowing was their generosity that the younger brothers who had not yet met Francis or seen his power were confounded.

I can well believe this pleasant "miracle." I walked through the same plain last year at the time of the *vendemmia*, or grape-gathering, and it was hot, and I paused to mop my brow and watch the men and women under the vines; and, seeing me, they immediately ran up and pressed bunches of grapes upon me; and when I offered payment, declined with smiles of courtesy. I walked on towards Assisi, eating blue grapes from the Lord's table.

Then there was a fine scene with Cardinal Ugolino as the central figure. He was coming to preside at the conference, and all the brothers, all five thousand of them, went out in procession to meet him. He came along the Perugia–Foligno road, in the midst of a cavalcade of nobles and high clergy; and when he saw coming towards him this brown "army of the Lord," bareheaded and barefoot, he was so moved that he reined in his horse, dismounted, cast off his fine cloak and his shoes, and insisted on walking in bare cassock and bare feet behind the last of the brothers. Nobly done, Ugolino: we wonder no more that Francis always loved you.

And the old, clean spirit showed itself when, in the conference, Francis called for missionaries who would go to the Saracens, and large numbers volunteered, though they knew that, in all probability, their only means of conquering would be martyrdom.

All this was of the old inspiration; but the mutter of the new spirit could be heard beneath it. It rang through Francis' outburst when he learned that some of those brothers who wanted to approximate their Rule to that of St. Augustine or St. Benedict had been to Ugolino and said, "My lord, we want you to persuade Brother Francis to follow the counsel of wise brethren, and to allow himself sometimes to be led by them." Ugolino told Francis of this, and Francis, having listened, answered nothing, but took him by the hand and led him straight into the Chapter, and there addressed the assembly.

"My brothers, my brothers," he said, "the Lord called me by the way of simplicity. And therefore I desire that you speak not to me of St. Augustine, St. Benedict, or St. Bernard, nor of any rule of life except that which was shown to me by the Lord. And the Lord said to me that He wished me to be a new covenant in the world, and that He would lead me by another way than by this science. . . ."

And the Cardinal, says the *Speculum Perfectionis*, "was much amazed, and all the friars feared greatly."

It echoed again in the sorrow that underlay his last words to the missionaries who must face the perils of Africa.

"My sons, God has ordered me to send you to the land of the Saracens to make known there His faith. . . . Dearest sons, so that you can better fulfil His will, see that there is peace and unity among you, and invincible charity; be patient in tribulation, be humble in success. Copy Christ in poverty, for He was born poor and lived in poverty and died in poverty. And this I beg of you that you may always have the sufferings of our Lord before your eyes, so that you will want to suffer for Him."

And the brothers answered [so the story goes on] "Father, send us where you desire, for we are ready to do your will. But you, Father, help us with your prayers. For we are young, and have never been out of Italy, and know nothing about the people we go to, except that they rage against the Christians. And when they see us in our poor garb and our rope, they may laugh at us as crazy men; therefore we shall greatly need your prayers. Ah, good Father, how shall we be able to do God's will without you?"

At this Francis was greatly overcome, and said, "Cast all your fears upon God, for He who sends you will also give you power and will help you." And they all fell on their knees before him and kissed his hand and asked his blessing. And he blessed them, saying, "The blessing of God come upon you as it came upon the Apostles. And fear not, for the Lord is with you and will fight for you."

Yes, the rumble of the conflict can be heard in these incidents and words. But it can be heard loudest of all, I suggest, in Francis' announcement that he too was going to the Saracens. While the brothers listened in consternation, he told them quietly that he was going to the crusading army now outside Damietta.

CHAPTER XVII

I

As we journey to Damietta we will consider what were the motives for this move.

Unless I am wholly wrong, the master motive, of those above consciousness, was his stable resolve: "I will not fight them nor force them nor argue. I will teach by example rather than by word. I will not dispute like a pamphleteer, but just create my vision as an artist creates, and leave it for those who can see." As Celano put it, Francis' method was "to make a tongue of his whole body."

Linked to this motive was the persistent thought—and how it must have pierced him when he blessed and bade farewell to those boys going to Africa!—"If I am to be an example, I must go too. I cannot send them into possible martyrdom and remain in security myself. I desire always to lead my sons from in front." And it is noteworthy, as indicating his growing doubt of Ugolino, that the Cardinal could not stop him this time.

So far he enlists our applause. A third motive which I shall suggest may silence our applause, till we understand it. Francis was driven towards Damietta by a desire for martyrdom. Not, however, as a form of suicide by which to be done with the battle, but as a rush into it to find its heart. So only could he copy Christ completely. Some of this motive may have sprung from the mediævalism which he never quite lost, but not all; and the better parts were of all ages, and lovely. We do not understand because we have never troubled to understand Calvary; we do little more than accept Calvary as a moving but remote and (between ourselves) not very comprehensible tale.

Francis knew, in a way which we will study later, that Calvary was the heart of the matter. And he really and actually loved Christ—a Christ as vivid and warm to him as Leo and Clare. He loved him, not in the way of duty, but in the way of young love. Therefore the agony of Calvary was something terrible to him, and the thought lived with him always, "I do not suffer enough." To understand this, to believe it, and to sympathise with it, will you go back to the days when you were young and loved someone with a monopolising love, and will you imagine yourself obliged to witness the execution of your loved one? Would not the cry have rushed through you, "Oh, what can *I* do? Let me share it! Let me have my share!"

Lastly, in this journey to Damietta the idea which had haunted him since Las Navas was incarnating itself at last, as all haunting ideas will. It was his own idea: Christianity must conquer Islam by love, not force. Impossible? Nay, "but if you have faith, you will say to this mountain . . ."

Christianity must have that faith. *He* was going to have it. He was going to make his way into the lines of the enemy and speak to them of Christ. So far the Cross had saluted the heathen only with the sword's point: through his lips it should now give them his own salutation, "Il Signore vi dia pace." He would take it into the presence of the Soldan himself. So likely, Francis, isn't it? So likely that you, ragged and barefoot friar, will get yourself into the tent of the Master of the East. "On the contrary, it is very likely, if I have faith . . ." and, as we shall see, he did it.

High above the vision of Innocent III, whose preaching had whipped up this Fifth Crusade, high above the vision

209

of Ugolino, who later agitated for bigger and better Crusades, Francis' idea was also high above the sight of the saints of his time. St. Dominic, heroic and devoted soul in many ways, believed in argument first, and if argument failed, in the sword and the rack. His Dominicans were *domini canes*, the dogs of the Lord, not the merry-men of God. St. Louis, King of France, a Bayard among crusaders, and undoubtedly one of the noblest figures of the century, proclaimed his opinion that a Christian should argue with a blasphemer only by "running his sword through his bowels as far as it would go." The Templars' banner was white and black: white for their service to the friends of Christ, black for their savagery to his enemies. Francis alone, though his head was full of knights and adventurers as any of theirs—and these were fantasies carrying him to Damietta—Francis alone had discovered the secret of elevating crusadism and combativeness above the mess of fratricidal war into the eternal battle of Love against Hate. He did this in the twelfth century, and it remains the only lesson we need learn in the twentieth.

But why Damietta? Why was the crusading army outside that sandy seaport town, one of the gates of Egypt at a mouth of the Nile, instead of on the seaboard of Palestine? Because the crusadism of those days, like the Imperialism of our own, was a convenient blend of patriotic fervour and commercial greed, and Innocent III, born Duce that he was, discerning that the heart of Saracen influence had shifted from Asia Minor to Egypt, had directed the patriotic fervour straight at the heart, while the trading cities of Italy, their greedy eyes on the Red Sea route, supported him with ships and money and materials. Few men being wholly bad, we may believe that the city merchants mingled some Christian motives with their commercial acumen. We need not suppose that they watched with nothing more than cynical amusement while the pride of mediæval chivalry hurled itself at Damietta and perished under the palm trees, in order to open a caravan track for their bales.

But that was the position, in the main. There on the flats of the Nile delta, at the fringes of Egypt, a host of German fighting men (much better employed there than in harrying Italy), a motley force of Burgundians, Franks, Normans, and English, a power of prelates and clergy, a Papal Legate, a Duke of Austria, a King of Jerusalem, and a King of Hungary had been besieging Damietta for a year and a half, while the Venetian ships watched and encouraged them from behind.

And now Francis of the Friars Minor, with a band of his own crusaders, was coming from Ancona to join them.

Travelling with a convoy of transports, he was carried first to St. Jean d'Acre, or Acre, as we now know it, on the Palestine coast. This great trading port and wholesale mart was acting as the Intermediate Base for the operations at Damietta; in fact, it was to Innocent's Egyptian Expeditionary Force exactly what, in 1915, Alexandria was to the invaders of Gallipoli. On his arrival at Acre, Francis, as Head of the Order, was certainly met by the Provincial Minister for the Brothers Minor in the Holy Land.

This man was one of the bright hopes of the Order. He was of the type of whom people say, "That young man will go far," and "That young man will carry all before him." A self-made man, he had already raised himself from the humblest beginnings, and against heavy odds, into a person of culture and power. His name was Bombarone, and it suggests the man: a squat, thick charge of power and purpose that might be directed to good ends, but, if mishandled, would explode dangerously. As a lad, whatever he undertook he brought with a kind of Scotch dourness to success. Born of poor parents, his father a mattress-maker and his mother a woman of Assisi, he had lived at his birthplace, Beviglia, and practised the trade of his father. But he seems to have worked with one eye on the mattress and the other on a book, because soon he was able to add to his earnings by acting as schoolmaster to the poorer boys of Assisi. He was of about the same age as Francis, but it is probable that in those youthful days when Bernardone's son was plunging Assisi into indignation and alarm, the young Bombarone was at Bologna where he had achieved the first of his ambitions and was getting education at the university while he supported himself as a scriptor. Leaving the university town, he went to Cortona, and while he was in Cortona, wondering where next to make his way, he met Francis, who was preaching there after his Lent on Isola Maggiore. Some have supposed that he had known Francis as a young man in Assisi, but, whether or not this was so, the power of this new Francis overwhelmed him, and, possessing a strong religious bent and believing that he could elevate ambition into aspiration, he became a Franciscan. Such a man, even when trying to be spiritual, does not stay long on the ground floor of any institution, and in a few years he had risen to be Minister Provincial of Syria. So striking was his efficiency in all he undertook that some already looked to him as the natural successor of Francis. Bombarone was a marked man among the Friars Minor—but they did not call him Bombarone: they called him Brother Elias.

And now Brother Elias and Brother Francis met once more on the quays of St. Jean d'Acre. They had a few days together, and then the convoy put out of the harbour with sails set for Damietta. And one day a square-sailed ship, bearing Francis and his friars, careened out of the Mediterranean and came between the lips of the Nile.

2

I approached Damietta from the opposite direction, in an Egyptian train grumbling through the cottonfields on a single-line track. From Tanta northward our business seemed to be the shedding of the last Europeans, so that from El Mansura onwards the train held nothing but brown faces, red tarbooshes, and long white caftans. And with the last European the train seemed to lose all sense of time. It ambled on, halting sometimes to quarrel with a wayside station, and then ambling on again like a string of camels grazing.

But for me the prospect from my window was entertainment enough. Somewhere between Mansura and Damietta the Sultan must have pitched his General Headquarters, and therefore I was looking out at the theatre of Francis' one-man crusade. What was one to call this crusade that he ran concurrently with the Fifth Crusade of Innocent III? It has no number or name in history. I decided that the ridiculous and splendid little affair was best called Crusade Five A.

From my window to the horizon all was flat. The country was level as the floor of a mosque, beneath the shallow dome of the sky. And it was a hesitating, indecisive country where cultivation met and languidly argued with the desert. The maize and the rice wandered up to the

fields of dust and petered out. Or they met the rushes
and the wide sheets of water; for there were deserts of
water here as well as deserts of sand. The far-flung levels,
with their beauty of changing light, reminded me of the
Middle Western prairies, except that they lacked the
shadowed rhythms of those uneven floors. And at the
moment there was a prairie sunset in the sky.

But abruptly, as we rambled on, there broke new cultivation upon us. Palm groves, red with dates, filled the
land between us and the lakes; and under or among the
palms were mud villages and maize fields and patches of
brilliant green near the water's edge. And the sun chose
this moment to sink into its last brilliance, so that the
reflection of the palm-trunks lay striped upon lakes of
gold. A cool, soft breeze bent the pampas grass and the
reeds.

Il clima ed il bel cielo di Damiata. I remembered how the
old historian told us that the climate and the beautiful
sky of Damietta had disarmed the crusaders by alluring
them from war into softness, voluptuousness, and rape.

And there behind the palms were the white buildings of
Damietta, with the Nile before them and Lake Menzaleh
behind.

Now, could I have flown across the thirty miles of
Lake Menzaleh and over the Suez Canal just beyond, and
then have taken horse or camel and paddled some fifteen
miles into the sandy wastes of Sinai, I should have come
upon a long, low mound which—but hold! I have
described this mound long ago in another book, and I
cannot be plagued to make new phrases about it now.
Besides, as I read the material paragraphs, I do not see
how they could be bettered. They seem to me quite
excellent paragraphs.

Two soldiers (for it was a tale of the Sinai desert in the War), two of those half-forgotten jesters of 1914–1918, had ridden over the sand-dunes and on to the salty flats near the sea. The hoofs of their horses were stumbling in the crisp, brittle plain. And in front of them, trembling in the mirage, was a long, low mound.

They were now nearing the mound, and they observed that the face of the waste was peppered with red brick-chips and powdered with red brick-dust. What was this man-made substance doing here, broken into a million fragments and broadcast over the plain? The closer they came to the mound the thicker were the brick chips; was the mound their source? Yes, the long, low oval hill was red with them, the chips covering it like a brash. Riding round the hill, they found on its northern side a width of wall still standing, whose bricks were like those seen in Chichester or St. Albans. They put their horses to the gentle slope and found here and there a recumbent pillar, broken where it fell. At one place many massive columns lay parallel, the tops of their bases still showing at their feet, and the ponderous pediment which they once supported lying half buried along their heads. The wreck of a temple entrance, it seemed. Such tumbled majesty to find in the midst of a desert!

It was all that was left of the ancient imperial city of Pelusium, once the eastern key of Egypt. Here a Pharaoh, Psammetichus, met the Persians under Cambyses and was defeated. Here the armies of another king of Egypt faced those of his sister Cleopatra, while Pompey, the fugitive, was seeking to land here from the sea. In those days an arm of the Nile flowed this way and watered a flourishing town; but desiccation won, and in the fullness of time the desert devoured Pelusium.

And to-day as they rode round the low hill that was Pelusium's grave, the desert stretching all around them, they came suddenly upon the bivouac of a Bedouin. It was made of desert rushes, and not six feet long nor five feet high. A pleasant sight, but why? Why pleasant to see the proud erections of the brick-builders and the masons overthrown, and the simplest dwelling that man could fashion pitched among their ruins in unoffending triumph? Perhaps because the inner heart of man rejoices in every testimony that pomps shall wither but simplicity endure.

Admirable.

It was the bankruptcy of Pelusium which made the fortune of Damietta. The Levantine trade swung to the town on the other mouth, and the Saracens, coming down into Egypt, quickly made it the third largest town in that land, while the Italian cities, watching the flow of trade, looked upon it with crusading eyes. Damietta was now the eastern key of Egypt. But that ancient Damietta—Francis' Damietta—was not in quite the same position as the little riverside town I was peering at now through the palm trees. I will explain to you why.

Some years ago a motor-car was found abandoned in the gutter of a Hampshire lane. The police, much stimulated, sought the owner with great activity and traced him after many days. He was a young officer, and he seemed vexed that the police should come worrying him about the car. The whole business was perfectly simple, he said. The engine had given him so much trouble that he had got bored with the whole damned outfit and left it in the ditch for anyone who would like to have it. In much the same spirit the Sultan Bibars, about the year 1260, got so bored with the repeated visits of the Crusaders to Damietta that he smashed the city up, blocked the mouth of the Nile, and moved the inhabitants four miles up the stream.

And here in the twilight, as I stepped out of the train, was the new city before me, stretched along the opposite bank of the river. Having no idea where I was going to live, for if there were hotels in Damietta they had not risen to the modernity of telephones, I got into a gharry at the pressing invitation of its white-robed driver and seated myself and said "Hotel" three times, and waved a hand airily. He nodded with a wide grin and, turning to his starveling pony, whipped and shouted it along the road. We clattered over an iron bridge into the streets of Damietta.

Damietta is Egypt unvisited by the West. There is but one Englishman in the place, teaching in an Egyptian Government school. On this evening, as I drove in, the crescent and stars flew everywhere, and Arabic mottoes and triumphal arches spanned the streets, because the town was *en fête* for yesterday's arrival of Nahas Pasha, the Prime Minister, and for to-morrow's feast of Abu Maha'ti, the old prophet, whose tomb they keep in Damietta. Every street was a bazaar: the booths gay with rugs, cotton goods, tarbooshes, caged birds, ice-cream, lemon drinks, and glistening sweets. And the whole town smelt of spice. White-robed men and black-shrouded women flowed in eddying streams on sidewalk and carriage-way; and the drivers of gharries or donkey carts scattered them with shrieks. My own driver shouted and argued and gesticulated a way through the main streets till he found the river-side again; and lo, there on the Nile, between the long bund and the high-sailed feluccas, was a string of floating hotels—long, wooden house-boats—for Damietta is a favourite watering-place of the Egyptians.

Much against my driver's advice, I determined to have a look at one of these hotels. I got down from the gharry, crossed the plank drawbridge, and peeped in.

The place seemed to be empty, and I was about to retreat when a woman in a dressing-gown emerged from a door along the corridor and begged me to come in. She was the proprietor's wife (or so I still trust) and she led me into a bare wooden room where the proprietor was already

217

in bed. These were the only people in the big, floating ark, but they were quite ready, as far as I could understand, to take me in at the fairest of prices. The man in the bed and the woman at its side explained this to me simultaneously, and to each other simultaneously, and to me again, and to each other again—at which point my driver entered the room and opened a battle of words, gesticulations, and menacing advances. All shouted and threatened at once, except myself, the trophy of the tournament.

The driver won, it appeared. He led me away, firing words at them as we went, and even stopping sometimes to say a heap more, or returning a few steps to relieve himself of a particularly good point; and it was all to the effect that the Captain could not sleep in a beastly place like that. "Come, Captain," he said to me outside. "Come to the Grand Hotel Egyptien."

The Grand Hotel Egyptien proved to be a river-side saloon with two or three bedrooms above. The proprietor, in tarboosh and long white skirts, led me up the stairs and showed me his state bedchamber, and I remembered Francis and how he had slept harder than this, and decided to take it. I offered the proprietor two thirds of his "fixed price," and this so surprised and delighted him that he went out with bows.

Having unpacked my rucksack, I stepped out on to a little balcony which looked over the river. Beneath me, under lamps suspended between trees, the Egyptians sat at their café tables playing backgammon or draughts, and talking noisily all the time. It was as if they talked with their conscious mind and moved the draughtsmen with their subconscious. A few old solitaries sat alone, quietly pulling at their hookahs. From the bar behind came the clink of glasses and the drawling whine of an Arabic song. And beyond lay the broad Nile with a fringe of palms between it and the vast, empty sky.

I had not been looking over the scene for three minutes when I heard English words spoken below me in a voice that was undoubtedly bred in England. Eavesdropping, I leaned over the balustrade and realised that it was the single Englishman in Damietta, talking with one of his Egyptian colleagues in the Government school. Going down, I made myself known to him; and he explained that I had hardly arrived at the hotel before the news had come across the town to him that an "English writer" was staying at the Grand Hotel Egyptien. He could not imagine, he said, what an English writer was doing in Damietta. Was I writing for Baedeker?

Well, after all, Baedeker is a scholarly book, I suppose.

3

In the morning I drove through the noise and scurry of Abu Maha'ti's festival and, reaching the outskirts of the town, left my gharry and walked through the palm groves into the open flats beyond. I strolled on till I felt quite alone, and then stopped. I turned my face towards the sea. Here, somewhere between me and the coast, was the Crusader's camp. Somewhere in the hazy distance behind me was the Saracens' army with the Sultan himself in its General Headquarters. And thus, with the stretches of mud and sand and the ruined fields between them, the two halves of the world faced each other.

The Christian camp, since a crusade drained into its sump half the heroes, wastrels, and outlaws of Europe, must have been a kind of cross between one of the big Rest Camps of the Great War and a halt of the Foreign

Legion—with the contents of the Cave of Adullam thrown in. And to these "boys at the front," just as to our army halted along the Somme, came distinguished bishops and leaders of religion, Francis one of them. We have a letter from the Damietta front, written home by a French prelate; and in it, quite casually, he mentions Francis.

"Rainer, the Prior of St. Michael, has gone into the Order of Friars Minor, which is spreading over the whole world because they imitate the lives of the first Christians and of the Apostles. The master of these brothers is Brother Francis: he is so lovable that he is worshipped by all. After arriving in our army, he was not afraid in his zeal to go on to that of our enemies. For several days he preached to the Saracens, but with little success . . . Colin, my English clerk, has gone into the same Order, and so have Master Michael and Dom Matthews to whom I had given the rectory of Holy Cross, and I am having a task to keep Cantor and Henry back. . . ."

As we see from this letter, Francis preached Christianity first to the Christians, and, from all we know of this crusade, they needed it. His heart must have sickened at the morals of the camp. In his imagination he had pictured an army of Arthurian knights, and he found a rabble of looters and brawlers and lechers. The great knights and princes were the "film stars" of that age, and the disappointment of their uncritical worshipper from Assisi, on his arrival at Damietta, must have been like the shocks sustained by a film-fan during a visit to Hollywood. There were a few Galahads among the leads and the supers, of course, but so few! And he had his usual success with the Galahads, as the letter shows; but he sorrowed, after a time, to think that he could no more than touch the fringes of Wrong.

I walked on and on, over the mud flats and the maize-fields, trying to experience in myself the feelings of Francis. Sometimes he would wander away from the camp in his disappointment and his need to be alone. Did he look over these dun flats and miss Umbria in his sadness? Did he often see Assisi on its hill? And what did he feel about the animals that he saw? Instead of the milk-white oxen of Italy, with their full, swaying flanks, he would see the black, lean kine of Egypt. He would see them yoked to the water-wheels, their eyes blindfolded, their flanks beaten as they paced ever round and round, round and round, drawing up life for the earth and the men upon it. And in these suffering beasts did he see the Word, crucified and scourged, but ever turning creation's wheel? Comforting them with his hand, did he understand Calvary in a way that we do not? Did the longing come more and more upon him to share the yoke and the scars of Christ?

He had been here but a little while when the camp came astir with talk of a great "new push." On the 29th of August, at zero hour, they were going to launch one of the biggest offensives of the war. And this time they would break through. Damietta captured, and the enemy in rout, they would march along the banks of the Nile to Cairo. I think of the Fourth of June on Gallipoli, and how we expected to break through and capture the hill of Achi Baba and then march on by the bank of the Dardanelles to Constantinople. And once we were in Constantinople, the enemy's resistance would collapse all over Europe, and the war would be over by Christmas. The Crusaders' attack of August 29th was no more successful than ours, and, oddly enough, their losses were just about the same—some five or six thousand men. They fell back defeated, and the lines of both armies consolidated as before. When the sun dropped behind the palm groves, the war was just

221

as it had been in the morning. It still had long, monotonous years to run.

4

Very good: now let Francis try *his* way. After the
massed assault of the regal and papal armies the visit of
the whisper of love. Taking one brother with him,
Illuminato, he passed through the crusaders' front line
and walked straight on into the broad no-man's land. If the
humour of soldiers was the same then as now, the outposts
of Christianity must have blasphemed with admiration as
they watched that tired little figure, with his one follower,
go on and on towards the Turks and dissolve into the
mirage. Of course, as we know, the Crusades were remarkable for much fraternising and feasting between Christian
and Saracen princes, out of fighting hours; but it is evident
from the sequel that the friendly visit of Francis was un-
arranged and unexpected. And the watching soldiers
knew that the Sultan, who was of a satirical disposition,
had offered to buy the heads of Christians at a golden
ducat apiece.

"Well, there go a couple of ducats for someone!" Do
you not hear the words from a Christian trench? "Some
bloody misbelieving bastard is in luck to-day."

And what was Francis thinking as he walked on?
Martyrdom any moment now? "So now Christ shall be
magnified in my body, whether it be by life or by death.
For me to live is Christ, and to die is gain. . . ." None the
less, his heart must have beaten rapidly, and his voice
tripped over itself sometimes, as he spoke to his brother
Illuminato. One record states that he encouraged him
with his favourite maxim, "Cast your care upon God, and
He will protect you."

And so these two of Christ's fools came to the frontiers of Islam. Why they were not there and then destroyed and turned into ducats is a mystery—if it's not a miracle. Perhaps the Angels of Mons marched abreast in front of them. Perhaps the Angels bewitched the heathen dogs into thinking them an embassy of peace. Francis was calling out, "Soldan, Soldan," to explain that he wished to be taken to the Sultan, and they seized him and Illuminato and took them to General Headquarters. To the staff officers here Francis, speaking the *lingua franca*—that medley of European and Eastern tongues which was the currency of the Crusades—expounded his desire to preach the Gospel of Christ to the Soldan.

Now, those who live about the Court catch the custom of the King, and Malik-al-Kamil, King of Syria and Egypt, was a ripe fruit of Arabian culture: cynical, witty, courtly, tolerant, and restrained—at least until he was in the mood to be savage. In fact Malik-al-Kamil reminds us of a later Crusader who was to come face to face with him and discuss pleasantly, as between one man of culture and another, the stupidity of their followers and the desirability of two intelligent men talking this quarrel over. I refer, of course, to the Emperor Frederick II, *Stupor Mundi*, "The Wonder of the World"; and we shall remember how Arabian culture had invaded his Court in Sicily. It is sad to think that there was more real civilisation (if not as much as the Sultan thought) in the tents of Allah than behind the pennons and lances of Christ. The smiling courtiers of Malik-al-Kamil saw at once that this unforeseen visit would provide an acceptable diversion for their master; and they did not hesitate to escort the two barefoot Nazarenes into the pavilion of the King of Kings.

Francis came into the presence of Malik-al-Kamil, and

in that minute, for the first time and, as far as I know, the last, perfect Christianity met and bowed to Islam. And Malik-al-Kamil, in the tradition of Saladin's house, bowed to bravery as it came in.

And very soon, strangely soon, the native charm of Francis, together with the extraordinary power which a mystic draws from his unity with Reality, began to work upon the Sultan. He leaned back and stared with interest. He watched the sparkling eyes and the fervid, stuttering lips. He listened. In his turn he argued. He encouraged the argument: how better spend an empty hour than in an academic defence of Mohammedanism against Christianity, with some dubiety in his mind about both? He was much pleased with his new friend, and though he sent him away directly serious business called, he commanded that this Christian legation was to be accorded every comfort until he should be ready to resume the agreeable debate.

When he summoned Francis again, he had around him quite a large audience, which he had assembled to see this droll Christian mollah and to hear him unfold the teaching of Issa Ben Miriam. Issa Ben Miriam was Jesus, son of Mary. And he had a little joke all ready for their entertainment. He had caused a large Oriental carpet, whose pattern was all crosses, to be laid before his chair. And to his guests he had pointed out that if the little Nazarene trod on the crosses, he insulted his god, and if he declined to do so, he insulted the Soldan and his host. Let him be called in.

And Francis, brought in, saw the crosses, and the trick too, and immediately walked over the carpet to the Sultan's throne.

"But how now, Nazarene?" laughed Malik-al-Kamil.

"Do you not perceive what you have done? You have trodden underfoot the emblem of your religion."

"Sire," answered Francis, who, if it came to wit, was a match for most, "there were three crosses on Calvary, one belonging to the Saviour of the world, and the other two to two robbers. Ours is the true cross, so I can only conceive that yours——"

And this retort, all the more appropriate since Saladin had captured the True Cross in 1187, finally conquered the Sultan. Laughing loudly, or as loudly as was consistent with culture, he suggested that Francis must remain permanently at his Court.

"That I will willingly do," replied Francis, "if you and your people will accept Christianity."

At this the Sultan could only smile and shake his head, so Francis (according to another and very popular story, less convincing than the tale of the carpet, though I pronounce no final disbelief: these were strange days, and strange things are done in the East)—Francis, passionately anxious to be taken seriously, offered, in the spirit of Moses and Elijah, to submit to the Ordeal by Fire. If the Sultan would have a great fire lighted, he and the priests of Islam would both pass through it, and let the True God stand by His own.

Again the Sultan shook his head and smiled, while he answered cynically (and *this* sounds convincing) that he could not believe that his priests would be enthusiastic about such a proposal.

"Very good," answered Francis (I follow Father Cuthbert), "then if you will promise for yourself and your people to come to the worship of Christ if I come out of the fire unhurt, I will enter the fire alone; but if I am burnt, impute it to my sins, and if the divine power protects me,

225

acknowledge Christ to be the True God and Saviour of all."

But Malik-al-Kamil was not going to let things get as serious as this, so he closed the interview, though not without the fine courtesy of asking Francis to pray for him that God would show him the truth.

He seems to have added other courtesies. He seems to have granted Francis a licence to preach to his soldiers for several days, a safe conduct out of his camp, and a right of free access to the Holy Places of Palestine.

He was a very courteous gentleman. These smiling concessions to an unofficial but, as far as he could gather, highly celebrated Nazarene read like a foretaste of the concessions which he granted, ten years after, to the Emperor of the Christians himself, Frederick II; for that astonishing Crusader, in the course of his satirical chat with the Sultan, induced him to cede Jerusalem, Bethlehem, and Nazareth, together with a corridor of territory from the Christian coastwise kingdom in Palestine to the Holy Places —in fact, almost all that the Baldwins, the de Bouillons, the Raymonds, the Cœur de Lions, and the Innocents had been fighting for during a hundred and thirty years.

But Frederick and Francis were a hundred years before their time—or was it a thousand? The Crusaders stormed Damietta again, and this time carried the defences and entered the city in triumph. But the triumph was a greater disaster to the Crusaders than to the Saracens. Drunk with victory, their army fell to pieces, and the sundered ranks rushed forward into looting and butchery and rape. Loyal Christians exulting in revenge, they turned Damietta into a winepress of the Lord and tramped and paddled in the blood of the unbaptized. They quarrelled and fought among themselves, and no exhortation could bring these enthusiastic churchmen back to "the peace of Holy Church and our father the Pope." And the spring came, and the warm air; and, "forgetting the inconveniences and the perils of war," says the old chronicler, "they gave themselves into the arms of voluptuousness and softness and all the pleasures which could be inspired by the climate and the beautiful sky of Damietta."

And Francis left them. Boarding an early ship for the Holy Land, he passed out between the lips of the Nile. A sorrow must have sat upon his weary face as he sailed away defeated, but perfectly certain that his Master's way was the right one. His crusade had achieved nothing. except a licence for him to visit the Holy Places. And a story.

5

Francis left Damietta; and I, having thought my thoughts, returned into the modern town. The crescent and stars flew everywhere: the fair and festival of Abu Maha'ti filled the waste places, the white-robed men lounging about the booths, the white-robed children screaming around the conjurers, the black-shrouded women walking to the old saint's tomb; and it was all a little like the festa of San Francesco in Assisi. In the cafés the prosperous citizens sat by their backgammon boards, smoking their *chicas* or their *gozas*; and in the evening, at the proper hour, the muezzin cried from the minaret, and the faithful sank to their heels and, turning towards Mecca, bowed their foreheads to the ground.

For all its effect upon Islam, Francis' message had been writ in water. He had set his footprints in the sands of Damietta, but the first advance of the Crusaders had. trampled them to nothing.

CHAPTER XVIII

I

I SAID earlier that whenever Francis sailed from Ancona he disappeared, except for reappearances at Damietta and St. Jean d'Acre, into a mist. We possess nothing but rumours and guesses as to where he went. It was therefore with little hope of illumination that I followed him to Palestine. And yet, when I arrived there and wandered from Jerusalem to Jericho, and from Bethlehem to Nazareth and Galilee, I felt as certain that I was in the tracks of Francis as ever I did on the field-paths of Umbria. On the summit of Mount Carmel I felt that he had been here before me as surely as on the mountain above Poggio Bustone.

Francis went in a ship over the surface of the sea. I followed him, a few thousand feet in the air, looking down upon the tiny feluccas below me, tranced on a sea of glass. And as our frail wings passed over the strand of Palestine, and across the green plains of Philistia and Sharon, and then circled to land upon the airport of Lydda, it occurred to me that this was a most appropriate way to alight upon the Holy Land. It was like an angel out of the Old Testament. Peering down, I remembered Elijah and wondered if he too peered down from his chariot of fire.

And like any of those angels I sank upon a land of trouble. The ancient fires were smouldering still. As we grounded, I saw that the offices of the airport were a blackened and gutted shell, with the smoke twisting from one of the corners. Moslems in rebellion against the Christian Government of England had fired them the previous night. My trunk had to be examined and my passport endorsed in a hangar. They could not stamp the passport because all the stamps were ashes or char on the burned office floors. The passport officer printed in block capitals, and with laborious pen, my permission to stay in Palestine for a given period provided I behaved myself: a hand-made endorsement which afforded interest and delight to every passport office I visited thereafter.

Putting the endorsed passport in my pocket, not without likening it to the permit which the Soldan gave to Francis, I went out of the hangar and glanced round the Holy Land.

The Crusades were over and won. They had been finished just twenty years ago, when Cœur de Lion's children, good men in khaki and Christians of sorts, had captured Jerusalem and the rest of the contentious country. They had taken it by the sword and, as I was soon to remark, they seemed apprehensive of perishing by the sword. Leaving the airport in a car, I passed by Ramleh, which to-day was to have some of its houses blown up by the English as a retaliation for the burnings at Lydda. Even so Saladin destroyed Ramleh because it had been the headquarters of Cœur de Lion. A little way beyond Ramleh a lorry raced past us, loaded with England's Arab police and armed with a machine gun. It was hurrying down from Jerusalem towards Lydda to discipline the plains. Yet a little farther, and my Arab driver pointed out to me a place where some of the police had been ambushed by the rebels and slain.

My car sped on towards the hills of Judea. It passed up the valley of Ajalon, where Joshua commanded the " sun to stand still and the moon to stay " that he might get on with the slaughter. And I reflected that since Joshua's day the sun had indeed stood still and the moon stayed, in the sense that I had breakfasted in Alexandria and would be an hour too early for lunch in Jerusalem. Heading fast for Jerusalem, we shed the green plain beneath us and wound up into the rusty hills. The Syrian sun had burned them to rust and rose and white and gold, under a glazed, blue, porcelain sky. Approaching Jerusalem by the Ramleh road, one receives the impression (I know not if the configuration of the land justifies it) that one has to top the highest crown before one can look over the rim of a cup and see Jerusalem on its hills. One remembers pictures, perhaps, and thinks of it as moated by the dark valleys of Gehenna and Jehoshaphat, and encircled by a chaplet of mountains. But it does not reveal itself quite like that. The romance of your first view of Jerusalem is somewhat flawed by the modern suburbs which litter the summits between you and the Jaffa Gate; yet, even so, nothing can make it less than one of the greater moments of your life.

That first view of the walled white city, spread on its hills, breaks the rhythm of your breathing and commands you to silence. "O Jerusalem, Jerusalem, thou that killest the prophets and stonest them which are sent unto thee. . . ." And if it so stirs the least sensitive of us, how did it stir Francis when, approaching by another road, he reached it at last? He stood there gazing, I know, silent upon a peak in Judea. "O Jerusalem, Jerusalem. . . . Behold your house is left unto you desolate. For I say unto you, ye shall not see me henceforth till ye shall say, Blessed is he that cometh in the name of the Lord."

The vision was very near to Jerusalem when the Italian Christ stood looking upon it.

City of vision and storm. It seemed fitting that I should

ST. STEPHEN'S GATE, JERUSALEM

THE OLD GATE OF ST. JEAN D'ACRE

find a curfew order reigning over Jerusalem. They told me in the Hotel Fast that if I wanted to walk abroad that afternoon, I must see to it that I was back by half-past seven, for then the curfew would shut the citizens within their doors and allow nothing but silence to occupy the streets of Jerusalem. Behold, her streets would be left unto her desolate. It was now noon, and I went to the window of the Hotel Fast and looked out. I could see the khaki police patrolling the streets in pairs, with pistols slung, and the highlanders of the Black Watch guarding the Jaffa Gate. But for the present these were only quiet units in the many-coloured and hurrying multitude. The barter and traffic of the city were pursuing their noisy way, heedless of them. All fashions of Eastern wear and head-dress thronged along the roads, and the European suits and hats drifted among them. The laden donkeys of the first century passed the lorries and cars of the twentieth. The klaxons of the cars grated harshly across the tinkling bells of the donkeys and the clinking cups of the drink-pedlars. After all, what were to-day's little shootings and stabbings compared with the splendours of suffering which these streets had known? They were nothing. Nothing but a little smoke from the old glowering ashes.

And indeed, as the day wore on, it appeared to me that there was more of rumour than revolution in Jerusalem. Rumour ran through the streets and up the stairs of the hotel: an Armenian photographer had been shot in David Street; a lorry of police had been ambushed between Hebron and Bethlehem; an Arab bus filled with Jews had been fired on . . . and all the time the business of Jerusalem went on, noisily, indifferently.

Twilight, however, brought an experience different

231

from any I have known. The curfew order descended upon the age-old city and touched it to silence. It was as if the Angel of Death, he who passed through the land of Egypt on the first Passover night, had dropped upon Jerusalem.

The balconies of the Hotel Fast are at the point of a wedge-shaped block, so that they command streets to left and right and the main road in front that dips to the Jaffa Gate. I stood there for much of that silent, empty night, watching; and I give as they stand the notes which I put down in my diary, since they have a truth and an immediacy which more careful writing might lack.

"Curfew in Jerusalem, October 17th, 1937; 8.0. onwards. Complete silence in the streets. Like midnight. Moon looking down. Extraordinary stillness between the stars and the domes and towers, as if an enchantment held the city mute, like the palace of the Sleeping Beauty. Time itself might have heard a stand-still order. Shuttered shops. Lamps alone possess the streets. . . .

"Every now and then a lorry rushes by, loaded with Palestine Police. . . . A rifle shot far away. Incessant chirp of crickets. A cat alone defies the curfew order, wandering out of a side street and crossing the empty highway.

"9.15. Not a dog barking. Just at the end of the road in a pocket of darkness I can see figures pacing. They are the North Staffords, or the Black Watch, guarding the Jaffa Gate. . . . Occasionally a closed car travels fast as if afraid of an ambush or a shot. A solitary figure comes from the Jaffa Gate, his steps echoing on the sidewalk. Who can it be, since he is not in uniform? But he disappears into the shadows before I can know.

232

"10.25. Firing just begun and continuing spasmodically. The dogs bark at last.

"11.3. A distant explosion somewhere. Bethlehem?"

2

No one knows how long Francis stayed in the Holy Land. It was a considerable time, and every learned authority has a different estimate to bedevil the unlearned and lazy. But there are two things that will hardly admit of dispute: he knelt in the sacred places, and he walked with his dreams in the tracks of his Lord. Remembering his sense of dramatic fitness, who can doubt that a Lenten day of 1220 saw him in the wilderness beyond Jordan, or that Good Friday of that year did not close before he had walked along the Via Dolorosa, trying to think it all out? And I dare almost assert that the same Good Friday saw him kneeling before the Sepulchre and reaffirming with a new passion the vows he had made before the little altars of San Damiano and the Portiuncula.

With these convictions in my mind, I took an Arab car and drove from Jerusalem to Jericho and the country about Jordan. That wild road, tilting down and down the defiles, has been too well described by other travellers, and especially by Mr. Morton, for me to attempt a small echo here. Besides, my search was different from theirs: I was looking for Francis, not for Christ. Or I was looking for the Christ that came this way in the heart of an Umbrian friar.

The friar first seemed close to me when I stood on the bleaching levels between Jericho and the Dead Sea and realised that this was an old lake-bed. On one side rose the mountains of Judea, lifting steeply from the plain; on

233

the other the mountains of Moab; between lay the stricken valley, and behind me that lifeless and imprisoned sea which was all that remained of the lake-waters. Jordan brought a ribbon of verdure down from Galilee till the salt killed it, and all was waste. And yet, desolate though it was, I murmured instantly to myself, "The Vale of Spoleto."

Spoleto's vale and Jordan's vale were alike in this, that each was a lake-floor walled in by mountain ranges, and each was the theatre of a great decision.

In all else they were each other's opposite. The Umbrian vale was green; this one was white and gold. The Italian basin was one wide vineyard and fertile market-garden; this long depression, except for the banana groves of Jericho and Jordan's fringe of feathery trees, was a wilderness of stones and ghostly salt mounds and bewildering glare. The mountains of Francis carried the green things almost up to the sky; the mountains of Christ were empty white heights, rose-tinted. The stage where Francis fought and conquered his lower self was a very human place, with little farm-houses among the stacks, and a balmy air among the vines, and the unearthly light on the hill-tops only; this stage where a greater conflict swayed to its decision was, most fittingly, a stark desolation, inhuman, eerie, and sublime. One could imagine that the alighting feet of God had burned it, so that it could never bear again; or that the Evil which came here one day had blasted it with Its passage. It was a wan, empty valley, tumbled, tormented, and ashen.

There, rising behind Jericho, was the Mountain of the Third Temptation. And the Third Temptation, we agreed, was exactly the same as Francis overcame on the heights above Assisi. "All things will I give thee, if thou wilt fall down and worship me."

It is a temptation which must assail every man upon whom breaks the consciousness that he has good gifts and a talent for success: the temptation to prostitute one's genius for the sake of a numerical triumph, to sacrifice quality for quantity, to win power and applause and the kingdoms of the world by a deserting of the higher for the lower self. In the hearts of the best it may sometimes whisper like this: "If I lower the ideal a little, I can win the people for it. Surely that would be statesman-like. Surely that would be wise. But if I pursue uncompromisingly the highest of all, if I preach only perfection and the completeness of self-conquest, I shall limit the power of the message of God, and even, perhaps, slay its hope of success. Would it not be wise to compromise a little if by so doing one could capture the kingdoms of the world?"

Mohammed yielded to it. I hold it fair to say that he compromised with the sensuality and the combativeness of men and so won the kingdoms of the Arab world. And in a pregnant sentence, which may or may not be true, but is worthy of consideration here in the wilderness under the mountain, Dosotievsky wrote, "The Church is Christ yielding to the Third Temptation."

But the man Jesus did not yield, nor the man Francis, whatever their followers may have done. The greatest have always seen that to trim their ideals in the name of expediency is to bow to Satan; while to follow the brightest light within them is to worship all they can see of God, and Him only must they serve.

And, mark you, it is a temptation which returns again and again, though its power is diminished with every defeat. It did not leave Christ forever after the repulse up on the mountain. "The devil departed from him *for*

235

a season." It came whispering again when the people demanded a sign from heaven. It attacked Him severely enough to try His temper when Peter, after declaring his conviction that He was the Messiah, refused to believe that He would forswear everything and, if necessary, die. At that moment it was so close as to re-create the whole scene on the mountain and to make Jesus say, "Get thee behind me, *Satan*, for thou savourest not the things that be of God but the desire to please men." And its last echo is heard in the last moments of His life: "If Thou be the Son of God, come down from the cross, and we will believe." But He stayed.

Nor did it desert Francis, though he defeated it once on the hills above Assisi. It was present with him now as he stood in the wilderness, looking up at the mountain where Christ defeated it. Were not his brothers, were not his ministers, was not the Protector, Cardinal Ugolino, urging compromise upon him and calling it Prudence and the way to influence and power? I think that Francis looked up at that peak and drew strength not to yield. I think that he decided anew, with an uprush of love and consecration, to resist it to the end. And I think that, immediately after his decision, immediately after his "Get thee behind me, Satan," he felt an elation and a unity with God; for that is what happens to the least man among us in his moment of triumph over temptation. And is this, perhaps, all that is meant by the old Bible words, that "angels came and ministered to him"?

3

I suppose it happens to every pilgrim that the first time he treads the Via Dolorosa he goes in the reverse direction to that of the Master, when He came this way bearing His cross. Attracted before all places to the Holy Sepulchre, he will, after mingled emotions in that place of darkness and tinsel where all the quarrelling churches of the East crowd about the Tomb like wasps about the honey, come out into the narrow street and, learning that he is at the end of the Via Dolorosa, will walk back to its beginning. Like most of the streets in Jerusalem, the Way of Sorrows is a series of narrow corridors either roofed in by vaults to keep out the sun or arched over by buttresses which fly from one side to the other. In some places it is a stepped slope, to fit the fall of the hill; in others it is a cobbled and level street. The Arabs, Jews, and Christians stream along it, some on foot, some on donkey-back, some goading their laden beasts before them; just as if a procession had never come this way, following with jeers, exultation, or compassion a condemned man carrying his gibbet. Unless they are pilgrims led by an Arab guide, or by a Baedeker in the hands of one of them, they do not pause to look at the inscriptions on the walls which mark the stations of the Cross. Of course, if the Church of the Holy Sepulchre does not really cover the site of Golgotha, then this is not the road of Christ's passion at all; and in any case the earth that took the imprint of that shouting procession must be many feet below the street levels of to-day.

But neither of these points mattered anything to me, when I left the Holy Sepulchre and walked for the first time along the Via Dolorosa, going from its end to its beginning. All that mattered to me was that Francis, who would never, in that uncritical age, have questioned its authenticity, certainly wandered up and down the same series of streets, trying to picture the scene of twelve hundred years before. *He* pictured Christ; I pictured *him* going up and down it, and trying to think it all out.

Failure? The utter failure of purely pacific resistance and of love? The abject defeat of a great attempt to prove that only love could win in the end? The mockery and deriding of the doctrine that forgiveness, even to seventy times seven, was the true grandeur, strength, and practical wisdom for men? Was this what that old procession of the lynchers meant? Was it history's classic announcement that force is this world's victor, and not love; that the men of hard common sense are right, and the dreamers are pleasant, sentimental fools; that there is little wisdom in leaving the field open to the coarsest bully and suffering him to silence you for ever? Was it a coronation procession, going with execrations or laughter, to crown the futility of a dream?

No! The truth which now dwelt forever in Francis would well up in him with the cry, *No!* I *know* it is not so. Let argument say what it will, my heart knows. Let appearances be what they may, I *know* that He was right, and that I am right. I know it as I know that the sun is light, and that the night brings the dark.

And, looking upon that derided and rejected figure, his gibbet on his shoulder as the banner of his lonely loyalty to the truth as he saw it, Francis would receive from it, suddenly, flashingly, joyously, a new assurance that he was right. Just as Christ turned and looked upon Peter, so He, going by, would turn His face upon Francis; and Francis would not deny Him. Just as He turned and spoke to the women by the way, "Daughters of Jerusalem, weep not for *me*, but weep for yourselves and for your children," so He would turn and say to Francis, "My son, weep not for *me*. This is the road of victory for me, as it is the way of defeat for them. Those who seem to have the victory have it in the eyes of a little time only; the victory is mine in the eyes of the ages. If I abandon love and forgiveness in this of all hours, my teaching is lost; but if I stay loyal to them through all, if I forgive even as the nails are hammered home, I shall raise my cross, not only upon Golgotha, but in the heart of all good men to the end of time. I, being lifted up, will draw all men unto me."

And Francis: "My Lord and my God."

4

I had reached the Ecce Homo Arch. And the Ecce Homo Arch, which spans the street above the place where Pilate said "Behold the man," and Christ first took up His cross, was the end—or, rather, the beginning—of the Via Dolorosa.

But, lost in thought, I did not pause here. I wandered vaguely on and, after a few paces, saw that I was approaching the city wall. Straight as a corridor, the narrow road was leading to a shapely arched gate. Through the gate I could see, brightly lit by the sun, like a scene behind a proscenium arch, the stony hillside dipping down to the Brook Kedron. And the background was the white harshness of the Mount of Olives, and the turquoise sky.

It was St. Stephen's Gate: the gate through which they cast out the first martyr to stone him with those white stones from the hillside. And to-day it was guarded above and below by figures in khaki drill and topees. Young lads from Staffordshire, England, were seated on its roof about a gun: others of them stood within the arch or patrolled the street below. And the wicked round eye of the gun looked straight down the Via Dolorosa. It commanded it. It enfiladed it. It dominated the Ecce Homo Arch and the site of Pilate's Pretorium. The 7th North Staffords had succeeded the 12th Legion.

Returning to the Ecce Homo Arch, I rang the bell of the Convent of Notre Dame de Sion. It is a surprise to me that Mr. Morton, in his erudite and reverent book, does not mention the Arch of Ecce Homo and the convent at its side, because the convent holds for a man faintly distressed and disappointed by much that he has found in Jerusalem a pure, unspoiled emotion; and had Mr. Morton but known it, while he was passing under the arch, Gabbatha itself, the pavement where Pilate set up his judgment seat, was lying open and visible and waiting to be visited, a fathom below his feet. It is, in my view, the most authentic thing in Jerusalem, and therefore the most moving. That the siting is right, that Pilate's Pretorium was really here, hardly a student will now dispute; and you have but to look at the stones themselves to believe that at last, and in very truth, you are standing in the steps of the Master.

The convent door opened, and a sister welcomed me in with a smile full of kindliness. She could do nothing else: her face within its white wimple and black veil was made only for kindliness and love. It is just possible that this book may one day fall beneath her eyes, so I will say no more than this, that as she led me through the corridors I felt very near her Lord. When she learned that I was a writer, she asked me to send her some of my books, and, as I was made happy by such a privilege, I drew out my notebook and asked for her name and correct address. The note-book was crowded by this time with descriptions and records and comments, many of which, at the moment of jotting down, I had thought very fine, but it contained no poem quite like the one she dictated to me now.

"Your address, Sister?"

"You wish to write it down?"

"If I may, Sister."

"Why, certainly. Here it is. 'Sister Mary of Sion, Ecce Homo, Via Dolorosa, Jerusalem.' "

"Thank you, Sister."

She took me into the clean, white basilica which is above the sacred pavement as a church is above its crypt. She put me into a pew about half-way down the nave and, sitting beside me, explained the church and its meaning.

It was designed, she said, to give Him eternal love and honour in the place where He was mocked and scourged. Here where the Jews raised the terrible cry, "His blood be upon us and upon our children," the Rev. Father Marie Alphonse Ratisbonne, himself a converted Jew, had arranged for this basilica to be built as a church of expiation. It was to be served by "Daughters of Sion." As he said, "There where the terrible words were pronounced, *Sanguis ejus super nos et super filios nostros,*' may there be souls whose lives are devoted to love and reparation. I and my people are Jews, and my desire is to see erected here a sanctuary bearing the inscription, 'May His blood be upon us and upon our children in a dew of benediction.' "

No garish decoration here, no tinsel, no swarming guides to sting you like wasps for money, no dens of the money-changers; nothing but a clean, sweet whiteness, and one sentence running above the altar, "Father, forgive them. . . ."

Then she led me down the stairs to the crypt. She touched a switch, and the light fell on the stones of the Antonia fortress where Pilate set up his tribunal and curule chair. Those old brown flagstones carried conviction at a glance. They lay side by side, unmortared, but resting in a bed of cement. The gutters were still there, which drained the rains of two thousand years ago. They drained them into a deep reservoir, and Sister Mary, lifting a trap-door, showed me the reservoir below, which archæology had recently unearthed. But my eyes returned to those flagstones. The patina of thousands of years was upon them, like a brown glaze. On some of them you could see the striated grooves worked into them to keep the horses from slipping, and on others the tracings, overwhelmingly moving, of the games played by the Roman soldiers, including mazes, hopscotch, and the "game of the King." The tracings for the "game of the King" included a rude crown.

It was very quiet down here. Very different from the bustle and noise of the Church of the Holy Sepulchre at the other end of the Via Dolorosa. It was even a little cold, but with the coldness of purity. There was no orna-ment except the neat marble plaques on the walls, given by those who wanted to offer honour to Christ in the place where He was spat upon. There was but one picture: a large mosaic in one corner which showed Christ putting the cross upon His shoulder, with the old Pre-torium in the background.

"It is there in that corner," said Sister Mary, "because we believe that that must be the actual spot where He first lifted up the cross."

"I understand, Sister."

We went towards it. And there, standing before the picture, she asked me what I thought of Christ. I said my stumbling words. I told her that to me in my later life the best revelation of Christ had been Francis of Assisi; and with some diffidence I told her that I, a heretic, was trying to write a book about Francis, because I felt that, in a world jaded, confused, weary of butchery and grab, and dimly perceiving that Man without a God of some sort sank into childish barbarity, but troubled and even repelled by some of the traditional representations of Christ, the little compassionate Umbrian man was a fresh avenue to His meaning. Because the meaning of Francis must surely be the meaning of Christ.

Sister Mary of Sion thought for a minute, gazing at the mosaic of Christ putting the cross to His shoulder. Then she looked up at me (for I am tall, and she was not) and asked, "Would you mind if I knelt down here and prayed for the success of your book?"

So complete was the sympathy she had established between us that I felt no embarrassment at all, but only answered, "Please do this for me, Sister."

And there on the brown stones, where perhaps Christ lifted up the cross and made His great trusting gamble on a goodness in the human heart, she knelt down and prayed that my book might be of help to many.

Amen.

CHAPTER XIX

I

ACRE sleeps on a low promontory by the sea and remembers her past no more. With her long headland for a couch, she lies, a chain of cream and pink buildings, between the blue of the sky and the blue of her own bay.

She is like some aged lady who has had many husbands in her life but can hardly remember the names she took from them in days so far away. What was she called when those bricks of sand and cement which are still to be found among her possessions were dried in early Biblical suns? Acco? Was she Acco then? Or when those old marble pillars that still support some modern vault were first set up, was Rome her husband then, and her name Ptolemais? Paul passed through her streets in those Roman days, but she recalls nothing of that half-blind, half-lame figure, or of the "beloved physician" who was with him. But, then, I don't suppose he looked very important, and he only stayed to salute the brethren in Ptolemais, before going on to be bound at Jerusalem. She remembers the Crusaders coming to woo her, because the tall, square citadel in her midst will not allow her to forget it. But she is confused about it. Was the citadel built during her first marriage to the Crusaders, before Saladin threw them out, or during her second marriage, after Cœur de Lion had snatched her back again?

Cœur de Lion. He was her greatest lower, counting her worth a two years' siege and a hundred thousand men. And he opened for her her greatest period, her hundred years union with the Crusaders, when she was capital of the coastal "Kingdom of Jerusalem," and defended by the Knights of St. John, and called St. Jean d'Acre. In her present lonely retirement she recollects but hazily, or not at all, how prosperous and well dressed she was then, and what a fine establishment she kept up. She had barracks and war hospitals, churches and chapels, docks and caravanserais. And, jostled among her crowding guests in those full times, though she remembers him no more than the apostle of twelve hundred years before, was a brown-clad friar who had come from Jerusalem or Nazareth; and, later, a "young bachelor," as he would call himself in his memoirs, or Marco Polo, as we call him now, who used her hospitality before starting upon his journey to Bagdad, and the Oxus, and the kingdoms of the Great Khan.

If these hundred years were her most prosperous period, her grandest moment was at their end, in 1291, when the Sultan Khālil, after a bloody siege, expelled the Christians and marched his Saracens in; for with the fall of Acre the old crusading "Kingdom of Jerusalem" crashed, and the Kings of Frangistan went from the Palestine coast for ever, leaving only their castles and citadels along the shores, as monuments to the ruin of a fine dream.

After that she was St. Jean d'Acre no more: she became Acca of the Saracens and Turks. And her prosperity fell from her, because she had always been a war profiteer, and the wars were ended. For many hundred years she was just the ancient gentlewoman in adverse circumstances that she is now. Only a mosque and the citadel and a few poor dwellings brooded over the ruined harbours. She picked up some of her old position in Napoleon's days, offering a decent resistance to that imperial seducer who liked to put in his call where the great Captains had been before him.

But it was only a transient recovery of the old dis-

245

tinction, a momentary flash of the old spirit. Her day was, and is, over. All her estate has gone to her great-granddaughter or grand-niece or distant relative—I know not what to call her, but her name is Haifa, and she lives under Mount Carmel on the other arm of Acre's bay. And Haifa is developing the very promising property in the energetic and vulgar modern way, while the little old disinherited lady lingers in her dower house on the hill.

Acre is the widow of the Levantine sea.

2

And just as Acre saw the dramatic and decisive moment in the Crusades, so she saw a dramatic moment in the life of Francis—a moment heavy with hints of the end.

Let us go in and learn what she has to tell us. Leaving Haifa, we shall need to drive only a dozen miles on a level road by the sea, but that road will take us out of modernity into history. We leave behind us the hotels and cinemas and white villas of modern Haifa, which climb to the very ridge of Carmel; we pass the arrayed oil-tanks, which are the true symbols of our present age; we pass the pioneer settlements of Zionist Jews, which mark the latest invasion of the Hebrews; and then we are driving by the palm groves where Richard of England bivouacked his army. And the first thing we see of Acre proper is her ancient gate. It is very ancient, and we wonder if its wood is the same as that which shivered beneath the shock of Richard's curtal axe. Turning under it, we drive into a small oriental boulevard and see at its end the grey citadel towering above a press of cafés, shops, and tumbling houses.

Now we park the car, that we may look more closely at

the citadel. Walking up to it, we peer through its ground-floor windows, which are heavy and menacing. At first, thanks to the glare from which we have brought our eyes, we see nothing except darkness, but after a time we discern Gothic arches in the gloom. The picture heightens in definition, and we see vague aisles stretching into obscurity. The floor clarifies itself, and we observe that it is dusty, uneven, strewn with rubbish, and some way below the level of the street.

At this point an Arab guide who is pestering us at our shoulder informs us that we are looking at the sunken crypt of a Crusaders' chapel, and we remember that he is right. Yes, this was the crypt of a chapel, and here knelt the Knights of St. John, for the citadel was their Residency. The arches seem a little flattened now, as if they could hardly sustain the weight of the old bastille above. And well they may sag, since the old fortress is now a prison, vengeance sitting above sanctity, retribution above ruth—no bad picture (as it seemed to me, looking in) of the way the nations of Christendom have always superimposed their systems of judicial torment upon the religion they profess.

We leave the citadel and continue walking northward. Only a minute's walking, so small is the city now, and we come upon the crenellated walls again. Though young compared with the gate, these fortifications wear the patina of time and the peace of forgetfulness. Nothing assaults their repose except the long, slow Mediterranean breakers that scale the lower courses and languidly retreat. The deep embrasures for the guns are still there, and the Arabs use them as impromptu latrines—which will make a simile for a prophet.

But the most wistful experience of all, to us who have

247

a feeling for the lost past, is to stand on the eastern wall and look down on the old, broken harbours. To-day only a few fishing-boats sleep on their sides among the fallen stones, while the lazy water laps against the old stairs. Standing there, I fill my eyes with memory, and restore all this to what it was when Francis was here. I re-people it with the restless figures who brushed his shoulder as they passed. I see on the water the galleys of Venice and Genoa, and the high-masted merchantmen from the mouths of the Nile. The bum-boats of the East peddle their silks and fruits among the ships from the West. Down from the town come the carts and camel caravans, bringing rugs and spices, dyes and Damascene blades, which will return in the empty bottoms. On the burning quays stand piles of merchandise and stacks of munitions for the war. The coolies and stevedores shout at their lading and un-lading, while the knights and men-at-arms disembark, with the priests and the monks and the traders and the tourists. Jugglers and tumblers entertain the idle crews, and the water-sellers, with their dropsical skins, do a brisk trade. And in the heart of the hurly-burly I see a little group of friars of whom one is the son of Bernardone.

It is a summer day that I have in mind, and I conceive the group as consisting of Brother Elias, Syrian Provincial Minister, Francis, who had reappeared here, Peter Cataneo, who had joined him, and Cæsar of Speyer, who was Elias' most remarkable recruit in Palestine. Brother Elias, I suggest, was doing all he could, in these days, to help, care for, and impress the Head of the Order. His strong affection for Francis, and his strong ambition for Brother Elias, would both prompt to such a course.

Well, Francis and Peter left the harbour to return to the house they were living in and partake of a meal. And Elias and Cæsar went a different road. And Francis and Peter, when their table was spread, sat down opposite each other. For a moment, just before eating, Francis screwed up his eyes and kept them tight shut, to ease a pain there. Opening the eyes, and straightening out his face, he persuaded himself that the pain was less. But in that moment fear had constricted his heart. That discomfort in the eyes again! That stinging and watering! It did not mean—oh no, it could not mean—that the sun and the dust—no, God could not have allowed the sun of His Holy Land to strike him in the eyes! Eastern eye sickness? Blindness? All the loveliness of God's creation to fade slowly into darkness? . . . Ah, well, if it were so, it would be his testing; it would be a chance to practise what he had always preached to his brothers—that every trial and temptation could be turned into a source of joy. "Thy will be done. . . . Write, Brother Leo, that this is the perfect joy."

And so, smiling, he spoke of other things to Peter. For the present this pain in his eyes was his secret.

And he and Peter were just about to begin their meal, when the door opened——

Now, some of the foregoing is obvious guesswork, but the opening of that door upon Francis and Peter seated at table lets in the clear light of recorded fact. The two brothers looked up. An excited figure had entered. What? Brother Stephen? Brother Stephen in Acre of the Holy Land? How was this? They had supposed him a thousand miles away in Italy.

Stephen, a lay brother, explained, a little breathlessly, no doubt. He had come secretly, and without authority, but at the instigation of a number of the brothers, to search out Francis, wherever he might be, and beg him to return. Terrible things had been happening to the Order (there is no reason to suppose that Brother Stephen, proud to be King's Messenger, would let his story suffer in the telling), and all the old original brothers, and many of the new ones who desired to follow Francis only, wanted him back at once. Leo wanted him, and Angelo and Rufino and Masseo; and Sister Clare.

But what—why—what had happened? What could be bad enough to justify this hot-foot and stealthy journey?

In summary, this is what Brother Stephen answered. The whole spirit of the Order was being subtly slain. The two Vicars General, Francis' deputies in his absence, had accepted, under the influence of Cardinal Ugolino, letters of authority and protection from Rome for all missionary brothers; they were going to build large convents, where the brothers could live like the Benedictines or the Augustines; they had added new fasts and regulations to the simplicity of the first Rule (which had enjoined little more than a literal following of the Gospel words), so as to assimilate it to the Rules of the ancient orders; and they were enforcing obedience with the sternest punishments, even to expelling from the Order those who insisted on being loyal to Francis. Cardinal Ugolino himself had framed and published new Constitutions for the sisters of San Damiano, which turned them into Benedictine nuns, only Benedictines of a stricter and more formal type. And Brother Philip, the Superior of the Clares, in the same spirit of legalism and discipline, had sought a warrant from Rome that anyone who insulted the sisters should be visited with excommunication. The Order was split into two factions, but the Vicars General and the Ministers were being able to drive their systems through all opposition, because they had the Cardinal and a majority of the brothers with them.

In a word, Ugolino, had been busy organising.

Having delivered himself of his news, Brother Stephen spread on the table a copy of the new Constitutions for Francis and Peter to digest with their meal.

The response of Francis was as typical a thing as ever he did. He dramatised his answer in an action that was simple, quick, humorous, and straight on the target. Picking up the Constitutions and looking hurriedly through them, he read that this actual day was one on which a Brother Minor must no longer eat meat. He glanced at the meat on the table, and then at Peter Cataneo sitting in front of it.

"Eh, Lord Peter," he said. "To-day is a day on which, according to our new rules, it is a sin to eat meat. What are we going to do now?"

"Eh, Lord Francis," answered Peter, retorting in the same mood, "we are going to do what you say, for you are our authority."

(That was a kindly word of comfort, Brother Peter, but then you were one of his first two disciples, and always among the best of "those who were with him.")

"Then," said Francis, "let us in accordance with the Holy Gospel eat what is set before us."

And he helped himself to meat.

My industry in Acre (and it was great) was not rewarded by discovering the site of this almost sacramental meal. But I will tell you this. A Christian Arab who spoke English stood talking with me on the harbour wall. I spoke to him of Francis and Brother Elias but he only listened with confused eyes and a shaking head. Then I used the word "Franciscanism," and he brightened

251

with understanding and delight and, starting off at a quick step, beckoned me to follow him. He led me over the broken quays, indicating where I must walk delicately, and brought me down some ancient steps into a jumble of buildings behind one of the old harbours. Here old chapels and vaults and derelict harbour offices (or so they seemed) had been adapted into dwellings for the very poor. Acre is a jumble of history like the blurred muddle in a child's mind—Phœnicians, Romans, Apostles, Crusaders, Marco Polo, Napoleon—and this huddled Syrian slum expressed the fact very well. Washing hung from wall to wall; fly-blown children played among the smells; the old Roman sea beat against the quays behind; and over a door, in a stray corner which only a wanderer would find, was a shield bearing the crossed arms of the Franciscans and the five-fold cross of the Holy Land. The door stood ajar, and within I could see a slatternly woman preparing a meal.

Who knows? Perhaps some old Franciscan *luogo* stood here even in Elias' day, and I was not far from the place where Francis ate meat as a signal that he would stand by his own.

His meal had not been many days eaten before he took the first ship for Venice. I also took ship for Venice, but I sailed from the upstart port on the other side of the bay. My majestic ship came out of Haifa's new harbour and headed northward for Beyrout. We passed Acre on our starboard, and I stayed leaning on the rail to see the last of that pink-and-white town sleeping above the sands. And as I thought of Francis looking at it for the last time from the gunwale of his boat, I remembered, suddenly, that, in his simple trust and affectionateness, he was taking home with him the able Brother Elias.

CHAPTER XX

I

THERE is fitness in the fact that while word was running down the length of Italy that Francis had returned to deal with apostasy, he should first be seen approaching Bologna. Because Bologna might almost be styled the Captain General of his foes. It was more his enemy than the Pope or the Cardinal or the Ministers, who all had a love for him, and at least a dim sight of his vision. It was more his enemy than Brother Elias or Peter Stacia (whom we shall now meet) because it was the great master that trained them and sent them forth. It was more his enemy than the other great university city of Paris (which the Franciscan zealots of later days indicted as the destroyer) because it was so much less remote than Paris. Bologna, chosen seat of the Pride of Learning, created the time-spirit that fought him. It produced nearly all those men who first invalidated the Franciscan ideal by succumbing to the Third Temptation and compounding with the world. It produced Pope Innocent III, Cardinal Ugolino, Brother Elias, and Peter Stacia.

And for a day, on his arrival there, it overthrew Francis himself. It changed him into an angry avenger, ready to use force and retribution against his foes and to call down solemn curses upon them. It was the scene of the one hour in his life when the delicate stairway which he had built to scale Heaven completely collapsed, and we see him on the earth like ourselves, furious, vindicative, and sullen. It was the story of the Stone House at the Portiuncula over again; only this time he lost his temper so completely as to be hard put to find it again. I will tender no justifications for him, because he would have tendered none for

253

himself; I will only remind you that he was heart-sick and ill and worried about his eyes.

This is what happened. Travelling from Venice towards Bologna and nearing the university city, he learned that the Minister Provincial of Lombardy, Peter Stacia, with the encouragement of Ugolino, had collected great sums of money and built an imposing convent for the brethren which was to be a kind of Legal and Theological College affiliated to the university.

This was to challenge with one toss of the gauntlet every article in Francis' creed. It was to contemn and discard the poverty, the simplicity, the homeless wandering, the Christ-copying, the moneyless-ness—in fact, the whole world-challenge of Franciscanism. Furthermore, the defiance of the Bolognese brothers was flying like a pennon from the turret of their building, in the name they had given it: "The House of the Brothers." The *House*! And *of*, or *belonging to*, the Friars Minor! Such a house had been built by the Dominican, or Preaching, Friars in the previous year, and Peter Stacia's copying of them was a sop to the jealousy and competitiveness in the Friars Minor. But the clear sight of Francis perceived at once that what was life for the Preaching Friars, who were vowed to Science that they might combat heresy, was death to the Friars Minor, who were vowed to poverty that they might combat pride. And he exactly expressed this by refusing to enter "The House," and going to live with the Dominicans instead.

So far he had done well, and was without sin; but in that Dominican home his vexation festered and soured till it permeated his whole being, and he was Francis no more. Like any king of the Gentiles, who exercises lordship over them, he summoned Peter Stacia to wait on him in the Dominican house, and there called down Heaven's curse upon him; and, when the frightened brothers begged him to lift it, he would not. More, he issued an order that all the brothers in that house of sin should do heavy penance. All this from the man who, years after, wrote an anxious and poignant appeal to Brother Elias to refrain from harshness. "If any brother sin mortally . . . let none of the brothers cause him shame or slander him, but let them have great mercy on him, and keep very secret the sin of their brother. And let the Guardian care for him mercifully, as if he were in like case. . . . And if he should fall into venial sin . . . let them have absolutely no power of enjoining other penance upon him, save only this, 'Go and sin no more.'"

It fell to a Dominican brother who, as a disciple of Dominic, "Hammer of Heretics," must have believed in force and stern punishment, to plead with Francis, who believed in neither, that he should deal more gently with his children. Truly things stood topsy-turvy for an hour in Bologna. But though Francis remitted the penance, he commanded all the brothers to quit immediately, and in the name of holy obedience, that iniquitous house, and even to take their sick members with them, though they carried them out on litters.

Contrary to all his creed, Francis had joined battle with the rebels like any angry potentate, and Cardinal Ugolino himself had to hurry in to sweeten his wrath and establish peace. Ugolino was in Bologna at the time, and some of the brothers, smarting under chastisement, ran with their tale to him, their natural protector; and we can imagine his muttered displeasure when told of the unreasonableness of Francis. Really this Francis, saint though he undoubtedly was, could be a little difficult at times. To come lowering in like a thunderstorm, just when we were beginning to trim his incoherent and impossible Order into something really fine! But tact was needed; tact. Sending for Francis, and using all his charm, he explained to the dear fellow that he had got it all wrong; that the House of the Brothers didn't really belong to them at all, because, remembering his strong feelings on the matter, he had caused himself to be registered as its proprietor.

And, as before at the Portiuncula when Francis came wearily down from the roof of the new stone house, he accepted this excuse and went from Bologna.

Besides, like a man to whom consciousness is returning after anæsthesia, his true self was coming back into him with pain. He knew that he had sinned against the highest in him. He knew that he had blundered; that this was no way to deal with opposition. And he knew that he must go away and wrestle with doubt and indecision as to how best to cope with the wide recalcitrance in his Order.

He must face and worry out the everlasting problem of every man, be he statesman, teacher, or parent, who is cursed with the knowledge that retribution only increases the evil it seeks to amend, and force is sure only of failure. Somewhere in a solitude Francis stared into the dilemma with straining eyes: to refuse to fight and use force seemed to hand the prize to the enemy, and yet—and yet—to fight and use force was to achieve nothing in the end except the opposite of what you sought. He had done more harm than good by his angry dragoonings at Bologna. Harm? Why, very likely he had damaged irreparably the ideal which through years of struggle he had been building for his children. "God pardon me, and lay the guilt on me if any of these little ones stumble hereafter through fault of mine."

Ah, yes, the more he thought, or, rather—since thought had long passed into knowledge—the more he stared at the knowledge within him, the more he knew that to meet the foe with his own weapons would be to betray his Master. Perhaps he saw again the Via Dolorosa twisting between the houses of Jerusalem. Perhaps he saw again the face of his Master turned towards him as He went by with His cross, and read again the message in His eyes: "My son, you must teach only by persuasion and example; never by coercion or angry punishment. Listen, Francis; you are one who has eyes to see and ears to hear. You cannot teach peace by war. You cannot teach gentleness by violence, nor love and forgiveness by retribution and wrath. The citadel that you have to capture is the heart, and no man carried it yet by repression and reprisal. These do but harden the defences against you, which will succumb only to the slow siege of love. Fare you well. I go on to Golgotha. May good fortune and victory abide you too. Be you only lifted up—that is all—and you will draw them unto you."

Then Francis, in the contrite accents of Peter: "Leave me, Lord, for I am a sinful man."

For it is often in repentance after sin that a man sees most clearly the truth that is Christ for him; and loves it best, and resolves most passionately to be worthy of it.

Good: so let it be: he must do nothing to coerce the brethren. Gentle rebuke only, a clear and uncompromising statement of his position, and thereafter the lesson of his life. Those few who could see the ideal would come with him at once; the others—well, he must keep it aloft before them in the hope that one day they too would see.

Nolebat contendere cum ipsis, says the narrative, *sed . . . volebat in se illud implere.* "He was unwilling to contend with them, but wished to fulfil in himself the ideal."

For his part, he saw *their* idea with painful clarity. They wanted to keep him as a figurehead, an ornament, and a "draw," but not as a governor; they wanted a practical, level-headed, worldly-wise man to govern them: one who would allow them to have sensible houses to live in, and libraries and cloisters for study like the Dominicans, and a reasonable amount of common property to secure them from care. And one who could make the law, enforce obedience to it, and give them a dictator's peace.

It was what the Church, however kind and encouraging, had wanted to do with him from the beginning: always it had wanted to force his free limbs into the old monastic habit. "Back to the old, the customary, and the blessed of the Church," was its cry, while his was, " Forward to something new and nearer to Christ. Forward into an adventure. Not for us, the tried, the proven, and the safe."

But they wouldn't have it: they wouldn't have his free poor men, wandering the world in the likeness of Christ, and refusing money, privilege, protection, and any shield or sword but love. He had wanted to change the self-seeking competitiveness of Society by flooding the world with men so new that they esteemed as vulgarity the pursuit of personal eminence. But they wouldn't have it: they wanted something familiar and easier to understand. His Order was afraid of Calvary. It had forsaken him and fled.

2

But while his faith in his vision was so lofty as to have become knowledge, his faith in himself was as low as clear sight and complete humility could make it. He saw that he had poor powers of thought and that therefore it was not in him to solve this problem of how to govern a world-wide order without discipline. Without external discipline, that is. Discipline willingly accepted he knew to be lovely, and preached continually; but discipline enforced from without—with this he could not come to terms. He could countenance a mild and loving discipline which an offending brother would accept as just—but there! he was back at accepted instead of enforced discipline. All that he could see with clearness was that, if a minimum of enforced discipline was necessary, he was not the man to inflict it. "It is not in me," he said, "to act the sergeant of the Lord." And again: "If I am not able to correct and amend them by preaching and admonition and example, I will not become an executioner, punishing and flogging them like the magistrates of this world." How wonderful that Francis should have said these words in that savage and torturing century! Not till the beginning of the nineteenth century did we English, a kindly people, begin to dislike executions and floggings and torment, and our eyes are not very wide open yet.

And this distrust of his mind was reinforced now by distrust of his body. He knew that his eyes were smarting and failing, and that the vigour of his early years was in him no more. Either he had burned it all up, or, as I am inclined to think, this time of conflict and strain was one of those periods common to all mystics, when God seems to have withdrawn from them for a space, and all is very dark, and the energy of the great union is lost. Apart from this energy his body had always been frail—the thin glass of a lamp too bright for it. Nor does it appear that the greatest mystical energy always spares the body it possesses. Many of the greatest mystics have been enabled by it to live dynamically (and generally on nothing at all) for seventy or eighty years, but others of them have achieved their dynamic reconstructions in one lively decade or so, and then laid down happily to die. Francis was built for the latter company: energy used him up; its loss left him limp. His collapse at Bologna may have been a cause, or an effect, of his loosening grip upon God, but it had shaken him.

And so his position in this darkening hour may be summed up thus: "The rightness of my message I do not doubt, and it is of its essence that I coerce none, but teach only by example. My mind I have always doubted, and now I doubt my body, and even my spirit till I shall be one with God again. I begin to see my way. For their sakes I must concentrate all my poor power on living the life I believe in; on making a tongue of my whole body. But another must be their shepherd to guide and, if in his wisdom he think fit, to correct them with gentle discipline."

Some peace settled upon him: he knew his road.

And behold the issue. It is the Michaelmas Chapter of 1220. A great multitude of the brothers had assembled, drawn from every part of Italy by the word that Francis was home again. All had come with joy, both the few faithful who looked upon him as their saviour and the many dissidents who, however they might disagree with him, loved him and looked upon him as the noblest man upon earth. Not a soul there who wanted to be without him as a leader, though some desired that the leadership should be nominal only. The alarms which had been theirs during his absence, when rumours had rushed among them that he was drowned or imprisoned or martyred, were the measure of their relief and happiness now. As before the Chapter of Mats, every road in Italy had seen the friars tramping over mountain and plain to meet again a beloved father.

And when they were all assembled to hear him, he rose. He rose from the seat of the president. Silence awaited his words, but when the words came, when he began to tell them all that was in his heart, the silence, as we know from a chronicle which may derive from Leo himself, was broken by sobs and sighs. He told them how he was fit no longer to govern so great a body, and that in future he desired to be among them as one that served. He called God to witness that he cared for nothing except to lead them in the way which He had shown him, and that he believed he could do this best by abandoning command and trying only to walk that way before them. He told them that he had consulted long with Cardinal Ugolino, who had been unsparing in counsel and sympathy, and that these were the decisions they had come to together. Peter Cataneo, a man of learning, who had been a juris-consult of the Church, and one of his first and dearest followers, would succeed him as their leader. Peter Cataneo, God be with him, would be his Vicar General. And he, Francis, was going away into a solitude to see if he could amend the Rule in the interests of peace, and he was going to take with him their good brother Cæsar of Speyer, another wise and learned man, to help him.

Let the *Speculum Perfectionis* write the conclusion.

To observe the virtue of holy humility he resigned his office in a certain Chapter before the friars, saying, "From henceforth I am dead to you, but here is Brother Peter Cataneo whom both you and I will obey." And bowing himself before Brother Peter, he promised him obedience

261

and reverence. And the friars could not forbear weeping and sighing when they saw themselves in a manner becoming orphans of such a father; but Francis rose, and with his eyes raised to heaven, and his hands joined, said, "Lord, I return to thee this family which thou hast confided to me, for now, as thou knowest, I have no longer strength or ability to keep on caring for them. I confide them therefore to the Ministers. May they be responsible before thee in the day of judgment, if any brother by their negligence or bad example, or by a too severe discipline, should ever wander away."

CHAPTER XXI

I

As I proceed with my tale, and as the stature of Francis increases, I begin to query my position in the record. I no longer want to speak of an unimportant and sometimes frivolous traveller and his wanderings. The grandeur of the subject, and the looming of La Verna, turn the traveller's discourse into triviality.

But let us pause a moment: Don Quixote had a coarse figure on an ass beside him. Sancho Panza, jogging along beneath his master, served a purpose in the tale, his clumsy questionings illuminating nobility on the highroad. And the princeliest troubadour from Provence took his jongleur with him, that the fellow's interlude of lighter song and ruder entertainment might throw into relief the splendour of the real singer. Therefore I will take heart, and go on. But I must speak more soberly now, when there is occasion to speak at all.

All mystical writers agree that the aspiring soul, just before that complete and lasting union with the Infinite which most of them call the Mystical Marriage, must experience a time of darkness, loss, and loneliness. St. John of the Cross and others have called it the "dark night of the soul." In it God seems (the word is only "seems") to have withdrawn from sight, and the soul must stumble blindly forward, with only its faith, its memories, and its hope to guide it. Why this experience should be necessary it is not within my purpose to discuss. Here I shall only suggest that, since the fall of the darkness means the approach of the union, and since its lifting finds the union perfected and indestructible, we may speak of it as the shadow before the embrace of the Beloved.

"Halts by me that footfall? Is my gloom, after all, Shade of His hand outstretched caressingly?"

And I must always feel that this night was gathering about Francesco di Pietro Bernardone now. He is stumbling in a twilight, though there are moments of brightness before the nightfall is complete. Soon on the summit of La Verna the darkness will deepen to an intensity so absolute that no human eye may discern what happens within, not even the loving and saintly Brother Leo, whom we see hovering anxiously on its outskirts and peering for an assurance of his master's safety. It lifts, and the mystery of Francesco di Pietro Bernadone is achieved.

Hesitation, despondency, and even some irritability shackle his steps in the months before La Verna. And very true, human, and moving they are, though they may flaw his sanctity for a while. How revealing it is that Brother Giordano da Giano, who first met Francis at this time, should write in his Chronicle that he did not at first think him "altogether free from human weaknesses," and that it was only afterwards that he knew him for a saint. Or hear a story, freely translated, from the *Speculum Perfectionis*.

But once, when Francis was returned from oversea, a certain Minister wished to know his understanding of the prohibition in the Rule, "Take nothing with you by the way." And Francis answered, "I understand it to mean that the brothers must have nothing besides their habit, cord, and breeches and, if they are forced by necessity, sandals." And the Minister said to him, "What then am I to do, who have so many books that they may be worth more than fifty pounds?" And Francis answered, "I neither will, nor ought, nor can go against my conscience and the perfection of the Gospel, which we have professed." Hearing these things, the Minister became very sad. And Francis, seeing him, cried fervently before them all, "Oh you who would be seen of men as Friars Minor and yet wish to keep your treasure chests! The Brother Ministers think to deceive God and me, but look: you may do as you will, but not with my consent. I desire it written in the beginning and end of our Rule that Friars are bound to observe the fulness of the Gospel, and that the brethren are forever without excuse, since I have announced, and announce again, those things which the Lord for their and my salvation placed in my mouth."

"You may do as you will. . . ." O Francis, where is thy laughing challenge of yesterday; where is the perfect joy?

We know of wise but very bitter sayings uttered by him at this time. "These sons of a father who was a beggar will not be ashamed one day to wear the scarlet cloth of gallants." Or, "Would that there were fewer Brothers Minor, and that the world, seeing one but seldom, should wonder at their fewness!" Or hear the sorrowful resignation that embitters the loyalty in his letter to Antony of Padua: a letter which consents, after all, to the opening of the school at Bologna and sanctions the appointment of Antony as its Reader in Theology. "Brother Antony, my bishop—" it is good to see that the old banter is not wholly silenced—"Greetings in Christ to my dearest brother from Brother Francis. It pleases me that thou readest in theology for the brethren, provided they do not, for the sake of the study, give up their prayer and slacken the spirit of devotion. Farewell."

It is Francis coming down from the roof.

And do you remember the young novice who asked that he might possess a psalter of his own, and whom Francis teased, saying, "When you have your psalter, you will want a breviary, and when you have your breviary, you will think yourself a great prelate instead of a Brother Minor, and sit on a throne and call for your breviary." Well, about this time the novice, a full brother now, came to Francis and broached again the subject of the psalter.

Very different is the note in Francis now. Very weary. With a sigh he says, "Go and do in this matter what your Minister tells you." Hearing which, the brother hastened away in surprise and joy.

But Francis, standing in the same place, considered what he had said to that young brother and immediately called after him, "Wait for me, Brother, wait for me." And he ran up to him and said, "Turn back with me, Brother, and show me the place where I said to you that you could do as the Minister decided." And together they went back to the same place, and there Francis kneeled before the young man and said, "*Mea culpa*, Brother, *mea culpa*, for whosoever would be a Brother Minor should have nothing but his clothing."

But what need we more, to see into his heart, than his own statement when a certain friar asked the meaning of his abdication? "My son," he answered, "I love the brethren as much as I can, but if they would follow in my footsteps, I would love them still more. But there are those amongst your superiors who draw towards the old ways and think little of me and my teaching." "And a little after," says the same story, "when his exceeding great infirmity weighed upon him, he rose upon his bed and cried out, 'Oh, who are you have dared to take my brothers from me? If I come to the Chapter, I will show you what spirit I am made of.'"

"My son, I love them as much as I can. . . ." That was in the darkness before La Verna. In the white radiance beyond, on his suffering but triumphant death-bed, he uses similar words, but with what a change of accent! Love is frustrated no more: it knows no barrier that can beat it back. His brothers beseech his blessing as he goes from them, and he answers, "I bless them as much as I can, and more than I can."

Plusquam possum. It was in that bright last hour, and not

266

in this time of darkness, that he sounded, unknowingly, the real motto of his life: "Always and in all things, more than I can."

2

Sometimes one may learn the nature of a great pain by considering a little one. Many years ago I wrote a play and thought it good. The years have passed, and I think less of it now, though I still believe it had some good lines, and was nowhere vulgar. A worthy management and a good company undertook to stage it for me. It was given to a competent and well-intentioned producer who—whether he or I was right doesn't matter, for it is only the artist's pain we are considering—saw in my words quite different meanings and possibilities from any that I had intended. As it appeared to me, he abandoned quietness for noise, and modesty for quick, cheap, easy effects. I sat at the rehearsals, contending, disputing, appealing, till I was a stench in the nostrils of producer and actors all. Then I went from the theatre for good and all, and left the play to them, to do their worst. And there the story may end. It is told only because it may help you to understand, as it certainly helps me to understand, a tithe of what Francis was suffering now when he believed that his producers and his company were vulgarising a creation that he loved.

It is now that we are grateful for those old first brethren who cried that he was right and supported him with their understanding—for Bernard of Quintavalle and Giles, for little Leo and the handsome, mocking Masseo, for Angelo Tancredi, the knight, and Clare in San Damiano, quietly confident that if all the world differed from Francis, then all the world must be wrong. All these, and others who are nameless, must have been to him now as a woman for his comfort. They surrounded him with sympathy; they made him an audience to which he could pour out his justi- fication, and be understood. To these, in long talks, he expounded how he would reconcile freedom with obedience and harmonise his loyalty to the Rule with loyalty to his erring family. When, less clear-sighted than he, they hinted at a breaking away from the dissentient Ministers, he shook his head and answered, "If a superior commands a subject anything against his soul, it is right for that subject not to obey him, but that does not mean that the subject should throw off his allegiance and sit alone in his pride. If, in consequence of his rightful dis- obedience, he is submitted by the authorities to mis- understanding and persecution, he must love them the more; for he who would rather suffer persecution than wish to be separated from his brothers remains in perfect obedience, since he lays down his life for the brothers. By any other means he might lose souls that he should gain."

Behind a letter to Leo we can see a picture of Francis walking in green places with these loyal brothers and being healed by their questions or their quiet listening.

Brother Leo, thy brother Francis wishes thee peace and health. I reply Yes, my son. That word sums up all we said while walking, as well as all my counsels. Whatever may be the manner in which thou thinkest thou canst please the Lord God, follow it, and live in poverty. Do this, God will bless thee, and I authorise it. And if it is necessary for thy soul, or for thy consolation, that thou shouldst come to see me, or if thou desirest it, my Leo, come.

And yet the truth remains that even these, when death had taken him from them, and his influence was withdrawn—even these with their sterling loyalty and their insight so much brighter than the others, fell, in their eagerness to defend his memory, into anger, combativeness, vindictive words, or schism. Giles lashed the betrayers with the sardonic tongue of an old countryman; Leo, the gentle and quiet, dashed to the ground a vase set up by Brother Elias to collect money for the great house and church of San Francesco; Jacopone da Todi burned the backs of the retreaters with the vitriol of his poems; and others in despair sought refuge in schism. Almost we may say that one only saw the father's ideal with completeness and failed it nowhere, contending for it with uncompromising firmness, but with love for all and impatience towards none; obedient always, but remaining alive till she got her way, and then dying. Clare. This woman waited in life till she had secured the last word. As I said in the beginning, it looks sometimes as if the Author had designed an æsthetic fitness for every detail of Francis' story. It is well that the woman in the story should be the perfect mate.

And so, with a few of the faithful, he betook himself to a solitary place, taking his Rule with him, to see if he could make it more intelligible to the rebels, more winning.

That he went up into a mountain we need hardly say. He went into his well-loved Vale of Rieti and climbed to a little hermitage on Monte Rainerio, now called Fonte Colombo after the Lady Columba who had given her house and the adjoining woods to the brothers. It is, I should say, the leafiest and most sylvan of all the Franciscan retreats. Like the Carceri, Monte Casale, Greccio, and the Celle of Cortona, it hangs on the rock face of the mountain, but all the slope and crown of the mountain, and the steep gorge below, are massed with trees. They make a continuing forest of beech and ilex and oak, with ferns to veil every wall and jutting crag.

Here in the hermitage clearing there stands to-day, still guarded by the brothers of the Strict Obedience, the little chapel of Santa Maria Maddalena, built by Francis' own hand some years before these events, and standing to welcome him when he came this way after his abdication. You may walk down a zig-zag path to the grottoes among the trees and ferns where he worked upon the Rule with Cæsar of Speyer, that learned man, to help him, and Leo, that fine penman, for his amanuensis. As I climbed up to Fonte Colombo, I thought of that slight, disappointed figure toiling up the path with Leo, and clasping his rejected Rule.

But if you pity him, pity him for his pain, not for any weakness of will. Though in our crudeness we may lose patience with such patience and cry for a little stern discipline on the refractory, though in our immaturity we may worship the so-called "strong man" and count all lenience weak, Francis was greater, righter, more adult, and, yes, stronger than we. His unwavering loyalty to his vision in this hour, his refusal to mar that loyalty (except in trapped, "weak" moments) by any anger, vindictiveness, or hurting word, or by anything that would *separate* him from unity with his brothers,—this strong, steadfast example has held up the heads of the noblest of his followers, has strengthened the brothers of the Strict Observance to this day, and has fed the fire of reform after reform. The just still live by his faith. And the sinners, many of them, are lifted a little way out of their hates, their self-assertiveness, their aggressiveness, their intolerance, and all their absurdly primitive and puerile passions. There is a cross in the courtyard of Fonte

Colombo's hermitage: let it be the symbol of this example which looks backward over twelve centuries to that other symbol on Calvary, whose stature it does not fail. It stands through the ages, a challenge to his friars, to us, and to all our quarrelling and separatist world. It stands uncompromised, and we, because we have a portion of his spirit, are left wondering.

CHAPTER XXII

I

NOTHING, it would seem, is spared the chosen soul before its admission to the Last Embrace. Francis' cup did not pass from him; it was filled to the top, and he was bidden drink it all. Peter Cataneo, who might have been a bridge between him and the rebel Order, died almost at once, and Brother Elias was appointed Vicar General in his place. Brother Elias, who had been Bombarone in the world! Here was the "realist" politician, the good business man, the "strong" dictator they wanted. Here was a real sergeant of the Lord. Here was a man very willing, in the best interests of the Order, to punish and flog like the magistrates of this world.

Had Francis any word in this appointment, or did he stare at it with confounded eyes? It is just possible that, longing to hope great things of Elias, whose kindness and whose administrative gifts had been proved in Syria, he refused to listen to the unkind whispers of intuition. But I find this hard to believe, first, because the subsequent collaborations between Ugolino and Elias suggest that the Cardinal inspired the appointment, and secondly, because whatever may have been Francis' love of Elias in the beginning, his penetrating eyes must have seen by now that the crowning of such a man was the very parable of what was happening to the Order. Eternal forces had met and clashed within it: law against love, security against adventure, the dictator's peace against liberty, self-aggrandisement against self-abnegation; and the lower forces had won. They had cast Brother Elias on to the throne.

That Francis saw all this, very soon, if not at once, and

that he feared for his brethren, seem proved by the Letter of Appeal which he sent to the new Vicar.

> To Brother Elias, Minister. The Lord bless thee. I speak to thee as I am able concerning the condition of thy soul. If there be persons, whether brothers or not, who are a hindrance to thee in loving the Lord God, yet shouldst thou count all such trials as favours. And let this be to thee a command from the Lord and from me. . . . Love those that do such things unto thee. . . . And by this I shall know that thou lovest God and me, His servant and thine, if there be no brother in all the world, let him sin as deeply as he may, who shall go away from before thy face without thy mercy . . ."

There follows the beautiful appeal, which I cited a few pages back, for tenderness to the mortal sinner and no penance for the venial sinner above "Go and sin no more." "Keep this letter by thee," concludes Francis, "that it may be better observed."

But Elias did not keep it by him. He thought it the impracticable dream of a visionary, and admired it as such, and wished the world fitted better to the pretty dream, and got on with his stern task.

And yet, if we read him aright, we shall fill with compassion rather than condemnation, even as we do (did we speak the truth of our hearts) for Judas. How can we condemn a man too like ourselves, who are not malignant people, but just blind, well-meaning, cocksure blunderers? Elias had his higher side: so have we; but neither he nor we will let it break through our tough egotism and our iron-hard self-justification. He and we, and Francis too, are mixed characters; and the only difference between Francis and us is that Francis early enabled his higher self to conquer, at whatever cost, while we too early sounded the retreat. And thereafter Francis is troubled only by pricks from the lower self, while we are troubled by pricks from the higher.

Many things in the life of Bombarone, Frate Elia, show that these nobler parts were in him, though baulked and silenced. In the first place he succumbed to the appeal of Francis at Cortona, which must mean that after a youth of dour ambition and social climbing, he was able to fall in love for a little with the sweetness of service and self-giving; and I have not the least doubt that he strove hard in his first year to be worthy of this new idea. Then there is the hermitage of the Celle near Cortona to tell us of a gentler Elias. As it stands to-day, humble and retired among the trees of its hillside, it is largely the creation of Elias, and no man who created this quiet place could have been blind to all that Francis saw. The remote, sequestered Celle exactly expresses the lost side of Elias as the magnificent San Francesco in Assisi, also his creation, expresses the side which triumphed. Proud upon its mountain, lifted high above a hundred, soaring arches, dominating the valley, San Francesco is a monument to his love of pomp and power and place.

But it is also the monument to his love. Let him disagree with Francis as he might, let him despise his patience and lenience, he never lost his love and worship for a man much greater than he. He only thought that he could organise his ideas for him so much better than he could himself. (Was not this what Judas thought?) Like Ugolino, like many dictators, he could be affectionate to those near him. In the long months of Francis' last sickness he cared for him like a mother: the word is Francis' own, who said that Elias was to him *in loco matris*. In the last journey from Siena to Assisi he fussed about him and guarded him like a faithful dog. Indeed, throughout all these last years, the larger half of his determination to organise the Order was a desire to spare its frail and failing creator all unnecessary trouble and worry. Here is the letter which he wrote to the brotherhood in the hour after Francis' death. His parade and pompousness are in it, but something else is in it too.

I sigh before I utter word, and what wonder? For the thing I feared has come to pass, for me and for you. Far from us has gone the consoler, and he who carried us like lambs in his arms has set forth, a pilgrim into a far country. The beloved of God and men, he who taugnt the law of life and discipline to Jacob and gave the testament of peace to Israel, has entered the mansions of exceeding light. Greatly should we joy for him but grieve for ourselves: now that he is away the darkness surrounds us, and the shadow of death covers us. A calamity to all, but a singular danger to me whom he has left in the very midst of night, beset by many occupations and oppressed by innumerable cares. . . . Before he was taken from us, he blessed all his sons and forgave all faults of word and thought which were committed or conceived against him by any of us. . . . For his soul pray to God. Let the priests say three masses, the laics five paternosters, and let the clerks say vigil solemnly in common. Amen.

BROTHER ELIAS, Sinner.

The pricks, the pricks!

And, Francis dead, he set about building a sepulchre which should be worthy of such a man. With his immense energy and organising ability he ransacked the world for money and raised San Francesco upon its high place, almost before the body of his saint was cold. The body of the Little Poor Man, who had commanded his children to raise no fine churches but to build, rather, the church not made with hands, he laid in the finest Gothic church of Italy. (I am sure Judas would have raised a tomb of equal majesty for the saviour of his people.) And he buried the body so secretly and so deep that no one knew where it lay for six hundred years. Thus the strong hand of Elias guarded his master for six hundred years. And to this day his arches of San Francesco stand like a fortress round the thing that he loved. And that is why San Francesco is no monument to the Poverello, but to Frate Elia, his poor, blind caliph. It is the monument to his blindness, and his love.

Nor is this all. Some years after Francis' death the Order rose against Elias' tyranny and expelled him, and the Pope excommunicated him, and he, indignant at such ingratitude, deserted the papal cause and went over to the Emperor, whose trusted ambassador he became; but all the time he still wore, defiantly, the grey-brown habit and cord of Francis. And before his own death, while still in excommunication, defying them all and believing himself a true Franciscan, he built a convent and church high up above Cortona, and called it San Francesco. And here, absolved at the end, he died. In this other church of San Francesco, high up among the storms, his brothers laid the proud Elias to rest, in the grey livery of a master he had loved.

Let us bury his faults there too, covered by that grey robe.

2

As I mediate on Elias, I seem to see what had happened. According to the issue of his inward struggle such a man must either become Francis or the opposite of Francis. He tried to become Francis, and he failed. And because this failure set him free to use his native gifts for his own aggrandisement, he climbed easily to the generalship or the Order. As its general though all the while persuading himself for his own peace that he was serving his master

276

better than he could serve himself, he marched the Order away from him. He collected vast sums of money and built them great houses and churches; he encouraged them to pursue learning and beat the Dominicans at their own game; he introduced strict discipline and stern punishments, even to the scourging and banishing of Leo, who had overthrown his *offerte* vase; he persecuted the zealots; he allowed the *minores* to become *majores* and take high posts in the Church; and he himself rode through the world, a mighty potentate, master of a world-wide disciplined Order, and famous for his fine palfreys, his liveried lackeys, and his chef.

In a worldlier sphere, or on a lower level where they still suppose that strength lies in ruthlessness, and that virility consists in crushing your opponents, Elias might have been honoured for his great abilities and pardoned for the few weaknesses that went with them. His tragedy was simply this, that, in a moment of bright vision he entered the Franciscan Order, but, the blindness closing upon him immediately, he became one of the least Franciscan persons who ever lived; thus winning from history the name of Judas instead of the name of Napoleon. Had more of his Franciscanism survived to do battle with his haughty impatience, he might have been called Paul.

And it is constructive to consider how completely, because he became the opposite of Francis, he failed. Elias craved power and position and the praise of men; Francis abandoned all these. Elias had splendid confidence in his common-sense and realism; he called his own stern discipline strength and the lenience of Francis softness; and yet it was the dreamer, the forgiver, who won all. It was Francis who saved his fame and his power by throwing

277

them away, and Elias who lost them by seeking them. Elias conquered a little fragment of time; Francis conquered the ages. The world gave Elias power and place for a few quick-passing years, and then forgot him; it lifted Francis to a place of worship and continuing sway. Francis is perhaps the only figure in human record whom everyone has always loved. But Elias! Like all those who compromise with expediency and content themselves with less than perfection, Elias forgot Time: he forgot that the mills of Time grind quickly, and grind exceeding small.

Who really remembers Elias? Who climbs to his tomb, high above high Cortona? Only a wandering historian who chances to be considering the victory of Francis, and has time, and the mind, to pay to failure the passing tribute of a tear. I got Natale to drive me through Perugia and along the shores of Trasimene and up and up to the mountain city of Cortona. Cortona, says Anne Macdonell in her fine study of Frate Elia, is the right tragic setting for the last years of that arrogant soul, the best high place to hold his dust. "It sits there on its mountain, strong and isolated. There is something sinister in its pride of place. . . . The great hills menace you, and the kindly plain and placid Trasimene are far below." She might have added that it stands between the quiet glen of the Celle and the battlefield of Trasimene, even as the soul of Elias halted between Franciscan peace and the hot conflict for an empire in the world.

And the dust of Elias throws no light upon his city, unlike that dust which irradiates the towers of Assisi and draws the pilgrims towards it. When I alighted from Natale's car in the chief piazza, I could find no one who was interested in Elias' grave. No one knew of whom I

278

was speaking. A guide undertook to lead me to San Francesco, and together we climbed the twisting and stony streets, up and up, as if we had not already climbed far enough from the plain. We came upon a small, oblong, tilted piazza, and there at the top was the façade of San Francesco.

This second San Francesco of Brother Elias was like a small, dull copy of his masterpiece in Assisi. I passed into its dusty and deserted nave and with some difficulty conjured a conventual friar out of a side door. His black robe was as dusty and worn as the walls and furnishings of the church, but his manner was pleasant and welcoming: he seemed amazed that anyone should have come to look upon the grave of Frate Elia. He led me up into the chancel and into a room behind the high altar. Choir stalls furnished three of its walls, and in the midst of the floor was a small desk—or it may have been a harmonium: I could not see because it was littered with papers. The friar pushed this to one side and uncovered a small inscribed stone on the floor.

"There," he said.

There. Elias' path of glory had led but there. Francis was venerated at his tomb, Clare was venerated at hers, even Margherita, a later Franciscan saint, drew pilgrims to her own church in Cortona, but for Elias no one cared. Nor was it certain that more than a little of his dust lay beneath this stone, because they tell of an angry Guardian who threw out what he could find of his bones. But such dust as was there lay forgotten under a table. His sins of arrogance and hate had possessed only this much of strength, that they had hidden his body more securely than his love hid the body of Francis.

279

To the Chapter General of 1221 Francis brought the Rule which he had revised in the interests of peace. Some three thousand were gathered to hear it. He had a crowded house, much as a Cabinet Minister in the Commons will have a full house when he introduces the most contentious bill of the year. They sat in expectant silence. Elias, the new General, occupied the president's chair, and Francis, who desired to be among them as one that served, but who, nevertheless, was the figurehead of the Order, sat at his Vicar's feet, and when he wanted something said to the assembly, pulled at Elias' robe. And Elias bent his head and, having heard his comment, rose and announced, "Brothers, Brother Francis says . . ."

Brother Francis sat there, possessing the respect and love of all, but the loyalty of only a few. And so the stage was set for the reading of the new Rule.

The silence which awaited its reading became the silence of dismay as it was read. It left them speechless. For of course it was nothing but an impassioned restatement of all that had provoked their complaints. Was it likely that Francis would have learned in his lonely communion with God on Fonte Colombo how to come to terms with things he believed to be wrong? His conciliation showed itself only in the laboured efforts to state better an inviolable vision and in the hungry, passionate appeals for unity with which the document was punctuated from beginning to end.

The Rule of 1221 is surely one of the most astonishing scriptures in religious history. It is hardly a Rule at all; it is appeal, appeal, appeal. The fact is, as Sabatier well says, that Francis was about the last person in Christendom to invite to make a Rule. First, because he hadn't a legal mind, or even a mind that reasoned well, and secondly, and more fundamentally, because he didn't believe in rule, but in inspiration. This is Francis' idea of how to write a Rule.

> By the holy love which is in God, I pray all the friars, Ministers as well as others, to put aside every obstacle, every care, every anxiety, that they may be able to consecrate themselves entirely to serve, love, and honour the Lord God with pure heart and sincere purpose, which is what He asks above all things. . . . Let us then keep in the true way, the life, the truth, and the holy gospel of Him who has deigned for our sake to leave His Father. . . . Then let nothing again hinder, let nothing again separate, nothing again retard us, and may we all, so long as we live, in every place, at every hour, every day unceasingly, truly and humbly, believe. Let us have in our hearts, let us love, adore, serve, bless, glorify, exalt, magnify, thank the most high sovereign eternal God, Trinity and Unity, Father, Son and Holy Spirit, Creator of all men. . . . He is without beginning and without end [here the mystic has full rein], immutable and invisible, ineffable, incomprehensible, indiscernible, blessed, lauded, glorious, exalted, sublime, most high, sweet, lovely, delectable, and always worthy of being desired above all things in all the ages of ages. Amen.

The general dismay was only saved from rising to murmurs and mutiny by the tact of Ugolino and Elias. It is proof of the tremendous power of Francis' personality (however you may think he carried gentleness too far) that these men knew that they were nothing without him. Let the Order lose him finally, and it would be like some commonplace lamp in which an unusual light had gone out, or like the haft of a lance from which the shining spear-head had snapped. If Francis were to disown them, they could roll up their plans for a fine, disciplined army of Franciscan infantry. When he was dead and canonised, it would be different: then he would be their founder and father for ever, and they would be free to do what they liked. They would be free to alter or suppress much of what he had taught. But in the meantime he must be soothed and, as we say, "kept sweet." Ugolino, greatest bishop of the Church, and heir to the papacy, knew this: he knew that the compassionate little friar was more powerful than he.

So, in effect, this is what these two sagacious and exceedingly practical men did. Ugolino nodded to that good, understanding fellow, Elias, and whispered, "Leave him to me." And Elias nodded back understandingly. And Ugolino, taking Francis aside, suggested with much delicacy that he should have another attempt at amending the Rule, making it, for example, conciser before it was submitted for ratification to the Pope—and truly, we may feel some sympathy with Ugolino in his suggestion that Francis' prose style might be conciser. So back went Francis to Fonte Colombo, taking Leo with him, and clasping his unwanted Rule. And of course, in the quiet of the mountain with God, he did little but write the same statement in new words.

A legend of Fonte Colombo, which I for one cannot believe since, if it were true, the subsequent behaviour of Elias would be incredible, may be recorded here none the less, if only as a piece of imaginative drama which most effectively puts the conflict before us. The compiler of the *Speculum Perfectionis* sets it at the opening of his book, like an overture announcing the main themes.

> Francis went up into a certain mountain with Brother Leo and Brother Bonyzo to make another rule which by the teaching of Christ he caused to be written down. But many of the Ministers, being gathered together with Brother Elias (who was the Vicar of Francis), said to him, "We have heard

that Brother Francis is making a new Rule, but we are afraid that he will make it so hard that we cannot observe it. Therefore we wish you to go to him and say that we will not be bound to that Rule: let him make it for himself and not for us." But Brother Elias answered that he would not go without them, so all went together. And when they were near the place where Francis was, Brother Elias called him. And Francis, answering and beholding all the Ministers, said, "What do all these brethren want?" And Brother Elias answered, "These are the Ministers who, on hearing that you are making a new Rule and fearing lest you make it too hard, do say and protest that they will not be bound to it: you are to make it for yourself and not for them." Then Francis turned his face to Heaven and spoke thus to Christ, "Lord, said I not well that they would not believe me?" And all heard the voice of Christ answering in the air, "Francis, there is nothing in the Rule of thine but it is all mine, and I wish that the Rule should be obeyed without gloss." Then the Ministers, looking upon one another, went back, confused and terrified.

A fable, no doubt; didactic in aim. This, however, is history. Francis sent an amended Rule to Elias, and Elias, after he had read the irritating document, adopted a blunter method of temporising than Ugolino. He did nothing with the Rule at all, and when asked by the brethren where it was, reported that someone had lost it.

CHAPTER XXIII

I

FOR the rest, the simplest statement is that Francis left them to go their way. He went back to the mountains of Rieti, to be alone. He knew that something was being worked out in him, something strange and awful, but great. There could be no question now as to whether he should follow the active or contemplative life: he must be alone with God and a few disciples till this thing should be accomplished. "My soul is exceeding sorrowful, even unto death. Tarry ye here and watch with me."

The "dark night" was deepening. The bright morning of his mission, when he jested and sang with his brothers at Rivo Torto, was far behind him, and he was moving through a midnight cloud on a mountain height, but he knew that if he passed steadfastly through the cloud, he would see God beyond it, as he had never seen Him before. Or, changing the metaphor, we may say that his soul was darkened by excess of light. It was troubled and hurt by the light, and not until it was inured to it would it be able again to see.

Let us be nothing but humble now. Let us not be so bold as to deny the possibility, or to despise the quality, of experiences we cannot understand. The deaf should not deny music, nor the blind the luminous horizons which those who have sight can see. The very dogs have knowledge of fragrances, and the birds, flying south, have instincts of direction, and perceptions of their common unity, of which we know nothing; nay, a ribbon of film can apprehend a rarer light than any our eye can record. The world of our senses and our brains is but a small hollow sphere cut out of the vast Reality, and limited by the frontier of our consciousness. What if that frontier were extended?

As I said before, we may peer into the darkness but we can only guess at what was happening within it to old Bernardone's boy. Nobody could tell this part of the story in its fullness except Francis himself, or one who was the equal of Francis in consciousness. I can speak only in pictures and hints, themselves but darkly understood. But I will do what I can.

Time is no longer very relevant on such a plane, so I shall break with chronology and give you these pictures, not in the order of their happening, but in the order which will best unfold the mystery. And first, these words from the Fioretti.

> St. Francis being secretly in prayer within his cell, an angel appeared to him and said to him on the behalf of God, " I have come to comfort thee and admonish thee, that thou prepare and dispose thyself humbly to receive that which God shall work in thee." St. Francis answered, "I am ready to receive patiently everything that it pleases my Lord to do unto me." And when he had said this, the angel departed. The next day being come, St. Francis prostrated himself early in prayer before the door of his cell and prayed thus, "O my Lord Jesus Christ, I pray thee to grant me two graces before I die: the first, that in my lifetime I may feel in my soul and my body, so far as is possible, all the pain and grief which Thou, O sweet Lord, didst feel in thy passion; the second that I may feel in my heart, so far as is possible, that exceeding love by which Thou was driven willingly to endure so great suffering for sinners."

Here is a key to some of it, I think. Francis knew that Christ had passed through this darkness, and he was not unhappy to be passing through it too, since he desired so passionately to equal his Lord. His brothers had been taken from him, his health had been taken from him, his

eyes had been taken from him, and now his sight of God
was obscured, but if it were necessary for the final purgation of his spirit that he should be thus stripped of all,
amen, so let it be. "I must know in my soul and body
what Calvary was. I must suffer more and more. I have
suffered nothing so far, because I have not loved enough.
Did I really love the whole world, I should endure in
myself all the world's pain."

I suppose it is so. To a man whose love was wide
enough, and whose sense of unity was complete enough,
the pain of the world would be a personal pain: in our
moments of loving someone else we have intuitions of this,
but no more. To Christ it was so, and Francis was
determined that in him it should be so also.

The "dark night," apparently, may endure for months
or years, but it is not unbroken. Flashes of the old joy
illuminate it; shafts of the new and greater ecstasy break
through. "Flashes of light," wrote a fourteenth-century
English mystic, Walter Hylton, "shine through the chinks
of Jersualem's wall, but thou art not there yet." Once
Francis, still the same simple lad that he had been fifteen
years before, called Leo to him and asked him to open the
Gospel book three times at random, and tell him what he
read. Leo obeyed, and each of the three times the book
opened at the passion of Christ. "By this it was given to
him to understand," say these quiet, mysterious pages of
the Fioretti, "that as he had followed the teaching of
Christ in his life, so he must be conformed to Him in his
afflictions and his passion, before he should pass out of
this world. And from this time forward he began to taste
more abundantly the sweetness of divine contemplation
and of the divine visitations. . . ."

Or look at another occasion. Those who have had so

much as a tiny foretaste of the Knowledge of the Union with the All know that it is a bliss so overpowering that one almost gasps to escape from it. And just as the experience may clothe itself in the colour and terms of the religion in which one has been nurtured, so that for the Christian it is identified with Christ or Father or Spirit, for the Neo-Platonist with the Impersonal, Unknowable One, for the Hindu with Brahma-Shiva-Krishna, and for the Sūfi with the God of the Mohammedans, in the same way it may use for its medium of approach some sensuous form that the individual man has loved in the world. It will conform itself to the soul of the receiver. It may approach as music or as subjective or objective light. To the credulous and uncritical (and whatever intellectuals may suppose, intellectual simplicity is no handicap to spiritual genius, or Francis of Assisi and a thousand more could never have been), and to the highly critical and wise, for aught I know, it may come as visions and voices. These things being so, the following story, though it may be nonsense to scoffers, will make great sense to others. Doubtless it has the accretions of a legend, but its core rings true. Francis had loved music all his life, and—

Francis began to think of the incommensurable joy of the blessed in the life eternal and to pray that God would grant him the favour of tasting a little of this joy. And as he thought thus within himself, suddenly there appeared to him an angel who had a viol in his left hand and in his right hand a bow; and while Francis stood stupefied at the vision, the angel drew the bow once across the viol, and immediately was heard such sweet melody that his soul was inebriated with sweetness and he lost all bodily sense, insomuch that, as he afterwards related to his companions, he thought that if the angel had drawn the bow a second time across the strings his soul would have parted from his body.

And do not suppose that these periods of flash-lit darkness were not intermitted by long periods of subdued light and chastened calm. We have pictures of Francis at this time in which we see him almost happy again. Greccio is the scene of most of them, for Greccio was the place of his preparation for La Verna.

Come with me, then, to Greccio.

2

The hermitage of Greccio, in the manner of Franciscan *eremi*, clings to the mountain side like a white flittermouse against a wall. The mountains surrounding the Vale of Rieti cave in here to make a semi-circular amphitheatre, but the rake of the amphitheatre floor is almost as steep as its sides. Floor and sides are crowded with foliage from the edge of the plain to the ridge along the sky.

And it is mostly woodland. The close cultivation of the plain climbs a little way up the slopes, and then abandons the struggle. When I left the level highroad and began to climb, my way wound past lonely white farmhouses, each standing on a higher shelf than the last. Their fields of maize fought a losing battle with the oaks and the ilex, and the brush of bramble and thorn. Stair above stair, with the white cottages upon them, and then nothing but the wood, with the road winding through it to the hermitage.

And since I was thinking, less of tranquil than of troubled days at Greccio, perhaps it was well that storm-clouds should come marching up from behind the mountain in rapid and angry echelons, and hurry across the sky. Here and there they left an aperture through which I could see above them a heaven serene and luminous and blue.

Soon a storm of rain drove me towards an open cellar under one of the last of the farmhouses. Diving under its low arch, I met at once the bright hospitality of Italy. A woman within, sorting tomatoes, cried to me to come in. "S'accomodi, signore; s'accomodi."

And with a blithe smile she pushed forward a small barrel for my chair.

So I sat on the barrel, and smiled at my kind hostess, and she smiled back at me, and all was love in that dungeon-like cellar. The rain pelted outside.

I looked at my hostess. Thirty years of age (as she told me in five minutes' time), she was a woman who had exchanged the soft prettiness of youth for the beauty of toil-worn face and hands. Her dark eyes were tired, but they could light up with Southern laughter. The weather on the mountain had drawn her skin taut over her cheek-bones, but had also made it clean and brown. She wore a black dress and a blue apron, and padded about in ragged boots.

Her cellar floor was littered with barrels of wine, baskets of figs, and piles of tomatoes and onions. Tomatoes and onions hung in strings down the walls from the vaulted roof. A hen came in out of the rain, while a less sensible pig grunted and complained outside. And I sat there and asked her questions, which she answered volubly while her busy fingers continued the labour that must not slacken.

She told me of her husband and her boy, and of their struggle to pull a living out of the rocky fields. She told me of their battle with the autumn hails. Their little produce, she explained, was maize and grain, tomatoes and grapes and figs and wine; and I glanced around this dark little crypt which was so plainly the whole of her garner. Then she told me how all through her year of struggling with the earth and the seasons, she would see the pilgrims going by to the Convento above. Mostly French, she said, though sometimes the tall Germans went by. It was rare to see any English on the road, for the inglesi were protestants who cared nothing for San Francesco. Not so? Well, she was glad to hear it. Myself when I had turned in out of the rain she had taken for a German —so tall! so tall! my cellar is not big enough—but she was pleased to learn that I was English. (I don't know why.) She asked me many questions about England, and about the women of England, and laughed much at all I told her, for they seemed to her so masculine in their habits, almost as if they were not women at all.

And all the time I was wondering if she was very different from the peasants of this Sabine vale whom Francis had so loved. I suspected that it was peasants like this toiling woman and her man, now down among the vines, who had begged Francis to live among them and tell them how they could be better, and who had climbed in a torchlight procession to the hermitage one famous midnight of Christmas Eve. I believe I was listening to the eternal voice of the vale.

The rain stopped, and I told her that I must push on with my climb; and she thrust her dried figs into my hands as food for the way. Laughing, she said, "Addio," and I gave her Francis' greetings (just to show that I knew them), "Buon giorno, buona gente," and "Il Signore vi dia pace"; and that was the end.

I bent myself to the steep road. I was high up now, and at the bends I could see the white hermitage hanging above the trees. Soon I could make out its entrance door and the little forecourt in front of it. And because I was on this road and the front of the convent was visible, I met a little company of brothers coming down. If you will understand me, they were not real, because they were walking down the road seven hundred years ago. I think that Leo was among them, and Angelo and Rufino; but I could not see. I guessed them to be of the company because this was the year before La Verna, and Leo and the other *nos qui cum eo fuimus* were with Francis at Greccio then. On this day two pilgrims, young Franciscan brothers, had come from a distance to assure Francis of their loyalty and to receive his blessing. But when they reached the hermitage they learned from the friars there that Francis had withdrawn to some solitude to pray, none knowing where. Nor would any of them undertake to seek him out and disturb him; for at this time the brothers at Greccio seem to have had a sense that something inscrutable was drawing their father from them, and that their part was to guard like faithful sentinels all approaches to the mystery. No, they could offer no hope to the visitors that they could see Francis. The young men were much distressed because they had only a little while to stay. "This is punishment for our sins," they said. "We are not worthy to be blessed by our father Francis."

Troubled by their sadness, the brothers tried to show hospitality by offering to accompany them down to the plain. Sadly the pilgrims accepted this offer, and the little company set off down the mountain road. But when they had descended quite a long way, they heard a cry from the hermitage above and, turning and looking up, they saw Francis standing by the door. He must have returned and heard of the young brothers' visit and of their disappointment. The two pilgrims immediately dropped to their knees upon the road, for, as all saw, Francis was peering down it with his almost sightless eyes, and was blessing his two young brothers, who must be upon it somewhere, with large, slow signs of the cross.

3

By now I was at the door of the present convent. I pulled the bell-handle; a bell tinkled within; and steps approached. The door opened to disclose a dark young brother, who instantly gave me the welcoming smile of every Franciscan host. Hearing my mission, and pleased with it, he bade me come in and see all. He led me first to the cave of the Presepio, because it was nearest the door. And the chapel of the Presepio, of course, was the place which, above all, I wanted to see.

The word Presepio means "Crib." How many of you who go into a church at Christmas time to see the crib in one corner know that Francis gave us this custom, and inaugurated it in this dark little cave at Greccio? I daresay you know it no more than you know that the Angelus was first rung from Franciscan belfries; and yet, if you think of it, these two customs show very intimately how Francis, in an age that stressed the pomps and formalism of religion and the wraths of God, brought back the sweeter aspects of a Gospel which was the "good news" of God's humility.

One look at the cave of the Presepio and I knew, I was sure, that Francis had been to the grotto of the Nativity at Bethlehem, and that it was this grotto which had given him, either when he was kneeling in it and trying to imagine the first Christmas morning or later in Italy when he was meditating upon his hours in Bethlehem, the sudden, exciting inspiration for the crib at Greccio. Because the grotto at Bethlehem and the cave at Greccio were

292

almost the same! Both were arched caverns in the rock. Blackened with age and the smoke of candles, as I saw them, they looked exactly alike. And I guessed that Francis, on his return from the Holy Land, had been struck by this likeness and had conceived, of a sudden, with an artist's thrill, the idea of what was really the first Nativity Play.

He was at Fonte Colombo when he resolved to act upon the idea, and Fonte Colombo is only a little way along the mountains from Greccio. His first step, according to Bonaventura, was to secure the sanction of the Pope. His second was to summon to Fonte Colombo the most powerful person in the neighbourhood of Greccio, Messer Giovanni da Vellita.

Giovanni, a soldier and lord of Greccio, was yet another of the wealthy and aristocratic persons who had succumbed to the charm of Francis, and was now trying to live the Franciscan life within the rules of the Third Order. It was his happiness to do all he could to help forward the work of the brotherhood in his neighbourhood. And as Orlando of Chiusi had given them the mountain of La Verna, so Giovanni had made over to them that site on the mountain slope opposite his village, upon which they had hung their white cloister.

To him a summons from Francis was a command, and he hastened to the cell at Fonte Colombo where his master was. When he appeared, Francis said to him, "Listen, Brother Giovanni. We are going to celebrate the Christmas festival together, you and I, and I have thought out what we are going to do. I want your aid. You know our cloister in the woods. Well, there is a cave there, and you are going to turn it into a stable exactly like that in which our Blessed Lord was born. I want you to have a manger

293

built in it, and to fill the manger with straw and hay. Then I want you to send along an ox and an ass, which will stand on either side of the manger. And at midnight we will celebrate Mass over the manger before all the people. Do you see: for once in my life I want to realise, if I can, and to enable the people to realise, exactly what it was our God did for us, and how poor He chose to be for our sakes."

Giovanni promised to do his part. He went back to Greccio village and sent his carpenters to the cave to build a manger against its back wall; and I am pretty confident that he superintended the works himself. Then he sent the ox and the ass on the afternoon of Christmas Eve. I can see the two patient beasts, those perfect symbols of service, being led along the road which climbs up and down, round the hollow of the amphitheatre from Greccio town to Greccio convent. They were put in the cave, just as Francis had ordered, on either side of the manger; where, I doubt not, they began to nibble at the hay.

In the meantime invitations had been sent out to all the brothers in all the hermitages, to all the peasants in the valley and to all the hillmen of the small hill towns, to come and greet their Lord at midnight on Christmas Eve. No more in that day than in this were the Italian poor likely to absent themselves from such a ceremony. They came. They came through the woods, bearing their torches and singing their hymns. They came from Greccio in the tracks of the ox and the ass. They came across the plain from Poggio Bustone, where they loved Francis so dearly. They came along the road from Contigliano to the south and Piediluco to the north. And thus most of them must have come in torchlight procession up the same winding road which had brought me to the convent door. "The forest resounded with their voices," says Bonaventura, "and that memorable night was made glorious by many brilliant lights and sonorous psalms of praise."

The entrance to the cave, I take it, was open to the night in those days, and the multitude would have crowded the slopes about it, those behind craning their necks to get a view of what was happening within. They saw the priest start the celebration of the Mass, using the manger as the altar, while the animals watched at either side, and Francis filled the place of the deacon, and the tall figure of Giovanni da Vellita stood near by. All agree that Francis was as excited and happy as a boy in this new creation. As deacon he read the Gospel; and after the Gospel, he preached to the people, telling them why he had done this. Then the Mass went on; it approached the great moment of the Consecration; the people sank to their knees; the priest laid the sacred elements on the straw and bent above them; the sacring bell tinkled in that glimmering cave, and all heads bowed low, for the Lord was in the manger.

Francis was happy then. The dark night of the soul, if it was really about him now, was lifted for a space while that Christmas Eve of 1223 was turning into Christmas Day.

4

Nor was the old laughter always remote from him during these months. The very next chamber into which I was taken by Padre Sabatino, my guide, was the "refectory and kitchen of Francis," and it swept my mind forward to the Easter Day following the Christmas ceremony at Greccio. I remembered how on that day the brothers had thought to keep the greatest festival of all

295

with something like a banquet, and that this tiny, low-pitched, oblong room was probably the place where they had spread their table. Some kind friend—Giovanni, perhaps—had sent them good food and fine linen and cut glass. With some delight they arranged the table and rang the bell.

The bell brought Francis in for the meal. He saw the fine spread. His action does not suggest that he was angry: it suggests that he was amused but dubious. Did the table recall those old banquets in Assisi when he was a young gallant in fine clothes? Not the best of his disciples had his spiritual sight, and he alone saw the ancient temptation lurking in that food and that finery. His manner of pointing it out was very gentle, and typical of the actor (I had almost said the "comedian") in him. He went away and waited till all the brothers were seated around the splendid repast. Then he returned and knocked on the door. The brothers, who had begun upon the good things, cried to whoever knocked to enter, and turned their heads to see who it might be. It was Francis with an old beggar's hat on his head, hobbling in with the help of a stick.

"Per l'amor di Messer Domenedio," he wailed to them, "faciate elimosina a questo povero ed infirmo peregrino." "For the love of Monsignor the Lord God, make an alms to this pilgrim poor and infirm."

5

Ah, it is easier, as it is happier, to describe these lifts in the darkness, when Francis was almost the Francis of yesterday, laughing, creative, and enthusiastic. But, unless I am quite wrong, they are breaks, and nothing more, in the strains, the bewilderment, and the bodily distress of his last hour of purgation. A cry from Francis which the ilex groves of the Carceri heard one day expresses better his lost and wandering condition. He had wandered alone from Assisi to find Bernard of Quintavalle, who was in retreat at the Carceri, and to get some comfort from that faithful first friend. He had struggled there alone, and with difficulty because his eyes could barely see the path, and his heart was heavy in a body drained of vigour. But now the light of the hillside had given place to the darkness of the woody ravine, and as he addressed himself to the climb, fingering his way between the trees, he felt happier because soon he would be with Bernard. He called to him, "Bernard, Bernard."

No answer came back to him, because Bernard was in his cell, caught up in an ecstasy. Francis stopped and called again. Still no answer: only his own voice sent back to him from the opposite wall of the gorge.

Struggling upward again, he called, "Brother Bernard, come and speak to the poor blind man." I hear the old familiar banter in this, but when Bernard answered nothing, Francis, letting humour sink into self-pity, cried, "Bernard, come and speak to me. I need you. I am blind." Useless; and Francis, hurt, turned to wander back again.

But to this weakness of self-pity he accorded one moment only: then his conscience (and his humour) arrested and rebuked him. "What are you grieving at, you wretched little man? Bernard is probably speaking with God. Is he to dismiss such a guest that he may entertain a mere creature like you?" And at that moment, just as he was thinking this, Bernard came running down to him. Francis immediately prostrated himself before him and ordered him, by holy obedience, to put his foot three times upon him and to say, "Lie there, thou boorish son of Bernardone. Vilest of creatures, whence thy pride?" Which Bernard, since the words "by holy obedience" allowed no argument, did—very gently, I feel sure.

We must accept it, that his mind and body had paid a price. They must always pay at the present stage of human development, if a man will do violence to himself to make a way for Knowledge. By every record of the "dark night," whose soever the heroic spirit that ventured into it, we know that body and mind are rent by the travail of the spirit straining to break through. It may be that one day all mankind will inherit the new universal consciousness which Francis and other explorers of the mystical road could reach only with exhausted bodies and bleeding feet. When men first strove to fly, we called them madmen; to-day, when they have been proved right, we call them martyrs. These pioneers of earthly flight were fifty years ahead of their time; the pioneers of heavenly flight five hundred, a thousand, five thousand in advance of their race. (Or so it may be. I do not know.) The ambitious boy from Assisi is daring too much, if you like. He is adventuring too far. There is nothing temperate, nothing sane, in flying into the sun; but he cannot do else, because there is, within his soul, "the strong and stormy love which drives her home." He is ending what he began in the field-paths about Assisi: "the flight of the alone to the Alone." The tremendous knowledge which he is approaching shuts out all light, because it is a presence larger than the sun—larger than the brightest light he has seen so far. Body and mind can hardly bear it. The body—this is of little account in so great an audit, but the mind? The mind, we learn from those who have ventured where Francis was venturing now, is often harried by what may seem to our less sensitive perceptions exaggerated torments and neurotic fears. It may even shake on its seat; and then evil will seem an incarnate thing at one's side; its stealthy footfall is heard behind one as one walks, and its whisperings follow one on the air. But Francis is pushing on. His bodily eyes are darkened, but the eyes of his soul, are they blind too, or opening on his goal? Who knows? But the time came when he felt impelled to go to La Verna. Always the mountains had drawn him, but now he must go to the highest height of all. It is impossible to study the records without feeling that a great impulsion was upon him. It is as if he was sickening for the visitation. It is as if he felt he must cross, and cross quickly, this terrible last interval between himself and the *Other*.

Choosing a few brothers, and only those who would understand, choosing Leo, of course, and Angelo Tancredi, and Sylvester and Rufino, with their great gifts of contemplation, and dear Masseo, who had accompanied him on so many a long journey, he said to them, "Rise, let us be going."

And together they went north to La Verna.

CHAPTER XXIV

I

VERY early in the morning I left Florence for La Verna. I wanted to be on the summit of the mountain while the September morning was still there. The highland road went leaping over the necks of the nearer Apennines, westward towards the sun; and my little Florentine car flew along it. We left Vallombrosa down among the autumnal leaves, with the sun just striking the villas. As far as I can remember, we had to surmount two or three cols before we saw La Verna. Then from the top of the last we saw her, far away across the undulating land, a grey peak lifted above the morning mist. And, as was very comely, Brother Sun was blazing directly behind her.

La Verna is in the heart of the Apennines and the midst of Italy. It looks eastward to the Adriatic and westward to the Mediterranean; a man on its summit can see all the Franciscan country: Umbria, Tuscany, Emilia, and the Marches. It is not the tallest of its chain, but it seems to be, because its shape is the noblest: alone among rounded summits its slopes to a peak.

To all students of the story of Francis this first view of La Verna is a moment meet for silence. I stood looking at it, not without deep feeling, and the thought came to me, "If the woody hollow scooped out of the mountain at Greccio was the right theatre for the events that happened there, what of this proud, lonely crest?"

While we are drawing nearer to it from the direction of Tuscany, let us look at Francis and his few companions approaching it from Umbria, in the early autumn of 1224. A little company of friars, Leo, Angelo, Rufino, Masseo, and one or two others, is coming from the Vale of Spoleto to these mountains between Arno and Tiber. Masseo has been given the leadership: he is *in loco patris et matris* to them all, and what he directs must be done by holy obedience. Francis is jealously guarded from anxiety that he may be free for contemplation and prayer; the others, quiet, reticent, and wondering, surround him like a fugitive king.

Of Jesus going up to Jerusalem to die, Mark has a sentence quite masterly in its unconscious art. "And they were in the way going up to Jerusalem, and Jesus went before them: and they were amazed, and, as they followed, they were afraid." Something of the same wonder accompanies this little band approaching La Verna.

In San Francesco at Assisi you may see in Leo's neat, laborious script, on the most famous Franciscan relic in the world, his explanation of why they were going to La Verna. This relic, so deeply touching because certainly authentic, is a little piece of parchment, faded and breaking, but still showing on its brown face the benediction which Francis wrote for Leo one day on LaVerna, because he thought he looked unhappy. Almost more touching than the writing are the old breaking folds in the sheet, because they tell us how Leo, after Francis' death, carried it about with him always. And just as we will write on some valued autograph letter the name of the writer and the occasion on which he gave it to us, so Leo has carefully penned under the writing of Francis, "Brother Francis wrote with his own hand this blessing for me, Brother Leo," and above it the words, "Blessed Francis, two years before his death, kept on La Verna . . . a Lent from the festival of the Assumption of the Blessed Virgin to the festival of St. Michael in September, and the hand of God was upon him . . ."

Some of them had been to La Verna before. Soon after Orlando had offered the mountain to Francis some brothers had come to survey it. They had found Orlando's castle under its southern slope, dominating the village of Chiusi: its ruins are there still, but they have become one with the jutting crag on which they stand and the fallen boulders around. No doubt this most punctilious host entertained the visiting brothers before they went up into the mountain. And when they climbed up it they found it every bit as remarkable as he affirmed. It was very different from the kind, round hills that stood about their Umbrian and Sabine homes. Above pleasant woods at its base it sloped up into a mass of bare basaltic rock, split on its more precipitous side into fissures and gorges, so that whole sides of the mountain seemed to have parted from it and be poised to fall. But above the bareness, throned on a steep-tilted plateau, there was woodland again: a wood of beeches and pines and birds. Climbing through this isolated wood, pedestalled in the sky, to the highest point of all, they could see, as we have told, the breadth of Italy sweeping over the mountains to its two seas. They could even see Subasio and Assisi far away to the south.

Knowing that this high solitude was such as their master would love, they made rude huts and established an *eremo* there; and Orlando built for them a little chapel, and called it Santa Maria degli Angeli, after the mother chapel at the Portiuncula.

What a host was the Lord Orlando! Hearing that Francis himself had come to La Verna with a few brothers for this autumn Lent, he hastened up to them and insisted

that his services must be theirs to command. At Francis'
request he had a little cell built for him under a beech
tree; and, say the Fioretti,

> this done, because the evening was now approaching and it
> was time to go . . . Orlando took Francis and his com-
> panions aside and said, "My dearest brothers, I would not
> have you suffer any bodily want in this wild mountain, by
> which you might be less able to attend to spiritual things;
> and therefore I desire, and this I say to you once for all, that
> you will confidently send to my house for what you need;
> and if you do otherwise, it will give me very great pain."

The Lord's table on the crest of La Verna.

Francis had asked that his cell should be a stone's
throw from the lodging of the other brothers, because he
knew that he must be alone. Only Leo was to come near
to him. Leo might bring him a little bread and water
when he thought fit. And for a few days this was his
manner of life. But so imperious was the need for solitude
that he was driven to seek a retreat yet further from the
brothers. He summoned Leo and said to him, "Go and
stand in the door of the chapel, and when I call you,
return."

Leo went, and Francis climbed a little higher and
called, "Leo, Leo!"

And, Leo coming immediately, Francis knew that he
was still within earshot. So he sent Leo back to the chapel
door and went yet farther round the side of the mountain,
and called again, "Leo, Leo!"

This time there was no answer. He was alone. Opposite was one of those wooded plateaux separated from the
main mass of the mountain by a deep, narrow gash.
Francis peered at it; then, returning to find Leo, he
brought him to it, and together they made a bridge of
planks or tree-trunks across the narrow cleft. Then Francis

sent for all his companions and told them that he was going to spend the forty days of St. Michael upon this quiet plateau; and he asked them to build him a cell there.

And when they had done so, he said, "Now go to your own place and leave me alone. None of you come near to me, nor allow anyone else to come. Only Leo, and he but once in the day, and once in the night at the hour of mattins, can come as far as his end of the bridge. I want him to come quietly and, when he is on his side of the bridge, to say, *Domine, labia mea aperies*, and if I answer him, he can come over, but if not, he must go away quickly."

And, having made these requests, he blessed them; and they went their way round the side of the mountain.

No one was to come near him: nor can we. He must go to the great Encounter alone. The legends that have come down to us must have grown from the little he told, but *secretum meum mihi*. I think of a verse of my childhood:

> Perchance the bald old eagle
>   On grey Beth-Peor's height,
> Out of his lonely eyrie
>   Looked on the wondrous sight.
> Perchance the lion stalking
>   Still shuns the hallowed spot
> For beast and bird have seen and heard
>   That which man knoweth not.

All that follows is but my surmising and my poor effort to hint at ineffable things. Like Leo, I can only come as close as may be, and, standing on my side of the bridge, say, *Domine, labia mea aperies*: O Lord, open thou my lips.

2

I can describe to you the place which I saw. Of the convent buildings which now guard the sacred sites I need not speak, but only of those parts of the mountain which are much the same now as when Francis came. You may see his "bed": it is down in a gash, or small crooked ravine in the mountain's side. You twist down to it between rocks green with moss and fern and shaded by slender pines. A green submarine light fills the recesses, pierced by shafts of the sun. The place of Francis' bed is so far in the breast of the mountain that you feel he wanted to force himself into the very heart of nature.

Not far from the "bed," down a few steps, is that first cell under the beech tree: it is a chapel now, but a large beech still overshadows it. Go on down a steep, ragged stairway that leads inward into the bowels of the mountain, and you reach the gorge of the Sasso Spicco. This is a deep and narrow involution in the mass of the mountain like the impression one might make by forcing a pencil into a mass of putty. On one of its high walls hangs the Sasso Spicco, an immense rock which juts over the deep corridor. It looks as if it might fall at any moment, but it was hanging like that seven hundred years ago, and Francis would sit beneath it to meditate. The air down here is chill: it comes damply off the lichens; and the silence is like the everlasting silence behind the movements of Time. Behind you the rocky stairs climb like a Jacob's ladder to the patch of sky; and, towards midday, the sun, crossing that patch, looks in like a curious visitor.

When I was down there I stayed within its ray to keep warm, as I pondered upon Francis' meditations beneath the overhanging Sasso Spicco. And I remembered that Francis *knew* his unity with the whole universe, and not only with the sun, but also with worms and ferns and rocks. And for a brief moment I felt the almost intoler-

305

able joy which that knowledge becomes. And I thought I understood why Francis wandered here alone.

Then up on to the steeply inclined plateau with its woodland of beech and pine. I walked to the edge of the wood—which is to say I walked to the brink of the precipice; and there, away from the precipice, stood those slices of the mountain that have parted from the main body, their tops still bearing shrubs and trees. A little way below me, round the curve of the mountain, on a shelf, as it were, was the place of the Stigmatisation, enclosed now in a chapel. But one could not approach it from this side, so I went on, up and up, as I knew Francis did, who must always climb to a summit.

In the wood it was difficult to think that I was walking above high precipices: it might have been a beech copse on the slope of an English down. Beneath the trees was an undergrowth of beech-scrub and fields of dog's mercury, speckled everywhere with cyclamen. The winding path was stepped by tree-roots and carpeted with pine needles and beech leaves. (Bear those rustling leaves in mind for a moment: you will hear of them again.) Outcrops of stratified and moss-cushioned rock made seats by the path on which an exhausted climber, long ago, might have rested. And all the wood was stippled with sunlight and aflicker with butterflies.

It was very quiet. It was almost as quiet as the Sasso Spicco gorge. Where you have the quiet of a wood's heart married to the quiet of a mountain crest you have something very quiet indeed. I was picturing Francis sitting upon one of the rocks to delight in it all when I remembered that at the time he was nearly blind. He could hardly have seen it, but I think he delighted to feel the rooted steps beneath his feet and the trunks within his hands, to smell the fragrance of the firs, and to hear, now and then, the fluttering of the birds in the branches.

The thought of his blindness stopped me. It seemed to prove, for the first time, the purely subjective nature of the Vision which he saw. It sent me again to the precipice that I might look in the direction from which, as he believed, the Winged Seraph came. I looked out over a world of mountains, flattened because seen from a height. Little villages lay in the valleys, and tiny white roads ran over the passes. It was noon, and a brilliant light lay behind the farthest horizon. And I saw in imagination a Seraph coming out of the light.

3

Such is the place: what more? I can argue with you the probability of La Verna's miracle. I can tell you that for me the wonder is in the spiritual moment attained to, and not in its physical accompaniment. And yet I hardly think it a miracle at all, because I like to hope, as I have told you, that all men will one day attain to this transcendental consciousness of unity with the One who is the All. That the agony of Francis' passing into this unity should have left upon his body the scars of the wounds of Christ seems to me beautiful in its aptness but secondary in its importance, and not physiologically strange. When men of science, materially minded, tell me that it is quite possible to raise blisters on the skin of a hypnotised subject by touching him with a finger and telling him it is a red-hot iron, I am not greatly troubled by the stigmata of Francis. Nor by the fact that though they are the first recorded instance of the phenomenon, they are not the last.

Of course to the complete materialist who believes that

man's body is all, and that his mind is no more than a by-product of mechanical forces (if such a person still exists), the Event itself, the so-called Spiritual Marriage, can be nothing but the most pathetic, as it is the most grandiose, of man's illusions. To the rationalist who holds that man can know nothing except by his intellect, and that all talk of supra-rational perceptions is windy nonsense, it will seem like an aberration or sport of the mind. But to those of us who boldly infer that body and brain do not make up a man, it will be, at the lowest, a ground for trusting in our immortality.

I can give you glimpses of what Francis was doing as he awaited the Event in his cell, or in the neighbourhood of it, out of sight and earshot of his companions. He was not alone; by all the records a falcon kept him company, and was a comfort to him. I see him stroking the head of the falcon, as he remembered that it was his brother. And Leo stole another glimpse for us, as is exquisitely reported in the Fioretti.

> It came to pass that, at the approach of the feast of the Holy Cross, in the middle of September, Brother Leo went one night to the usual place . . . and, calling from the bridge according to custom, *Domine, labia mea aperies*, and, Francis not answering, he did not go back as Francis had ordered him, but with a good intention passed over the bridge and went softly into his cell, and, not finding him there, thought that he had gone into the wood to pray. Wherefore he went out again by the light of the moon, softly searching through the wood; and at last he heard the voice of Francis, and, approaching him, he saw him on his knees in prayer with face raised to heaven, and heard him say in fervour of spirit, "Who art thou, O my most sweet God, and what am I, most vile worm and worthless servant? . . ." At which Brother Leo, marvelling, raised his eyes and saw a torch of fire which descended and rested on the head of Francis.

(Religious history before and since the Gospel is filled with stories of the appearance of light about a person in the hour of transfiguration, but if you have no sympathy with such tales, then think only that Leo was a very simple son of the Middle Ages, and to such credulity as his all things were possible.)

And Leo departed, securely, and glad at heart at the vision he had seen, and returned towards the cell. But as he went thus, Francis perceived him *by the rustling of the leaves under his feet* and commanded him to wait and not to move. Then Leo stood still and waited with much fear at the thought that Francis was displeased with him, because he was wont with all diligence to guard against offending his father, lest for his fault Francis should deprive him of his company.

Then Francis, coming to him, asked "Who are you?" And he, trembling, replied, "I am Brother Leo, my father." And Francis said to him, "Why have you come here, Brother Little Sheep? Have I not told you not to come and observe me?" And then, kneeling down before Francis, Brother Leo confessed his fault of disobedience and implored his pardon. And afterwards he asked him earnestly to expound the words he had heard.

Then Francis condescended to reveal and explain to him that which he had asked, saying, "Know, Brother Little Sheep, that when I said these words, there was shown to me in my soul two lights, one of the understanding of myself and the other of the knowledge of the Creator. . . . But take heed to yourself, Brother Little Sheep, that you watch me no more. . . ."

And then came the morning of the Feast of the Holy Cross. And Francis knelt outside his cell to pray. I call upon one who had himself been into the union, St. John of the Cross, to speak for Francis now. Read slowly, read carefully.

> Upon an obscure night
> Fevered with love's anxiety
> (Oh, hapless, happy plight)
> I went, none seeing me,
> Forth from my house, where all things quiet be.

By night, secure from sight
And by a secret stair, disguisedly,
(Oh, hapless, happy plight)
By night and privily
Forth from my house, where all things quiet be.

Blest night of wandering
In secret, when by none I might be spied,
Nor I see anything
Without a light to guide
Save that which in my heart burnt in my side.

That light did lead me on
More surely than the shining of noontide
Where well I knew that One
Did for my coming bide;
Where He abode might none but He abide.

O night that didst lead thus,
O night more lovely than the dawn of light;
O night that broughtest us
Lover to lover's sight,
Lover to loved, in marriage of delight!

Upon my waiting breast
Wholly for Him and save Himself for none,
There did I give sweet rest
To my beloved one:
The fanning of the cedars breathed thereon.

Francis was struggling, struggling, to know in himself
the fullness of the Passion of Christ. Is it this, that if God
is immanent in all and a man would seek to be one with
God, he must be immanent in all too, and know the consequences of their sin, and their pain? Perhaps. And
there came a moment, a moment smaller, possibly, than
any measurable point of time, and yet a moment that held
a vision within its compass. Surely, knowing that the
union was upon him, he had been meditating on the awful
vision of Isaiah, "In the year that King Uzziah died I saw
also the Lord sitting upon a throne, high and lifted up, and
his train filled the temple. Above it stood the seraphims:

each one had six wings; with twain he covered his face, and with twain he covered his feet, and with twain he did fly." For it seemed to him that such a six-winged seraph was approaching from out of heaven with great speed; and in the same instant it revealed itself as a figure nailed upon a cross—does not this dream-like confusion mean that on this day of the Elevation of the Holy Cross he had been seeing Isaiah's God in the suffering Messiah?—and the moment of vision became, or was, a moment of piercing anguish, because Francis had made his heart one with the heart of Christ. Did he make his own in this moment all the sin and pain of the world—the sufferings of whipped negroes and martyred Jews, of frightened, neglected children, and of all people lonely and unloved—a harlot sighed along the street, a criminal gasped on the scaffold step, forgotten women waited for death in unfamiliar rooms, a shot bird tumbled through the air, the fox was torn by dogs in the spinney, the beast of burden felt the goad on the endless hill, and the captured animal shrank from the lash in the circus ring—did he grasp them all and cry, "Let me give myself for them, and for those who sin against them. Christ, my Master, not less than Thou!"

One moment only, but a moment that was swooning bliss as well as piercing agony. All who have been within the union tell us that it is bliss unspeakable, though none, I suspect, has known the pain that Francis knew. Dante sang:

> O eternal beam,
> (Whose height what reach of mortal thought may soar?)
> Yield me again some little particle
> Of what thou then appearedst, give my tongue
> Power, but to leave one sparkle of thy glory . . .
>
> Such keenness from the living ray I met,
> That if my eyes had turned away, methinks

> I had been lost; but, so emboldened, on
> I passed, as I remember, till my view
> Hovered on the brink of dread infinitude.
>   O grace! unenvying of thy boon! that gavest
> Boldness to fix so earnestly my ken
> On th' everlasting splendour, that I looked,
> While sight was unconsumed, and, in that depth,
> Saw clasped in one volume, clasped by love, whate'er
> The universe unfolds . . .

And if it was this for Dante, it was more, much more, for Francis, to whom Dante himself looked up as the greatest of the saints. Francis, besides the bliss and the anguish in his soul, knew a sharp, agonising pain in his body. Probably the pain slew the rapture, and he found himself kneeling upon the earth of La Verna. Kneeling there, conscious only of an aching on his hands, on his feet, and under his breast. He looked down and saw upon his body the five scars of Christ.

These, then, were the wounds that the ambitious young knight who rode out of Assisi twenty years before, had found in the end. *Tetelestai.* It was finished.

4

"If only someone might come back with news," we often hear it said, "and tell us what lies behind all!" But unless the testimony of some of the noblest who have lived, in every epoch and every clime, is to be scouted as a mass of delusion, we may answer that many have reached to the Reality that lies behind our world of appearances, and have come back to us, bringing their news with them. And all, be they Mohammedan Sūfis, Hindu sages, Greek or Christian mystics, report to us in their different idioms the same traveller's tale.

"All is love," they say. "The mind may not compass

the Reality, but the spirit can know that It is Light and Harmony and Love."

Francis set down with his own hand the exultation that came with, that *was*, the knowledge found upon La Verna. He wrote it in Latin, in glowing words, on a parchment; and it was this parchment which he gave to Leo, with a special blessing on the other side for that companion of his solemn hour. Leo kept it folded against his heart for fifty years till his death in 1271. Then it passed to the brothers of the Sagro Convento in Assisi where you may see it to-day, their priceless treasure, in its silver reliquary. You have but to read these "Praises" of Francis, spontaneous, repetitive, unrestrained, to feel the abounding happiness which forced them on to this parchment.

> Thou art holy, Lord God. . . . Thou art goodness, all goodness, the greatest goodness . . . Thou art love, thou art wisdom, thou art humility, thou art patience, thou art beauty, thou art security, thou art joy, thou art justice . . . Thou art infinite goodness, great and admirable Lord God Almighty . . .

We are reminded at once of that other passionate and uncontrolled writing, of which we spoke many pages back; that other folded parchment which was found, four hundred and fifty years after Francis, sewn into the doublet of Blaise Pascal, like a thing very precious and secret. "The year of grace, 1654, Monday 23 Nov . . . from about half past ten in the evening to about half past twelve midnight, FIRE. . . . Assurance, joy, assurance, feeling, joy, peace. *The sublimity of the human soul.* . . . Joy, joy, joy, tears of joy. . . . I do not separate myself from Thee."

In Francis' joy and certitude his one desire was to go down from La Verna and evangelise the world as never before. He was wounded, emptied, and unable to walk, but they could not stop him. And that perfect host, Orlando, hearing of his departure and of his wounds (though whether the truth was told him is not clear), came himself to say good-bye and brought an ass for the sick man's journey. And on the morning of the 30th of September Francis called all the brothers and gave them his blessing and bade them farewell. To Masseo, according to a letter of Masseo of which parts may be authentic, he said, "Brother Masseo, my will is that in this mountain there dwell always Godfearing brothers, the best that are in my order, and therefore it behoves the Superiors to station here only the best of the brothers. Ah, ah, ah, Brother Masseo! I say no more!" It sounds as if the smile were back about his lips. "Farewell, Brother Masseo, Farewell Angelo and Rufino. Addio, addio. Peace be with you, my dearest sons. I am going with Brother Little Sheep to Saint Mary of the Angels, and I shall never come back here any more. Farewell, farewell all. Farewell, holy mountain. Farewell, dearest brother falcon. I thank you for the love you bore me. Farewell, Sasso Spicco. I shall not visit you again. Farewell, little chiesina, St. Mary of the Angels. To thee, Mother of the Eternal Word, I commend these my sons."

There is an exulting triumph in these outbursts, but I do not find in them the perfect comment. More remarkable in its quiet assurance that all his life of poverty and self-offering had been proved right is a single sentence which came from him a little time after he had left La Verna. He was suffering much in his body, and one of the brothers asked him why he did not, according to his custom, seek some comfort from his bible. To which Francis answered only, "I need no more, my son. I know Christ, the poor man crucified."

314

CHAPTER XXV

I

FRANCIS came down from the mountain, Leo leading the ass. He came back into the world with his knowledge—back among us all with the challenge that we run from, because it bids us give up so much and be free. Whether Lady Margaret Sackville had him, among others, in mind when she wrote her sonnet, "Behold the Dreamer Cometh" I do not know, but it fits him well, as he comes down from the mountain.

> Behold the dreamer cometh. For his sake
>   Strew the long road with stones. Doth he not bring
>   Strange tidings of great joy? Oh, he would fling
> Our chains far from us. Slay him, lest they break.
> Watch closely. Is not all we love at stake,
>   Our old familiar servitude and sin?
>   The stranger's at the gate. Let him not in—
> Let him not in—lest all we dead should wake.
>
> This grievous torment surging up anew
>   Each generation, scarcely may we keep
>   Our beds, so near the dreamer comes. Alas,
> Beware lest, all unnoticed, he slip through,
>   For with no trumpet blare he stirs our sleep,
>   But very meekly, seated on an ass.

He is in the darkness no more. His body may be wrecked, but his spirit is exultant. The rest is a tale of suffering and singing and not a little laughter. He plays tricks upon the brothers. Having nothing to give a beggar whose wife had just died and who was in the last straits, he gives him a new cloak which the brothers had just procured for him, and, knowing that the brothers will not let the man get away with it, he makes him promise not to part with it except for good payment. And the brothers have to pay. When the physicians rebuke him for having over-driven his body so long, and ask him if it has not been a good servant to him, he admits that his brother the ass deserves a testimonial and its rest at last. And he apologises to it. "Rejoice, Brother Body, and forgive me, for now I am to be allowed to grant you all that you desire."

He is hardly back at the Portiuncula before he insists on setting out on the new mission. "We have done nothing so far," he says, with all the exaggeration of his new enthusiasm. They try to stop him; they remind him that he can see little and walk not at all, but he inquires what the saddle-ass is for, and sets out on its back.

But they know what he does not know—or what he does not worry about. Death has little importance to a man who has looked in for a moment upon the Ground and Meaning of Things. It is annihilated as a man's shadow is annihilated when he steps into the midst of the light. Like sickness, like sin, it is of a lower order of reality than the Reality which his eyes have seen and to which henceforward his spirit will be knit, let the body wither as it may. He knows that the innermost reality of every man, if he can but find it, is an aspect of God, Who is without sin and cannot die.

But if the Initiate may live thus rashly, the less enlightened very properly decline to act on such high assumptions. Vicar General Elias, the responsible captain, reasons with him, but is defeated by chaff. He writes to his understanding patron, Cardinal Ugolino, who is with the papal court at Rieti. He submits that their irrepressible and tiresome saint will probably listen to *him*. And Ugolino immediately sends a loving command to Francis that he is to come to Rieti and be properly looked after in the Bishop's Palace there and have the advice of the best physicians. Receiving this order, Francis accepts it with resignation and obeys.

But it is a strangely unhurried obedience. On the first day of his journey from the Portiuncula to Rieti he gets no farther than San Damiano, which is about ten minutes' ride from the Portiuncula. He has a fancy to go in and be with Clare for a little while; and he yields quite happily to this natural desire of a sick man for the sympathy and softness of a woman. (Every sick man is a boy returning to his mother.) None of the old fears and doubts are in him now; he just knows that he has a longing for Clare, and will be happy with her and amongst the good women around her.

And Clare no sooner saw him than she promptly put him to bed: that is the substance of the whole delightful story. She had a wattle hut made for him in the convent garden, but just under her own terrace-garden, so that she could keep an eye on it. It was summer, and she knew that this was the kind of sick-room he would like best. And it would appear that she stood no nonsense, for in that wattle hut Francis remained for six weeks. I feel no doubt that Clare was Matron of this small infirmary—had she not from the beginning run a hospital for the sick poor at San Damiano?—but she had good orderlies under her, and you will hardly need to be told their names. They were Leo, Masseo, Angelo, and Rufino: *nos qui cum eo fuimus*. Rejoice, Brother Body, for with Clare to fuss around you, and these old loyalists to do her bidding, you are as comfortable at last as a man in felt slippers. To be sure, the actual slippers which Clare made for her invalid at this time can be seen at San Damiano.

But if all external discomfort had been very sensibly put an end to by Clare, the suffering within his body could

317

not be so easily stopped and controlled. At times it was worse than it had ever been. And one night it was so bad that it almost dragged him down into self-pity. He was alone in the hut; he could not sleep for pain; and suddenly, to add to his distresses, some mice began to run about the place. His brothers the mice were being altogether too active, and for a moment he asked himself why, *why* he was tormented so? Was it quite fair——?

Now, this is an important moment, not so much in the life of Francis as in the history of literature, because if Francis, in answer to his own query, had swayed towards despondency instead of back into triumph and joy, the world would have lost something which was to prove almost as potent an inspiration to literature (and to religion too, for that matter) as the sermon to the birds.

But it was not likely that Francis, after La Verna, would have much difficulty in crushing this temptation. There in the darkness, alone, we are told, he crushed it with the words, "Now, brother, rejoice and be merry in your infirmities, for are you not as sure of the Kingdom as if you were already there?"

He lay awake thinking, while his blind, helpless hands felt the ground. Feeling it, he would feel one with the earth as it rolled round in the night. And he thought of the earth which he had loved and was leaving. He thought of it in all its aspects. He thought of the sun and of the wonderful light in the Vale of Spoleto. He thought of the moon and stars which, even if his wakeful eyes could not see them, were filling the summer night with beauty. He thought of the wind, gentle on the plain and brusque and hearty on the uplands. He thought of the streams in the hills, and of the lakes of Rieti, and of the seas which he had crossed.

He was dividing the world, as you see, into its "elements," earth, fire, air, and water. And he saw God in each of them apart, and in all of them together. Wonder and worship surged up in him; and words for their expression. And he began to compose a poem.

The happy work of creation numbed the pain in his body. He lost himself in doing what he had always wanted to do, the work of a troubadour, which was to compose a lyric of love. Francis, in his wattle hut, was creating the Canticle of Brother Sun, or "The Praises of the Creatures," as it is sometimes called. He whose eyes the sun had struck, so that even the light in his own vale hurt him, was making lines in praise of the sun. He who was shortly to leave this pleasant world was happily drawing up a form of thanks for all its creatures.

And in the morning, delighted with his creation, and impatient and impetuous as ever, he called the brothers to tell them about it. He wanted Leo to write it down before he should forget it. They came, and he told them of his distresses in the night, and how a poem had suddenly come to him. And after a little pause, he began to recite it to them. For the first time the world was hearing Il Cantico di Frate Sole.

"Altissimu, omnipotente, bonsignore . . ." began Francis in that wattle hut . . .

Most high, omnipotent, good Lord,
To Thee be praise and glory, honour and blessing:
Only to Thee, most high, do they belong,
And no man is great enough to speak of Thee.

Be praised, my Lord, with all thy creatures,
And most of all for Monsignor Brother Sun,
Who makes the day for us, and the light.
Fair is he, and radiant, and very splendid:
A semblance, Lord most high, of Thee.

319

Be praised, my Lord, for Sister Moon and all the stars.
In heaven Thou hast made them, precious, bright and fair.

Be praised, my Lord, for Brother Wind
And for air and cloud and every weather
By which Thou givest sustenance to all thy creatures.

Be praised, my Lord, for Sister Water,
Useful, humble, precious and chaste.

Be praised, my Lord, for Brother Fire
By whom Thou dost light up the night.
Beautiful is he, and joyous, robust, and strong.

Be praised, my Lord, for our mother, Sister Earth
Who doth support and keep us, and produce for us
Her varied fruits and coloured flowers and grass.

Oh, praise and bless my Lord, and thankful be,
And serve him all, with great humility.

2

The Canticle of the Sun is more than a poem written
during a night of pain. It is more than a simple lyric,
historically interesting as the first universally known poem
in the Italian language, the first spring murmurings of a
great literature, the head-waters that lead to Dante,
Petrarch, and Tasso. Whether or not its author knew
all that it was, is difficult to say; but those of us who
have watched the light in the valley of Spoleto and felt its
soft air, and at night have seen the stars mingled with the
lights of Perugia on a company of hills, will know that in
its simplest meaning it is the song of his own vale; while,
if we have ears for a deeper music, we shall know also
that it is the song of La Verna. It is the lyrical statement
of a knowledge attained there, which can be only suggested
by poetry and stammered by prose.

His pleasure in it was patent. He wanted to send

straightaway for Brother Pacifico that he might set it to music. And as this awoke the ever-present idea of the *jongleurs de Dieu*, his head filled with a scheme for selecting a troupe of preachers and singing brethren who would travel through the world, under the expert leadership of the old troubadour Pacifico, and sing to the people in the market-places this new love song. The plan burgeoned with pleasant detail, comforting his sick bed. "The best preacher in the troupe," said he to his nurses, "must first proclaim the meaning of the Canticle, and then all will sing it, and then the preacher must say, 'We are the minstrels of the Lord, and like other minstrels we want to be paid, but the only pay we ask from you is your repentance.' "

And like every artist well pleased with a new creation, he was constantly touching it up and adding to it. Things that impinged upon him from outside he would convert into material for its improvement. Just at this time his old friend, Bishop Guido of Assisi, was quarrelling again with the Podestà or "Chief Magistrate." In fact, he had brought the quarrel to such a pitch, the Podestà no doubt assisting, that episcopal palace and city hall were no longer on speaking terms with each other. Guido had excommunicated the Mayor and all his Corporation, and they had retaliated skilfully by an economic blockade of the palace—an interesting early example of the boycott. They had forbidden all citizens to trade with the Bishop or his clergy. To Francis, so filled now with his knowledge of the identity of all life and its coherence in one whole, so that all men were immanent in one another, this quarrelsomeness, this haughty exclusiveness, this shutting of oneself in one's anger, was bewildering in its childish immaturity and dullness. To a man who can see something with final clarity it is always a sick frustration that others cannot see it too. And that Official Christianity, whose duty it was to see it and to preach it, should be among the bonniest of the fighters seemed a blind negation of its own cause.

He considered what to do. He could not but know that nowadays his power over the citizens, both ecclesiastical and lay, was much greater than that of the Bishop and more certainly effective than that of the Pope, since they had lifted him into the mysterious region of the saints while he was still alive. He resolved to use this power. The resolve met and merged with the thought of his Canticle, and with the companion thought of Pacifico and his glee-singers; with the result that he set about composing a new verse. It came easily, because its subject could be made to follow naturally what had gone before. God was not only in the sun and the wind and the stars but, most of all, in the charity and forbearance of men. Was not goodwill the greatest of the Creatures? Of course! He composed quickly. . . .

The script ready, he sent a messenger to both parties to tell them that Brother Francis wanted them to assemble in the courtyard of the Bishop's Palace, for he had something to say to them. Strange inversion of power here! Nearly twenty years earlier, magistrates and bishop had been summoning Francis, and in the Bishop's case to the same palace; now Francis, an empty vagrant, possessing nothing in the world except his clothes, was summoning *them*; and without hesitation or indignation they came.

And when all were in the courtyard, the Bishop seated on his throne with his clergy around him, and the Podestà standing at a wrathful distance with his officials to support him in his rights, the two brothers whom Francis had sent, the first fruits of his new idea, stood up, and one of them said, "My lord Bishop and Excellencies, your brother Francis in his weakness has made a Praise of the Lord concerning His creatures, and he asks you to listen to it very carefully."

The brother explained the matter a little further, and then the two together sang the Canticle. And when they had sung of Sun and Wind and Water and Fire, they came to the new verse and sung to Bishop and Podestà about a greater creature than these.

> Be praised, my Lord, for those who pardon for Thy love,
> Who bear infirmity and tribulation.
> Blessed are they who keep themselves in peace
> *For thou shalt crown them, Lord most high.*

It proved one of Francis' happiest successes. How the news of its success must have pleased him! These hot-blooded but good-hearted Italians, a little pugnacious maybe, but as quick to appreciate all forms of beauty as they were quick to fight, and ready to acclaim, most of all, moral beauty which they found so sadly difficult, these honest fellows whose hearts yielded easily to song were won. The Podestà came forward and said, "I say to you all, and not only of my Lord Bishop, whom I wish and ought to have for my lord, but if anyone should have slain my blood-friend—more—if any should have slain my son, I would forgive him."

And in this sunny land of gestures he went forthwith and kneeled before the Bishop. "I am ready, my lord," he said, "to make satisfaction for everything as it shall please you, for the love of our Lord Jesus Christ, and of his good servant, Francis."

And Bishop Guido, stretching forward both his hands, raised him up and answered, "My office bids me be humble, but alas, I am quick to wrath! It is my part to ask pardon of you."

And both men embraced and kissed each other.

3

Happiness and success worked an improvement in the invalid, and he was able to resume his journey to Rieti. At Rieti he was welcomed into the Bishop's palace and cared for with every attention. Nothing could have exceeded the kindliness of Cardinal Ugolino. All these last months of Francis' life Ugolino is seen at his most attractive: august and puissant vizier of the Church as he was, he cared for a little sick friar as for a man greater than he. He brought the best specialists to him. He was for ever considering what next could be done to add to his strength or his comfort. A vigorous old oak of a man, more than thirty years older than Francis, he stepped into Pietro Bernardone's empty place, and was his father.

But Francis was never at ease in a palace, and they removed him, possibly on the advice of the doctors, to the nearest hermitage that was on a hill-top and among the trees, Fonte Colombo. Here the happiness continued to possess him. He composed new songs and, well pleased with them, sent them to Clare. Aware that his time was drawing in, and wondering when the end would be, he composed a letter to the whole Order and asked that it might be read at all Chapters after he was gone, as a last word from him.

To all the reverend and well-beloved Brothers Minor, to the Minister General, to all the ministers, guardians, and priests of this fraternity, and to all the simple and obedient brothers, and not only the oldest but the newest and most recent, Brother Francis, a mean and perishing man, your little servant, gives greeting. . . .

Knowing what his name could work throughout the world, and no longer afraid of pride ("One day I shall be a great prince") he composed another letter to "All Christians Everywhere."

> To all Christians, monks, clerics, or laymen, whether men or women, to all who dwell in the whole world, Brother Francis, their humblest servitor, presents his duty. . . Seeing I am too weak and ill to visit you in person, I have resolved to send you my message by this letter. Let all the podestàs, governors, and those who are placed in authority, exercise their functions with mercy, as they would be judged with mercy by God. . . .

And at Fonte Colombo there happened an incident which gave us one of the most celebrated sayings of Franciṣ. I can think of only two figures in history of whom it is possible to say, "he, and he alone, could have uttered such and such a sentence." They are Jesus of Nazareth and Francis of Assisi. There are sayings, not found in the Gospels but handed down by tradition, of which one must immediately proclaim, "Only Jesus could have said that." "Lift the stone, and you shall find me; cleave the wood, and there am I." Would anyone guess twice if asked who said that? It is so with the Logia of the Umbrian friar: his signature is stamped upon them. "My sister swallows, you have praised the Lord long enough; now it is my turn." Who but Francis? And it is one of these exclusively personal sayings that we are to hear now.

The pain in his eyes had been getting worse, and though he refused to worry about it, Ugolino and Elias insisted that if any alleviation was possible, it was to be found for him. They overcame his indifference by the old, smiling, loving command that he was to do what he was told "by holy obedience." They found the best oculists and sent them to him. And one of them, to their dismay, recommended a desperate remedy. This was to cauterise with a red-hot iron the side of the face from jaw to eyebrow. What they expected to achieve by this is beyond my knowledge to explain, but it was a treatment very fashionable at the time.

Was Francis a little afraid? For a minute, yes, I think. It is significant that he asked the Vicar General, Elias, to be present when the operation was performed, as if he feared what might happen to him under the pain. It is even more suggestive that, when Elias tarried in coming, Francis at last instructed the doctor to proceed, as if he could endure the suspense no more.

The doctor put the iron into the brazier; the brothers flung their hands over their eyes and fled from the room; but Francis, when the iron was ready, only stood up and said, "Deal courteously with me, Brother Fire, for I have always loved thee."

FONTE COLOMBO, WHERE FRANCIS COMPOSED THE RULE

CHAPTER XXVI

I

And now Ugolino, ever casting about for some new means of healing, tried the experiment of sending him to Siena in the charge of a devoted doctor. At Siena the air was supposed to be good for invalids, and there was an abundance of famous physicians. But neither the air nor the doctors could do anything for him, he grew steadily worse. He was now coughing blood, and one night the hæmorrhage was particularly bad, lasting till the morning. His brothers were filled with alarm lest the end was at hand. They sent at once for Elias, the Vicar General, and meanwhile gathered about his bed with white faces and many tears. They spoke to Francis of their love for him and of their fear for the future, and begged his blessing.

"Father," they said, "what shall we do without you? You have been father and mother to us, our shepherd and master and corrector, though correcting us more by example than by word. What are we to do without you to lead us, who are but rude and simple men? O Father, before you depart from us, give us your blessing, and leave us some statement of your wishes, that we may say afterwards, 'These are the desires our father expressed at his death.'"

And Francis, looking upon them all, said, "Call to me Brother Benedict of Pirato."

This Benedict seems to have been filling for a time the place of Leo. A priest, he said Mass for Francis whenever possible, and acted as his secretary. Where Leo was at the time I cannot say. The scene in the *Speculum Perfectionis*, to which Leo was probably a chief contributor, reads like

327

the description of an eye-witness—but it was Benedict of Pirato that Francis called.

He came quickly, and Francis said to him, "Write this. Write that I bless my brethren who are in the Order, and all those who shall come into it, even to the end of the world. And since, because of my weakness I may not speak much, I make plain my desire to all my brethren, present and to come, in these three brief words: that they shall always love one another as I have loved them, that they shall always love and observe our Lady Poverty, and that they shall remain faithful servants of our holy Mother Church."

But it was not written that Francis should die at Siena. Nor in any great town, nor out of his native Umbria. It was written that Francis, who did all things well, must die at his chosen Portiuncula, in the wood beneath Assisi, and just at the hour when the sun was going down.

In answer to the summons, Elias appeared post haste. One look at Francis, and he decided to get him back to Assisi. But not to the Portiuncula: that was not what he had in mind. He wanted to get him into the city itself, because it was a place with stout walls and strong men to guard them. When Francis died, his body must be secure in the hands of his Order, and protected by battlemented walls. Elias knew that, just as the living Francis was the ornament of the Order and its magnet, so the body of the dead Francis would be a source of distinction for it, and power—and wealth. And Vicar General Elias was not the sort of commander to let this strategic treasure fall into the hands of any but his own forces.

He must get him to Assisi privily, furtively, and by a circuitous route. He must get him there before the Perugians knew that he was dying. He must steal a march on them so that it would be too late for them to sally forth and despoil their ancient enemies of this, their greatest prize.

The complete Elias stands before us in this hour. While one half of him was ministering to Francis with a tenderness not less than Ugolino's, the other half was scheming for the future greatness of the Order—and of himself—and delighting in the tactical game and his skill at it. He plotted the route: round by Cortona and Gubbio and Nocera, and so into Assisi from the opposite side to that side which looked towards Perugia. He arranged with the magistrates of Assisi that directly he and Francis' litter crossed the boundary into their territory, the soldiers of the town should come out and guard it for the rest of the way. He arranged with Bishop Guido for the reception of the dying man into the palace.

Francis offered no resistance. First, because he had all a sick man's longing to be carried home. Secondly, if I am right, because he saw through everything: he saw the love and the blindness of Elias and smiled at them with patient and whimsical eyes. This is suggested to me by one or two things that happened on that extraordinary roundabout journey; by the trick which he played on the brothers at Cortona, for it was here that he made them pay up for the cloak, and by the chaff which he offered to the soldiers when they came to meet his litter at Bagnara near Nocera. I do not think it unbecoming in this context, Francis being what he was, to say that he saw the joke. All that Elias could make of his vision was to turn him—him who had vowed to have no property because it led to quarrels—into a piece of property for which soldiers would fight.

Perhaps he thought, with the sweet reasonableness of these last days, that now that his Order was so enormous, some modification of the rigid "no property" rule would have to be conceded, and that he wouldn't mind being a bit of the conceded property, if only Elias had got the spirit right. Perhaps he comforted himself by thinking that, whatever happened, he had lived out his challenge and been faithful to it to the end, and that there would always be those who could see. There were always Bernard and Leo and Angelo and Clare, and there would be others like them to the end of time. So with a faint, enigmatic smile he lay on his litter and enjoyed in his own fashion the long, stealthy journey through the mountains to Assisi.

I made my way along the last miles of this journey, rambling from Gualdo Tadino to Nocera, and on towards Foligno, just to see what those parts of Italy were like, on which Francis looked with eyes that said good-bye.

The road was the old Flaminian Way, coming westward from the Adriatic. The mountains to either side of it determined its course, as they determined the course of the Topino stream which it soon encountered and kept for its prattling companion. The stream created a narrow bed of cultivation all the way. Maize and corn and clover made patches of vivid green between the imprisoning hills; and all the meandering vale was like a traveller's song of Italy. It was castled peaks, white hamlets among the poplars, haystacks like Kentish oasts, and everywhere the tall dark pencils of the cypress trees.

And I knew that it was a happy man who came this road on his litter, with everything to thank God for, and little to regret.

But it was a very remarkable way round. A guilty

330

way for a saint to come home ! Let us then, since we have Francis' licence, and even command, to smile, consider in more detail the mediæval background which produced Elias and exactly explains his subtle manœuvring.

2

In the Dark and Middle Ages a saint's relics could be a cause of war. Armies marched to their capture, because these were the ages of faith. To-day we are more likely to fight for the possession of an oil-field, because this is the age of oil. Which of these two cravings suggests the lower spiritual development I leave it to you to decide. For my part I don't think there is much to choose between them. To me it seems that what our form of grabbing has lost in superstition it has gained in vulgarity.

And the methods employed in the Dark Ages were much the same as those we employ now. Men stooped to the meanest tricks of diplomacy to acquire a famous corpse, and were applauded as statesmen if they succeeded. Much as a modern nation demands colonies for its prestige, so a mediæval city-state demanded at least one valuable, miracle-working relic. And once it had got its trophy, generally by dishonest means, it would defend it ferociously for the sake of its honour.

Take Venice for an example. Venice on its tight little islands, with the best navy in the world and the best merchant service in the world, Venice whose capital city was the financial capital of Europe, and whose commercial resources enabled her almost always to swing a war in favour of her allies, Venice, this top nation, desired, acquired, and greatly prided itself on, perhaps the finest aggregation of corpses in the world. From the

Eastern Emperors it obtained amid national rejoicing a hand of John the Baptist and the body of his father Zacharias, for which it built the church of San Zaccaria. It stole the body of Stephen from Constantinople and that of St. Mark from Alexandria; which later, if the tale is true, was only saved from the Saracens by being suspended from the ship's mast and covered over with swine's flesh. Its Doge Michieli brought home in triumph the bodies of San Isidoro and San Donato, "the acquisition of which," says Cotterill in his *Mediæval Italy*, "was regarded as a greater triumph than the capture of Tyre and Jerusalem."

The lesser states had their sense of honour too. The Dukes of Benevento extorted from Naples and Amalfi the mummies of Saint Januarius and Saint Triphomena. One of these dukes, according to Gregorovius, "sent his agents to search all the coasts and islands of Italy for bones and skulls and other relics, and transformed the Cathedral of Benevento into a charnel house."

And every church within a city desired to have its own particular treasure. Many churches were not even started until a suitable corpse had been purchased, or, if a whole body was too dear, a portion of one. A good corpse was a source of immense revenue to any church, and consequently the demand was enormous, and the trade in relics was much greater, if no more roguish, than, say, the trade in antiques to-day. Gregorovius tells us that "about seven hundred and fifty long lines of waggons used to bring constantly to Rome great quantities of skulls and skeletons from the Campagna and the catacombs, which the popes sorted, labelled, and sold for exportation."

Catacombs and graves [says Cotterill,] were plundered by night, and the tombs in the churches had to be watched by armed men. Rome was like a mouldering cemetery in which hyenas howled and fought as they dug greedily after corpses. And these corpses were labelled with the names of popular saints and sold piecemeal to pilgrims. . . . Sometimes a pope would, as a special favour, present some foreign church or potentate with a valuable corpse.

These dead bodies were transported on richly decorated vehicles and escorted for some distance by the Roman populace in solemn procession with lighted torches and pious psalmody; and from every town, at the approach of the car, streamed forth the citizens, imploring and expecting miracles of healing. When it arrived at its destination—a city or a monastery of Germany, France, or England—the sacred body was welcomed with hymns of triumph and festivities that lasted many days.

Perhaps we shall understand all this a little better, though the parallel is far from perfect, since there was little superstitious and nothing sordid here, when we remember the bringing of the Unknown Warriors into the capitals of Europe.

And so, however strange it may appear to us, it did not seem strange to the people of Assisi, nor to Elias, nor to Francis, that, when they heard he was nearing the city, they streamed out of the Porta Nuova to welcome their precious relic while he was still alive. They escorted his litter in a triumphant procession, as if it had been the city's *carroccio;* and when it had been taken into the Bishop's palace, mounted a strong guard of soldiers outside; even as we mount a military guard outside the Bank of England where our treasure lies.

3

Within the palace relays of citizens kept watch. I conjecture that Bishop Guido, who would contend so testily for the rights of the Church, gave strong support to

333

a this, and, while sorrowing for Francis whom he sincerely loved, enjoyed like Elias the military game. Elias, as Vicar General, was in charge of the defence measures, with a small staff of brothers. Everything had gone well so far. Things did not usually go amiss with this Napoleon of the Brothers Minor. The only flaw in the general pattern was the deportment of the saint himself. He was not conducting himself quite as the centre of the picture should. His pains were now very great, for dropsy had developed at Cortona and grown worse on that long journey; and to ease his sufferings and keep his courage high, he would sing for much of the day, and often during the night. He would also call in the brothers and ask them to sing to him in chorus, so that his sick chamber at times sounded like the rehearsal room of a glee society.

Now, the Bishop's palace stood, and stands still, on a part of the old Roman wall. A window above the Roman stones, and plumb with them, was indicated to me by the Bishop's chaplain as the window of the room in which Francis lay. I found this hard to believe since that part of the palace seemed to be of much later date than the thirteenth century; but we can be sure that the room was sited somewhere here, and that its window looked over the ancient wall towards the health-giving sun. In such a case it is not difficult to imagine the crowds that would gather beneath the wall to stare up at the window or to watch the sentries going to and fro. We ourselves have seen similar waiting crowds outside a palace, during the sickness of a king. They would hear the brothers singing within, and strain their ears to distinguish the voice of Francis. And Elias would glance out of *his* window and see them there.

The sight fretted him. It frayed a kind of religious snobbery in him which wanted Francis, *his* Francis, the Francis of his Order, to be the most exalted saint in the calendar. Like most energetic and successful men of affairs, he had been much too busy all his days to query the conventions of his time, and to his conservative and traditionalist mind this frequent singing and occasional laughter did not sort at all well with the deathbed of a saint. Of course he himself could understand and tolerate it as an amiable eccentricity, but it was a pity the people should be hearing it. So, just as Celano and Bonaventura in their official biographies tried to force the awkward shape of Francis into the conventional mould of a saint, suppressing this and explaining away that, just so did Elias now strive to steer him into more traditional behaviour. He came into his room and reasoned with him in words in which we can still hear, after all these centuries, his nervousness and his careful tact.

"Dearest Brother," he said, "I am greatly consoled and edified by all the gladness which you show for yourself and for your fellows in your ailments. But though the men of this city venerate you as a holy man, yet because they believe you nigh unto death, hearing these Praises sung day and night, they may say within themselves, 'Why does this man show such light-heartedness who is near death? Surely he should be thinking of death.'"

But Francis, turning his bright eyes upon him, and seeing through all, answered only:

"Suffer me, Brother, to rejoice in my Lord, both in His glory and in my infirmities, since by the grace of His Spirit, I feel so united to Him that I needs must sing."

No, they could force his death, no more than his life, into the leaden framework of a stained-glass window: it stayed within the homely rooms of us men, the most human story of any saint's passing, and therefore the most convincing. What could you do with a man whose followers loved him so well that they persisted in reporting the smallest details of his last hours, even to his requests for a piece of fish, a little parsley, or some marzipan?

"I have not much desire to eat," he is reported as saying one day, "but if I could have some of the fish called squail, perhaps I could manage it."

And to the brother who was attending him one night: "I have a longing for a little parsley. Do you think it would be possible to get some?" Now, either the nursing brother was sleepy and did not want to go out into the garden, or Francis was over-sensitive, but he thought he saw a momentary creasing of the brother's brow, and it worried him. It worried him for the rest of the night. He lay thinking, "They are tired out. I must not be exacting just because I am in pain and unable to sleep, or I shall be a cause of their incurring an offence before God by reason of their impatience. They may be thinking to themselves, 'We have no time for prayer or contemplation, or even to think of ourselves. It is nothing but labour!' O God, do not let me be to them a cause of selfishness and sin."

And in the morning, when they were all about him, what a relief it must have been to his worry to say, as he did, "Dearest Brethren and my little sons, don't let it weary you to labour for me in my sickness, because the Lord will return to you the fruit of your works for one of his humble servants. If you spend yourselves now on me, I think the Lord will be your debtor on my account."

As often happens in the last days, his condition fluctuated violently: at one time the hæmorrhage and the exhaustion would be so alarming that all supposed the end to be

336

near; at another he would seem so much better that they dared to hope for a recovery, and he himself would wonder if, after all, he was to be allowed to live. The doctor attending him then was an old friend named Bongiovanni; and Francis, when playing with this hope one day, decided to ask him the truth.

"Old friend," he began, "what do you say? How much longer have I to live?"

And Bongiovanni, like all good visiting practitioners, dodged away from the truth.

"Well, Father," he replied, "I see no reason why, if God is willing, this sickness should not pass away in time."

"Now come, Bembegnato," objected Francis, employing as usual a nickname, "I am not a cuckoo, and I am not afraid of death. In the mercy of God I feel so close to Him that it means little to me whether I live or die."

"Well, then," said Bongiovanni, "I must tell you that, so far as our knowledge goes, your complaint is incurable, and it is my opinion that you can live only till about the end of September or the beginning of October."

Francis turned his eyes from the doctor and said, "Welcome, my sister Death."

CHAPTER XXVII

I

AND when the doctor had gone, Francis sent for Leo and Angelo and said to them, "Sing to me. Sing to me my Song of the Creatures."

And there by his bedside they sang his Praise of all Creation, while Francis lay listening, not adding his voice to theirs, but silently assenting to this gratitude for sun and stars and fire and water, and all the good things of an earth on which he had walked for a few years.

And when they had finished he preserved his silence, nor did they say anything to break it. But after a while, he said, "I have composed a new verse. Listen,

> Be praised, my Lord, for Sister Death,
> From whom no man living can escape.
> Alas for those who die in mortal sin,
> But happy they who find themselves within Thy will,
> On them the second death can work no harm.

So then? Was a good death the last and greatest of all the creatures?

And either at that time or later he turned to them and said, "I should like to die at the Portiuncula."

He could not die in a palace.

No man was willing to deny him his last wish. Certainly not Elias, for his master's death was shaking his pride and his self-confidence, stirring his early love, and awaking old aspirations which he could wish asleep. In such moments a man's longing is to ease his conscience by doing all that he can for the dying, while there is time.

Elias arranged with the magistrates for a strong escort of men-at-arms, and then gave the word for the transportation to begin. Bearers put Francis on a litter and carried him to the courtyard of the palace. Here they saw the military escort waiting, and a crowd of people who had been drawn hither by the sight of marching men and by the flying news that Francis was going down to the Portiuncula. Thus it was a large procession which passed sadly from the Piazza del Vescovado to the nearest gate of the city. All tradition, and all the later biographers, say that the litter with the soldiers around it, and the sorrowful procession following, passed through the gate called La Portaccia, whose picture I therefore took for you. But though it has stood there for nearly six hundred years, during five hundred of which it was walled up, only to be opened on the seventh centenary of Francis' death, I do not think it quite old enough to have seen Francis pass from Assisi. I think he went through the old Porta Sementone, of which traces can still be seen among the remnants of the ancient Roman wall now within the city.

But the natural fall of the ground would have guided the cortege to where the handsome Portaccia now stands, and on down the present path through the olive trees, till it came to the old highroad from Perugia to Foligno. Here Francis told the bearers to set the litter down, and when they had obeyed, he said, "Lift me up a little, and turn my face towards Assisi."

They did so, and the people, standing by, watched in silence. They followed the direction of his half-blind eyes and saw the hanging white city on its mountainside. They saw him lift his hand to bless the city he could not see. And they heard the words. "Blessed be Thou of the Lord, O city, because through thee shall many souls be saved. I beseech Thee, O Lord Jesus Christ, that Thou be mindful always of Thy own most abundant

339

tenderness which Thou hast shewn forth in her, that she may be ever the place and dwelling of those who acknowledge Thee truly and glorify Thy name for ever and ever. Amen."

Then he told the bearers to carry him on.

Very carefully, tracing my way by the fall of the ground through the farmlands, I came upon the place where I felt confident that Francis had turned to bless Assisi. It is not the traditional site. The traditional site is to the west of this, at the point where the Casa Gualdi stands upon the carriage road down from Assisi. But I must believe my choice to be the right one. It is exactly at the point where people, seven hundred years ago, following the configuration of the ground, would come upon the Perugia–Foligno road, which is now no more than this rutty cart-track through the fields. Even now a path, intersecting it here, shows that this was once a cross-roads for those coming down from Assisi. A wooden cross stands here, but that may mean nothing, for many crosses, and many Roman fragments too, stand along this old lost highway in the vineyards.

It is a truly Franciscan spot, with an oak overhanging it, and the maize-fields all round, and the wayside paths running by. It is such a place as we would like to think of Francis sleeping in, instead of up yonder in that mighty fane which is such an odd sepulchre for the Little Poor Man. But it was not to be; and I can understand that in those superstitious and body-snatching years it could not have been. But oh, that his tomb might have been small and gentle and empty of power and pride! Still, as we shall presently see, it is only his body that sleeps for ever in the proud embrace of Elias; his strong, vital, original spirit no stout walls, no single church, no official and approved biography, no order for the destruction of unauthorised versions, has been able to hold.

They lifted the litter and continued on their way. Their way would have gone along this old lost road to its junction with the high road coming down from Assisi. At this cross-roads stood the leper hospital of San Salvatore, and if Francis could not see it clearly with his eyes, he would know that he was passing it, by the familiar odour mingling with the scent of green things.

What memories must have come to him, borne upon that odour! A boy walking in a wide arc through the fields to avoid the dread but secretly fascinating place; a young man riding towards it on his horse, which shied at the sight of a leper; the young man leaping from his horse and kissing the leper, and in that moment discovering love; the same young man going daily under the arches to minister to the lepers, and to kneel with them in their chapel; Bernard and Peter and Giles coming too, and the pleasure of introducing these new brothers to the poor inmates, and all the well-nigh intolerable happiness of it all, and the wonder that he could ever have done anything else, or lived in any other way.

But now the hospital was behind him, and he had finished with it for ever. They were in the woodland, approaching the gate of the Portiuncula. No longer a little gate in a hedge, alas; for the Portiuncula by this time was an aggregation of buildings with the little chapel in their midst, and a convent wall all round. A little way behind the chapel, to its left, was an isolated cell known as the Infirmary; and into this they bore Francis, and laid him upon a bed.

He had returned home. And almost the first thing he did after this was to return to a mother. I said above, in psychological rather than sentimental mood, that every sick man is a boy returning to his mother; and it is deeply suggestive to read now that, just as Francis when he was sick went to Clare to nurse him, so when he was dying he sent a message to the Lady Giacoma da Settisoli at Rome, asking her to come and be with him.

Giacoma was a rich and great lady of Rome, whose devotion he had early won, and who thereafter loved to " mother " him and his brothers when they came to the capital. Because she was so good to them, her house being often their home, he would pretend that she was one of the original Order and address her as Brother Giacoma. And now he wrote to her, asking her to come to him, and to bring with her the clothes that would be necessary for his shrouding, and a few candles, and some of the marzipan she used to make for him and he liked so well.

This easy invitation of a woman into the walled convent, to say nothing of a request for marzipan, was Francis' last unconscious defiance of convention, and has been an embarrassment to his orthodox biographers ever since.

The letter was hardly written, and the messenger had not completed his preparations for the journey, before they came running in to say that the Lady Giacoma was at the gate with her sons, her servants, and a supply of almost all the things he had wanted. The whole Portiuncula welcomed this as a miracle, but surely it was no more than the old miracle of love. Rumour that Francis was dying, sweeping over Italy, had come to Rome, and the Lady Giacoma, hearing it, had there and then seized upon everything that would be of use—what would those dear, foolish brothers have about the place?—clean, good clothes to wrap him in at the end, some candles as her

342

SEPULCHRE OF THE LITTLE POOR MAN

own offering, and a little of that sweetmeat which he used to praise and like.

When Francis heard that she was at the gate, he was very happy. "Now blessed be God," he said, "Who has sent us our Brother Giacoma. Bring her in, for the rule concerning women is not for Brother Giacoma."

It may have dismayed the more rigid, but no one cared to disobey him. They opened the gate, and the warm-hearted, "managing" woman rushed into the little infirmary and, seeing Francis there, flung herself on her knees and buried her face in the bedclothes at his feet. She insisted that she was not going to leave him until all was over, and Francis—was there a little chaff?—promised that she should stay there till the day after he died.

She is with him still. For after his death she came and lived in Assisi, to give her life and her substance to his work (perhaps not quite trusting anyone else), and in Assisi she was very good to Leo and those other loyalists whom Elias was persecuting. I should like to have heard the Lady Giacoma on Elias. There is a document in existence showing that she obtained two pounds from somebody for a tunic for Brother Leo. And there are those who believe that when, nearly fifty years after Francis' death, Leo lay dying too, an old woman called Brother Giacoma smoothed his pillow for him, and when it was finished, closed down his eyes. Then she died herself, and the brothers took her body into the Lower Church of San Francesco, and buried it near the high altar, somewhere beneath which they believed the body of Francis to be. And when, a few years ago, the crypt around the exposed sarcophagus of Francis was reshaped into its present form, Giacoma's remains were placed down here, at the end of the crypt but opposite Francis. It is all as it should be: around him, each at one corner, lie Leo, Angelo, Rufino, and Masseo, guarding him still, and, at a little distance away, their brother, Giacoma.

But what of that other woman, Clare? Some seven years before, at the instance of Cardinal Ugolino, her sisterhood of San Damiano had been made into a strictly enclosed Order, and therefore she could not pass outside the walls to be with Francis now. This was Poverty indeed. Natural woman that she was, she was torn with misery, which she made bearable only by sending messages down to the Portiuncula, assuring Francis of her love, and the love of all her sisters.

These messages not only moved him greatly but filled him with pity for her, "for," as the *Speculum* says, "he loved her singularly, with fatherly affection," and he thought he would like to give to her, and to her family, as he had to Leo, some little writing as a memorial of him. So, calling a friar, he dictated to him:

"I, little Brother Francis, desire to follow the life and poverty of my Lord Jesus Christ and of His holy mother, and to persevere in it to the end. And I beseech you, my ladies, and I give you counsel, that you live always in this most holy life and poverty. And be very careful lest by the teaching or counsel of any other you depart from it."

This dying wish he told the friar to take to Sister Clare, "and to say to her that she is to put aside all sorrow on account of not being able to see me, because I promise her that she shall see me before the end and be consoled."

Which promise seems to show that it was Francis himself who instructed that after his death, when they were carrying his body back to Assisi, they should take it by way of San Damiano, and lay it before the sisters' grating, that they might see him for the last time and say goodbye.

And the third lady in his life, his fantasy bride, the Lady Poverty? He sought to make provision for her. He had called her the widow of the world, and, anxious that she should never be wholly widowed again, he wanted to make a permanent home for her at the Portiuncula. Having always thought of the Little Portion as a meet home for Poverty, he now summoned all his brethren and said to them, "See that you never leave this place, my sons, and if you are thrown out of it on one side, enter it by another"—was his mind wandering back to his merry quip with the Bishop of Imola?—"for this place is holy. Here when we were only a few the Most High increased us; here He enlightened the souls of us His poor; here He inflamed our wills with His love. For which cause, my sons, keep this always as a holy place."

And then, by a last grand gesture, this dramatist-poet-knight proclaimed that he was faithful to his *dame* to the last. And, in so doing, he issued his last challenge to all of us who, nowadays no less than then, measure greatness by the quantity of possessions. As at the beginning he had shown no fear of shocking anybody if thereby he could give force to his message, so now at the end: he told the brothers to take him off the bed, strip him naked, and lay him for a little while on the bare floor. And when he was on the ground, he accepted from the Father Guardian a tunic, breeches, cord and cowl, the Guardian saying as he handed them to him, "Know that this tunic and these breeches are only lent to you by me, and you have no right of property in them."

Francis accepted them as a loan, was clothed again, and replaced upon the bed. Now he could die, owning nothing at all, not even, as of old, his tunic and cord. No half-measures, even in death, for the lad of Assisi.

But it did not occur to him, probably, that in that minute when he lay naked, he had put off the thirteenth century and lay there, a man not of any particular age, but of all time. It is not as a cowled figure from some old tapestry that he challenges our greedy appropriations, but as our contemporary.

2

It may have been now that he made his will. Some place the writing of it a few days or weeks earlier when he was still in the Bishop's palace. Others believe that it was written in the Portiuncula. One likes to take sides with the latter, and indeed a rambling incoherence in it suggests that he was very weak, and composing with an effort. But, ill-ordered as it may be, it is, with the Canticle of the Sun and the Blessing of Leo, the most precious writing of Francis that we possess, because it is his autobiography, and holds his spirit. It became the rallying standard of the loyalists, who set it up as a standard against all the bulls of Rome.

I can give you only a few sentences from it.

> See in what manner God gave it to me, Brother Francis, to begin to do penitence: when I lived in sin, it was very painful to me to see lepers, but God Himself led me into their midst, and I remained there a little while. When I left them, that which had seemed to me bitter had become sweet and easy. . . .
> The Lord gave me so great a faith in priests who live according to the form of the holy Roman Church that even if they persecuted me, I would have recourse to them. And

346

even though I had the wisdom of Solomon, if I should find poor secular priests, I would not preach in their parishes without their consent . . . I will not consider their sins, for in them I see the Son of God, and they are my lords. . . .

When the Lord gave me some brothers, no one showed me what I ought to do, but the Most High Himself revealed to me that I ought to live according to the model of the holy gospel. I caused a short and simple formula to be written, and the lord Pope confirmed it for me.

Those who presented themselves to observe this kind of life distributed all they might have to the poor. They contented themselves with a tunic, with the cord and breeches, and we desired to have nothing more. . . .

We loved to live in poor and abandoned churches, and we were ignorant and submissive to all. I worked with my hands, and would continue to do, and I will also that all other friars work at some honourable trade. Let those who have none learn one, not for the purpose of receiving the price of their toil, but for a good example, and to flee idleness. And when they do not give us the price of the work, let us resort to the table of the Lord. . . . The Lord revealed to me the salutation we ought to give, Il Signore vi dia pace.

Let the Brothers take great care not to receive churches, habitations, and all that men build for them, except as all is in accordance with holy poverty. . . .

I desire to obey the Minister General of this fraternity, and the Guardian whom he may please to give me. . . . Though I be simple and ill, I would, however, always have clerks who will perform the office, as it is said in the Rule. . . . This . . . is my Will that I, little Brother Francis, make for you, my blessed Brothers. . . .

And I, little Brother Francis, your servitor, confirm to you as far as I am able my most holy benediction. Amen.

3

It was the first day of October, 1226, a Thursday, and the end was very near. Not knowing when it might come, the brothers gathered round his bed and could hardly be induced to leave it. Most of the first brothers were there. Leo and Angelo were there, and sometimes at his request they would sing to him, and he, if he could, would join in the singing. Giles was there. A rather silent figure among them was Bernard of Quintavalle, who was always a staid man and quiet. At one time when they brought to Francis a delicate dish which they had carefully prepared, he tasted it and said, "This is something that Bernard likes," and he made him come closer and share it. It was Bernard who, as the senior and the spokesman of them all, asked him to give them his last forgiveness for all the times they had failed him, and his last blessing. And Francis answered him, "See, my son, God is calling me. I forgive all my brothers, whether present or absent, all their offences and faults, and as far as I can, I absolve them. And I bless them as much as I can, and more than I can. Tell them this everywhere, and bless them all from me."

Then he seems to have placed his hand upon the head of each in turn and given him a private blessing. But in his blindness he could not distinguish between one brother and another, and when his hand was on Giles's head, he thought for a moment that it was Bernard's. It is evident that he was feeling round for Bernard. Gently feeling the head of Giles, he said, "But this is not my brother Bernard?" And so, at his desire, Bernard came close and kneeled down, and when Francis felt his hands upon Bernard's head, he was greatly moved. Turning to Leo, he said, "Write that I, as well as I am able, wish and command that all brothers in the whole Order shall honour Bernard as if he were myself, for he was the first who came to me and gave his goods to the poor."

They watched him all that night; and the first light of Friday, the second of October, began to come into that hut. But Francis could distinguish light and darkness no more, and thinking it was still Thursday, he said, "I should like you to bring a loaf which we will break and eat together as our Master did the Thursday before He died."

"But this is not Thursday," they told him gently. "It is Friday now."

"I thought it was still Thursday," said Francis.

Still, the loaf was brought, and he broke it for them, and each ate his fragment as a symbol of his share in their common love.

"Now read to me the Gospel for Maundy Thursday," asked Francis.

They fetched the book and read that Gospel for the Thursday before Easter.

All that Friday saw him slowly sinking, and most of the next day. But just as the sun of Saturday, October 3rd, 1226, was dropping down towards the mountains of Perugia, and, as all noticed with joy, the larks were singing loudly in the last of the day, Francis began to sing too. That last strong lift of life which often precedes its collapse was putting a brief vigour into his voice. They could hear that he was singing the 142nd Psalm, and they noticed that many of the words, as is the way with the words of the psalms, were ringing with a strange appropriateness.

> I cried unto the Lord with my voice: yea, even unto the Lord did I make my supplication. . . .
> I cried unto Thee, O Lord, and said, Thou art my hope and my portion in the land of the living.
> Consider my complaint, for I am brought very low.
> O deliver me from my persecutors, for they are too strong for me.
> Bring my soul out of prison that I may give thanks unto Thy name; which thing if thou will grant me, then shall the righteous resort unto my company.

These were the last words heard from the lips of Francis. Soon the watching brothers saw that he was dead. And they wrote afterwards of the peace and happiness in his face.

They wrote also that in the silence they heard the larks singing.

This strange man, from the beginning of his mission to its end, had been happy in the fantasy that there walked with him everywhere a companion whom he called the Lady Poverty. In his meekness he did not see another inseparable companion whose name was Poetry. Poetry followed the steps of Pietro Bernardone's boy as it has followed the steps of no other man: its presence filled that hut in the woods where he died; it made of his tomb in San Francesco a chair for itself, and from this seat it impregnated with a new beauty of gentleness and humanity the art, the literature, and the religion of the world. And not the least of its victories was to secure that Francis, as his brothers loved to tell to the end of their days, went out of life into death, singing like a troubadour.

FESTA DI SAN FRANCESCO

Unity, not separateness. That is the beginning, the end, and the whole. Or, to be more accurate, unity as well as separateness; because if our awareness of unity is almost as bright as our awareness of our selves, it will wither our grasping selfishness away. All that Francis did is embraced in his knowledge of his unity with all life, and his desire, not only to know that identity, but to live it. He saw that all grabbing appropriation of goods, all angry punishment, all aspiration after personal distinction, expressed only—well, distinction, in its sense of separateness and isolation from others. He saw that he could realise his unity only by loving with little thought of self; and he knew, as does every soul, either dimly or clearly, that this love was God in him trying to reach the God in All that is. He saw that the Ultimate Reality was Love, and therefore men were lower than the true reality of themselves when they sinned by self-centred acquisitiveness or haughty exclusiveness or angry vindictiveness; and he wanted to be, and to body forth, a real man, as Christ had done.

There was nothing original in his knowledge or in his desire: they are the possessions of every saint and seer, no matter what his religion, country, or age. They are also possessed by quite a few who, alas, lack the spiritual muscles to build their lives in accordance with what they see. His only originality lay in the fact that, a born artist, he was able to act out the drama of Perfect Love walking the vineyards and the streets better than any man except the Divine Actor whose pupil he was. And that he saw, as hardly any man before him, that if he compromised with poverty or with forgiveness, his drama would be hazed over and lose in power. Some property, loosely held, might be allowed to the members of his Third Order, some right of punishment, lovingly administered, might be conceded to the sergeants of this world, but for him and his troupe of players, their poverty must outstrip the poorest and their forgiveness outpace the worst.

And he acted it out for us; nor spoiled one line of his part. Almost alone he did it, because, as we have seen, even Leo and Giles and others succumbed at times to exclusiveness and hate. He did a thing clean, and his own; nor soiled it with other men's fears. He kept his poverty complete, and his forgiveness complete; nor would be defend the first by infractions of the second. He would hold both intact, if he had to hold them alone.

He defied all the logic of this world, and all the common-sense of the practical men; and yet all men know— dimly, clearly—that he was right: right in the ideal he set forth; and right in his unswerving allegiance to it. From pope to peasant they elevated the absurd, illogical dreamer for worship and not the practical men. However blind to Francis' vision Ugolino may have seemed from his outward acts, he was expressing the hidden truth of his heart when, as Pope Gregory IX, two years after Francis' death, he canonised him in the Piazza San Giorgio, his eyes streaming with tears, as he recounted to the multitude what manner of man was their father, Francis. And so with Elias. His magnificent temple of San Francesco may tell us of his ambition and his coarse insensitiveness to the real meaning of Francis, but it tells us also that below consciousness he worshipped him as a man who was all that he would have liked to be.

And the common people from that day to this. Only half understanding him with their conscious minds, clutching, no doubt, at every small gain, beating their children in anger and vigorously cursing their enemies, they come in their multitudes to worship the little, poor man who was so much better than they. He stirs in them the dregs of their holiness. And I am confident that he disturbs these divine deeps in us all, even in those who have yielded most completely, during these last dark years, to the weakness of hate and seizure and brutality. In all of us, wandering away from our greatness, he sounds the return home.

.   .   .   .   .

On October the 4th, which is kept as his feast, all roads ead to the church of San Francesco.

At the beginning of our tale, we saw Francis seeking the outcasts; first, the odd-man-out in the Perugia prison, then the beggars, then the lepers of San Salvatore. And now at its end we shall find him, if an ancient tradition is true, still among the outcasts where he sleeps in San Francesco.

The tradition asserts that when he lay dying, he asked to be buried on the "Collis Infernus," a hill just outside the walls of Assisi, because it was there they executed the criminals and sometimes buried them. This "Lower Hill" was a rocky outwork of Assisi's hill, with steep or precipitous sides and a gully separating it from the western gate of the city. To any but Elias the difficulties of such a site might have seemed too great, but he by some

353

masterly engineering, walling it about with lofty arches, one colonnade of arches imposed upon another, made it into a long headland and platform for the support of his proud basilica. On that platform, driving its foundation into the rocks, he raised San Francesco.

And San Francesco is acclaimed almost everywhere as the fairest, even as it was the first, among the Gothic cathedrals of Italy. No one has anything but praise for Elias as engineer, architect, artist, and organiser. To-day, since the enlargement and embellishment of the crypt, it is really three churches piled one above another; first, the crypt containing the tomb of the saint, then the Lower Church, large as a cathedral, and then the soaring Upper Church, almost equal in size to the Lower Church, and very much loftier.

And the two higher churches are all colour. Every inch of wall, every section of vaulted roof, every rib of the vaulting, is covered with frescoes. All the painters of the dawning Renaissance came to Assisi to spend themselves in honour of Francis—Giunta Pisano, Cimabue, Pietro Cavallini, Giotto, and their schools. San Francesco, if we compare the amount of priceless paintings with the compass of the building, is, I suppose, the richest treasure house of art in the world. It is the watershed from which fall the rivers of the Renaissance.

And on October the 4th, the Festa di San Francesco, the people who have come into Assisi from all parts, pour into the Basilica Inferiore, or Lower Church. Last year at five o'clock in the evening, we were all summoned to the Piazza del Commune by the ringing of the Lauds bell in the slender campanile that dominates the square. We climbed to the square through streets whose every house was hung with banners and flags. Pennons flew from the towers of the Rocca, just as they did in mediæval times. And assembled in the square we found the heralds and halberdiers of Assisi in their parti-coloured doublets and hose. The two colours in these pied garments were azure and rouge, the colours of the city's flag: azure for faith, and rouge for love. At their side, needless to say, stood the *pompieri*, shining with plumed helmets and brass epaulettes, for no festival in Europe can be begun without the firemen. And because in this year the festa coincided with the closing of some Giotto celebrations, the heralds and halberdiers of Padua and Florence were also there, the lads of Padua in yellow and red, and those of Florence in white and red, with liripipe hats. Can you not see that the mediæval piazza, with these quaint figures on its stones, made a picture by Benozzo Gozzoli?

The heralds stood on the steps of the Temple of Minerva, lifted their long trumpets to their mouths, and sounded the hymn of Assisi; and forthwith the procession began.

It was difficult to say who of the streaming people were in the procession and who were not; difficult to tell whether the heralds, *pompieri*, Podestà, and chief burgesses were leading the march or being led and escorted by it; because, while some of us tramped with dignity behind the great men, others trotted like terriers at their sides or tacked like hounds in the van. Every few minutes the heralds pointed their trumpets towards heaven and addressed to it the call of Assisi; and so, with music and voices and running, we all trooped down the sunlit chasms of the streets to the Piazza Inferiore. And out of its brightness we passed with some disorder, and some dodging, into the long dim aisles and the quiet of the Lower Church.

I, I am ashamed to say, had joined the runners at an early stage so as to get into the north transept, from which I could command the greater part of the church, see the procession come in, and watch the picture take shape before me.

Soon every transept and chapel, every aisle, stairway, and side-altar, was black and a-sway with people; and now above the heads of the multitude in the nave came the trumpets and the pikes and the banners. Heralds and halberdiers went to the left of the High Altar, the *pompieri* to the right, and the Podestà and chief men to important seats in front of it. Thus all colour arranged itself about the altar, and the altar itself was brilliant with five rows of candles and with flowers heaped upon its steps.

In the apse, behind a woodwork screen, a hidden choir of friars was singing an office all the time, so that the picture took shape against a background of music.

And we waited. With reasonable quiet we waited. We waited listening to the steps and shuffle of crowds still packing into corners, listening to the singing of the brothers, looking up at the many-coloured frescoes on roof and walls, and gazing round on the cramped multitude. The deep-toned bell of San Francesco rang above us, as the sun dimmed and the church darkened. It was sunset, and the hour that Francis passed from the world.

The bell stopped. A long procession of tonsured brothers in white cottas went to their places round the altar, the hidden choir burst into a new song, and a dazzling scarlet cardinal passed with his escort to the papal throne, sweeping the people around him to their knees, like a reaping machine ploughing through the wheat. And Solemn Vespers began.

After Solemn Vespers would come the function of the Transito, or Passing of Francis. Alas, my knowledge of Catholic ceremonial was not enough to tell me at what point, as the hours went by, we crossed from Vespers to the Transito. I cannot tell you for which solemn office they began the Vesting of the Cardinal. All I know is that I watched this ceremony with a gaping interest.

The Cardinal stood on the top step of the throne, a baldachino of red and gold above him, a carpet of red running across the "theatre" to his feet, and dignified men in dress clothes on either side of him, to act as flunkeys. Before him, in Indian file, stretched a long line of tonsured friars (white figures on the red carpet), each holding a different vestment for the clothing of the Cardinal. These friars seemed to have been arranged by the Master of the Ceremonies, a portly and peripatetic brother, according to their heights, so that they looked like a row of white organ pipes. And to an accompaniment of music and singing they arrayed the garments around the Cardinal, one over another, like the layers of an onion. I use this simile in my ignorance, not in my irreverence.

And it was just as the last vesture was being wrapped around him that I remembered we were celebrating a man who at his death had asked to have all his clothes removed that he might die faithful to poverty.

At first I considered this a witty reflection, till I remembered that Francis was as eager for the seemly glorification of Jesus in the churches as he was for the humiliation of Francis; and then I didn't know what to think. All his sons, hundreds of them, were watching the ceremony

357

and seemed to see in it nothing out of key with their father's poverty. And it was certainly beautiful. It was beautiful as a ballet, but of a different order of beauty from that of Francis giving his cloak away.

Now certainly it was the Transito. All the principal clergy were kneeling before the altar beneath which the little man lay; they were singing the psalm he sang as he passed from us; they were praying to him. One of them, standing by the altar, blessed the whole congregation with some holy relic in its reliquary. And then— magnificent moment!—the pikes and banners sprang to attention, the swords of the *pompieri* leapt to the salute, the trumpets turned upwards to the roof and sang the call of Assisi, and the huge choir behind the screen, as the last silvery notes died away, burst into Francis' own song, the Canticle of the Creatures.

Altissimu, omnipotente, bonsignore . . .

The moment overwhelmed me with its splendour. I listened in a spell to the waves of triumphant sound sweeping between the dusky vaults of the roof and the black sea of people. I stared at the tableau about the altar: the rows of lights, the heaped flowers, the heralds, the *pompieri*, the pikes, banners and swords; behind the altar I saw through the openwork of the screen the arms of Padre Maestro Maria Domenico Stella conducting with Italian vehemence his packed, excited, and exulting choir; and just as I was standing agape and dumb with the grandeur of it, I chanced to turn my eyes to the left, and there—there from his place in a huge fresco on the transept wall—was the Author himself, gazing pointedly at me.

There, life-size in a painting attributed to Cimabue, he

stood, in his ragged brown tunic and cowl, his face lined and haggard and kind, and his eyes fixed on mine. Fixed on mine (God pardon my presumption) as if he and I had an understanding! And I could have sworn that his right eye—but I suppose it was impossible. I stared back, and one thing was beyond question, that in Cimabue's fresco his left eye was wide open, while his right eye might have been beginning or completing a—but enough of this. I say it was impossible. Manifestly.

After the Cantico came Eucharistic Benediction, for our Holy Mother the Church does not spare her children, singing to them, praying for them, forgiving them, preaching to them, and blessing them; and when at last we came out of the basilica, it was night in Assisi. The night of the festa. From the top of the highest tower to the steps of the last building Assisi was a-flicker with little points of flame fanned by the breeze. Every inhabitant of Assisi had put out his chain of little flames; mostly they were home-made cressets, just wicks afloat in saucers of oil, but some were real "links" on their brackets of wrought iron. Every house was picked out in small flames. They stood in rows on every balustrade, in every loggia, on every sill, round all the fountains, along the cornices of the public buildings, and in the topmost windows of the tall campaniles. They burned along the streets where he rioted as a young man. The highest of all twinkled against the velvet sky. It is said that the brothers on La Verna look south on the night of the festa to see the lights of Assisi. The whole city was a constellation of scintillating stars—and all because a young man, once upon a time, dared to be real.

Lights overflowed the city walls on to the fairground outside the Porta Nuova, illuminating the swings, the roundabouts, the booths, and the Big Top where, with full appropriateness, the clowns and the tumblers, unshaven and ragged and lively, honoured the Great Romantic by doing their turns in the sawdust with a virtuosity as brilliant as their motley was faded and their jokes were rude.

Do not tell me that Francis failed. The Spirit of Compromise captured his dream and pared it down; it captured his Brothers whom he had wished to be a free and world-wide order of spiritual chivalry, and changed them, as it had tried to change him from the first, into good but commonplace monks; it captured his body and buried it in one of the greatest churches of Italy; it captured his dangerous life-story and put it into censored and adapted biographies; but it could not catch Francis.

His spirit slipped through the stoutest of these walls. It broke through the cracks in the immuring biographies. It emerged to be the head of an Invisible Order, the Order of those who, whether within or without his visible brotherhood, can see his vision in its fulness. As Angelo Clareno said, one of the doughtiest of his champions in the next generation, "Francis is not in the name of an Order, nor in walls, nor in anything outward whatsoever, but in his obedient sons and his lovers." Among these may we be counted. God knows that most of us are not his obedient sons, but we may claim a lowly place among his lovers.

And this, after all, means that he achieved exactly what in the first place he set out to do: he preached by his life, which is the best way, the most effective Christian sermon that has ever been preached; a sermon which still, after all the centuries, works its gentle ferment and attains its design, because if in reading it we learn to love

Francis, we must find ourselves loving also his Master and his Model. Francis succeeded; it was the others who failed. Behold the eternal paradox of the Cross: by betraying Francis and denying him and defeating him, they enabled him to rise higher, to set forth his message better, and to conquer. "No man took my life from me. I laid it down . . ." "Daughters of Jerusalem, weep not for *me*."

Good-bye then, my master; and well done. I have left Don Quixote dead, and Sancho Panza can go home. The troubadour has gone singing to his tomb, and the tumbler may depart. I left Assisi the next morning, Natale driving me away from it rather slowly, because we had to pass, on all the roads, the strings of white oxen which were being led to the cattle fair up in the town.

BIBLIOGRAPHY

I. Biographies and Commentaries (Ancient).

Doctrine Spirituelle de St. François, ed. Pere Appolinaire. (Paris, 1878.)
Giordano da Giano, Early Provincial Chronicles (Paris, 1908.)
St. Bonaventura's Life of Francis, trans. E. G. Salter. (Dent. Temple Classics, 1904.)
The Chronicle of the Twenty Four Generals. (Quaracchi, 1885.)
The Legend of the Three Companions, trans. E. G. Salter. (Dent. Temple Classics, 1903.)
The Little Flowers of St. Francis (Fioretti), ed. T. Okey. (Kegan Paul.)
The Mirror of Perfection (Speculum Perfectionis), trans. R. Steele. (Dent. Temple Classics, 1903.)
Thomas of Celano's First and Second Lives of St. Francis, trans. A. G. F. Howell. (Methuen, 1908.)

II. Critical Studies of the Sources.

Boehmer, H. *Analekten zur Geschichte des Franciscus von Assisi.* (Tubingen, 1904.)
Goetz, W. *Die Quellen zur Geschichte des hl. Franz von Assisi.* (Gotha, 1904.)
Jörgensen, J. Appendix to *St. Francis.* (Longmans, 1913.)
Sabatier, P. Appendix to *Vie de St. François.* (Hodder and Stoughton, 1912.)
Sabatier, P. *Le Speculum Perfectionis, Texte Latin.* (1928.) *Etude Critique.* (1931.) (British Society of Franciscan Studies.)
Tamassia, N. *St. Francis of Assisi and his Legend*, trans. L. Ragg. (Fisher Unwin, 1910.)

III. Historical Background.

Barker, E. *The Crusades.* (Oxford Univ. Press, 1923.)
Bell, M. I. M. *A Short History of the Papacy.* (Methuen.)
Belloc, H. *The Crusade.* (Cassell, 1937.)
Bryce, J. *The Holy Roman Empire.* (Macmillan, 1895.)
Cambridge Mediæval History.
Chaytor, H. J. *The Troubadours.* (Cambridge Univ. Press, 1912.)
Cotterill, H. B. *Mediæval Italy.* (Harrap, 1915.)
Creighton, M. *History of the Papacy.* (Longmans, 1901.)
Dante's Divina Commedia. (Many translations and editions.)
Fisher, H. A. L. *A History of Europe.* (Arnold, 1936.)
Haskins, C. H. *The Renaissance in the Twelfth Century.*
Heywood, W. *A Short History of Perugia.* (Methuen.)
Lamb, H. *The Crusades.* (Thornton Butterworth, 1930.)
Sedgwick, H. D. *A Short History of Italy.* (Houghton Mifflin Co., 1905.)

Stevenson, W. B. *The Crusades in the East.* (Cambridge Univ. Press, 1907.)
Symonds, J. A. *Renaissance in Italy.* (Smith, Elder, 1900.)
Trevelyan, Mrs. G. H. *A History of Italy.* (Benn, 1928.)

IV. BIOGRAPHIES AND COMMENTARIES (MODERN).

Adderley, J. *The Little Poor Man of Assisi.* (Arnold, 1926.)
Beaufreton, M. *Saint François d'Assise.* (Paris, 1926.)
Birkett. F. C., and others. *Franciscan Essays, II.* (British Society of Franciscan Studies, 1932.)
Boase, T. S. A. *St. Francis of Assisi.* (Duckworth. Great Lives, 1936.)
Bonnard, A. *St. Francis of Assisi,* trans. F. Simmonds (Medici Society, 1930.)
Bosio, G. *Frate Francesco Pacificatore.* (Coletti, Rome, 1926.)
Chesterton, G. K. *St. Francis of Assisi.* (Hodder and Stoughton, 1923.)
Cowley, S. *Franciscan Rise and Fall.* (Dent.)
Cuthbert, Fr. *Life of St. Francis of Assisi.* (Longmans, 1921.)
Cuthbert, Fr. *The Romanticism of St. Francis.* (Longmans, 1913.)
Day, E. H. *St. Francis and the Grey Friars.* (Mowbray.)
de Robeck, N. *Among the Franciscan Tertiaries.* (Dent.)
Devas, Dominic. *Franciscan Essays.* (Sands.)
Egan, M. F. *Everybody's St. Francis.* (Fisher Unwin.)
Felder, H. *Ideals of Francis.* (Burnes and Oates, 1926.)
Fortini, A. *Nuova Vita di San Francesco.* (Milan, 1926.)
Goff and Kerr Lawson. *Assisi of St. Francis.* (Chatto and Windus, 1908.)
Hase, Karl. *Franz von Assisi.* (Jena, 1856.)
Hooper, E. K. *The Troubadours of God.* (Rider.)
Housman, L. *Followers of St. Francis.* (Sidgwick and Jackson.)
Housman, L. *Little Plays of St. Francis.* (Sidgwick and Jackson.)
Housman, L. *Saint Francis Poverello.* (Sidgwick and Jackson.)
Jones, C. A. D. *The Lord's Minstrels.* (Heffer.)
Jörgensen, J. *St. Francis of Assisi.* (Longmans, 1913.)
Knox Little, W. J. *St. Francis of Assisi.* (Islister, 1897.)
Lempp, E. *Frère Elie de Cortone.* (Paris, 1908.)
Little, A. G. *Some Recently Discovered Franciscan Documents.* (Oxford Univ. Press.)
Macdonell, A. *Sons of Francis.* (Dent, 1902.)
Mackay, H. F. B. *Message of St. Francis of Assisi.* (Centenary Press, 1924.)
Oliphant, Mrs. *Francis of Assisi.* (Macmillan, 1889.)
Renan, E. *Nouvelles Etudes d'Histoire Religieuse.* (Paris, 1884.)
Robinson, Fr. Paschal. *The Writings of St. Francis.* (Dent, 1906.)
Robinson, S. *Short Introduction to Franciscan Literature.* (Philadelphia, 1907.)

Sabatier, P. *Vie de St. François d'Assise*, trans. L. S. Houghton. (Hodder and Stoughton, 1912.)
Saint Francis of Assisi, 1226–1926, *Essays in Commemoration*. (Univ. of London Press, 1926.)
Salvatorelli, L. *The Life of St. Francis*, trans. E. Sutton. (London, 1928.)
Smith, E. G. *St. Antony of Padua*. (Dent, 1926.)
Smith, E. G. *St. Clare of Assisi*. (Dent, 1926.)
Stoddart, A. M. *Francis of Assisi*. (Methuen.)

V. ANALYSES OF MYSTICAL EXPERIENCE, ETC.

Bucke, R. M. *Cosmic Consciousness*. (Dutton, New York, 1901.)
Chandler, A. *Ara Coeli*. (Methuen, 1908.)
Hugel, Baron F. von. *The Mystical Element in Religion*. (Dent.)
Inge, W. R. *Christian Mysticism*. (Methuen, 1899.)
Kingsland, W. *An Anthology of Mysticism and Mystical Philosophy*. (Methuen.)
Nicholson, D. H. S. *Mysticism of St. Francis of Assisi*. (Cape, 1923.)
Nicholson and Lee. *Oxford Book of Mystical Verse*. (Oxford Univ. Press, 1917.)
Peers, E. Allison. *Spanish Mysticism*. (Methuen.)
Underhill, Evelyn. *Man and the Supernatural*. (Methuen.)
Underhill, Evelyn. *Mysticism*. (Methuen, 1911.)

VI. FRANCISCAN INFLUENCE IN ART, LITERATURE, PHILOSOPHY, ETC.

Berenson, B. *The Study and Criticism of Italian Art*. (Bell, 1931.)
Bracaloni, P. L. *Arte Francescana nella Vita e nella Storia di Settecento Anni*. (Todi, 1924.)
Cavanna, P. *Umbria Francescana*. (Perugia, 1908.)
Crowe and Cavalcaselle. *A New History of Painting in Italy*. (Dent, 1918.)
Hutton, E. *The Franciscans in England*. (Constable, 1926.)
Little and Others. *Franciscan History and Legend in English Mediæval Art*. (British Society of Franciscan Studies.)
Martin, A. R. *Franciscan Architecture in England*. (British Society of Franciscan Studies, 1933–34.)
Morelli, G. *Italian Painters*. (Murray, 1900.)
Ozanam, A. *Poètes Franciscains en Italie*. (Paris, 1848.)
Salter, E. G. *Franciscan Legends in Italian Art*. (Black, 1905.)
Salter, E. G. *Nature in Italian Art*. (Black, 1912.)
Siren, O. *Toskanische Maler im XIII Jahrhundert*. (Berlin. 1922.)
Thode, H. *Franz von Assisi und die Anfänge der Kunst der Renaissance in Italien*. (Second Edition, 1904.)
Toynbee, M. R. *Italian Life in the Fourteenth Century*. (Methuen.)
Underhill, Evelyn. *Jacopone da Todi*. (Dent, 1919.)
Venturi, A. *La Basilica de Assisi*. (Turin, 1921.)

VII. Topography, Travel, etc.

Anson, F. *Pilgrim's Guide to Franciscan Italy.* (Sands, 1927.)
Cameron, M. L. *The Inquiring Pilgrim's Guide to Assisi.* (Methuen, 1926.)
Cameron, M. L. *Umbria, Past and Present.* (Sidgwick and Jackson, 1913.)
Duff Gordon, L. *Story of Assisi.* (Dent. Mediæval Cities, 1902.)
Faure, G. *The Land of St. Francis of Assisi.* (Medici Society, 1924.)
Goad, H. E. *Franciscan Italy.* (Methuen, 1926.)
Harrison and Austin. *Some Umbrian Cities.* (Black, 1925.)
Hutton, E. *The Cities of Umbria.* (Methuen, 1905.)
Jörgensen, J. *Pilgrimsbogen.* (Copenhagen, 1903.)
Ricci, C. *Umbria Santa*, trans. H. C. Stewart. (Faber and Gwyer, 1937.)

INDEX

371

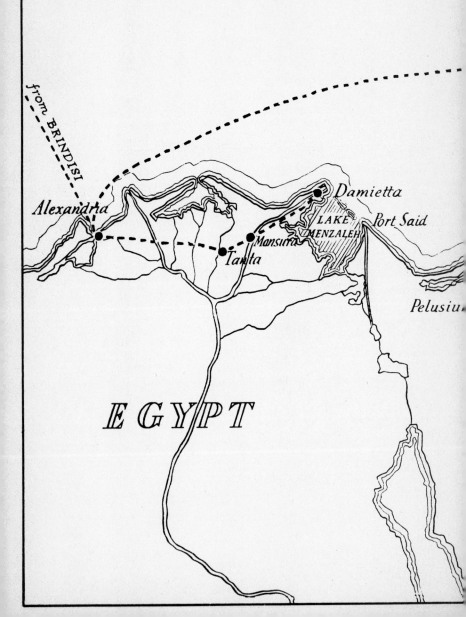

EGYPT and PALESTI

Author's Route - - - - -

from BRINDISI

Alexandria

Damietta

Port Said

LAKE
MENZALEH

Mansura

Tanta

Pelusiu

EGYPT

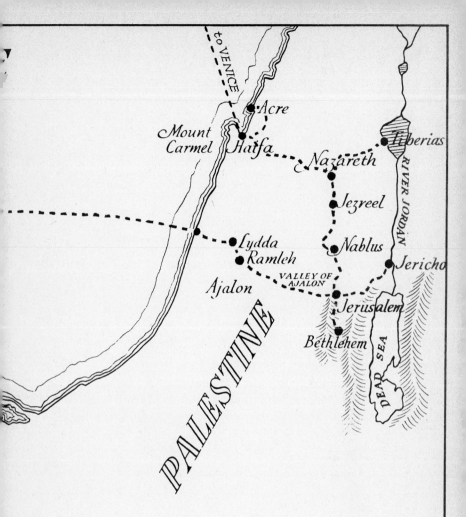